W9-BLW-128

HESITATION KILLS

HESITATION KILLS

Jane Blair

A Female Marine Officer's
Combat Experience in Iraq

ROWMAN & LITTLEFIELD PUBLISHERS, INC.
Lanham • Boulder • New York • Toronto • Plymouth, UK

BOCA RATON PUBLIC LIBRARY
BOCA RATON, FLORIDA

Published by Rowman & Littlefield Publishers, Inc.
A wholly owned subsidiary of The Rowman & Littlefield Publishing Group, Inc.
4501 Forbes Boulevard, Suite 200, Lanham, Maryland 20706
http://www.rowmanlittlefield.com

Estover Road, Plymouth PL6 7PY, United Kingdom

Distributed by National Book Network

Copyright © 2011 by Jane Blair

All rights reserved. No part of this book may be reproduced in any form or by
any electronic or mechanical means, including information storage and retrieval
systems, without written permission from the publisher, except by a reviewer
who may quote passages in a review.

British Library Cataloguing in Publication Information Available

Library of Congress Cataloging-in-Publication Data

Blair, Jane, 1972–
    Hesitation kills : a female Marine officer's combat experience in Iraq / Jane
Blair.
    p. cm.
    ISBN 978-1-4422-0876-6 (cloth : alk. paper) — ISBN 978-1-4422-0878-0
(electronic)
    1. Blair, Jane, 1972– 2. Iraq War, 2003– —Personal narratives, American. 3.
United States. Marine Corps—Officers—Biography. 4. Women marines—United
States—Biography. I. Title.
    DS79.766.B53A3 2011
    956.7044'34092—dc22
    [B]   2010047435

∞™ The paper used in this publication meets the minimum requirements of
American National Standard for Information Sciences—Permanence of Paper
for Printed Library Materials, ANSI/NISO Z39.48-1992. Printed in the United
States of America

BOCA RATON PUBLIC LIBRARY
BOCA RATON, FLORIDA

For my father

They [women Marines] don't have a nickname, and they don't need one. They get their basic training in a Marine atmosphere, at a Marine Post. They inherit the traditions of the Marines. They are Marines.

—Lieutenant General Thomas Holcomb, United States Marine Corps, Commandant of the Marine Corps, 1943

CONTENTS

ACKNOWLEDGMENTS

Without the help and support of my friends, family, fellow Marines, and book community, my book would not have come to be. There are many special people I met along the way who encouraged my vision to turn my personal journal—originally meant to get me through my time in Iraq—into this book.

I'm grateful that I was lucky enough to find my incredible book agent, Ellen Levine. Ellen and her staff worked tirelessly to find a spot in the publishing world that was right for my book. Thanks to the entire talented staff at my publishing company, Rowman & Littlefield. Susan McEachern and Janice Braunstein—thank you for patiently waiting while I lived through a revolution in the Middle East to get my proofs in on time for publication. Thanks also to Carrie Broadwell, Sam Caggiula, and Erin McGarvey.

Thanks to Clare Martin who was the first proofreader of my book and whose task of correcting my grammar and spelling mistakes was a big job. Thanks to James Wade who edited my manuscript and gave me such kind words of encouragement when we met at the Harvard Club.

Thanks to all my Marines, my colleagues, and leaders in the Corps—you will always be my tribe, and I am forever devoted to you. Special thanks go out to all the Marines at VMU-1; I hope that I have done justice in portraying our time in Iraq. I appreciate the leadership I came to know so well from Colonel Scott Mykleby, Major Sal Cepeda, and Sergeant Major Rew. Thanks also to my Marines for putting up with me—I learned more from all of you than you ever knew. To my officer peers, both in an out of the Corps, I truly value your friendship and camaraderie. I was lucky enough to have a chance to incorporate the stories of outstanding Marines such as Brian Chontosh, Seth Moulton, Pat Spencer, Paul Bock, Nicole Hembrick, Irving Stone, Ryan Ruehl, McNair, Jimenez, Carlson and others too numerous to mention. I hope that I have told your stories in a favorable and accurate light.

Thanks to my patient husband, Peter, who tirelessly edited my manuscript, infused my stories with life, supported me throughout the process, and borrowed a humvee. You have kept me grounded, sane, and, over the years, talked me out of countless crazy travel adventures that could have gotten me killed.

I can't leave out my mother who always inspired me to write, and who told me surreal but true stories about my family history in Puerto Rico: tales of sugar barons, ghosts in El Morro, and the beauty of her home at Al Cortillo Villa. Thanks also to my in-laws and relatives who always had kind words and unconditional love.

Thanks to all the Iraqis I met whose lives, I hope, have finally improved—I'm forever touched by your hospitality and hope in those uncertain times.

Thanks to the National Endowment for the Arts and your great seminars that encouraged me to turn my journal into a book. Also, thanks to the OpEd Project.

Frank Schaeffer, my friend and mentor, after all these years, you have been one of my greatest inspirations. And to Father Pavlos Bourgouris; you have taught me selfless devotion, compassion, spirituality, and how necessary it was to respect all of mankind. All my wonderful friends who always listened when I needed you: especially Penelope, Unni, Jennifer, and Blaine. To my doctor who showed me magic tricks at Setai, and who I hope will always have faith in me.

To my father, who never got to see me grow up, I wish you were still here.

1

A HOME AND A COUNTRY

Men who are capable of real action first make their plans and then go forward without hesitation while their enemies have still not made up their minds.

—Thucydides

War was inevitable. From the youngest Private to the base Commanding General, we all knew we were going, and where we went, war would follow. The Bush administration was ratcheting up the rhetoric. Instinctively, we knew our phones would ring, and we would be told that we had two hours to get on the bus. We'd grab our seabags, and we'd say good-bye to our loved ones and our comfortable lives. We'd be off to some foreign place where our only certain destiny was killing or being killed. So there I was, one Marine among many, about to deploy to Iraq and wearing a camouflage uniform—designed to both hide me from the enemy and to make me blend in with Marines headed for combat.

The post-9/11 world had many Americans fearful about future terrorist attacks. They bought security kits equipped with everything they would need to survive in their homes. They were prepared to trade certain liberties for security, sacrificing 229 years of national character on the altar of the moment. The Middle East, which had posed endless problems for U.S. foreign policies and those of other Western nations, was now at the center of a full-blown crisis. Iran and Iraq were included in what President Bush called the "axis of evil," a phrase designed to inspire fear in the United States and to let everyone know who was on our shit list. All it seemed to confirm was what some pundits and historians called a "clash of civilizations" between East and West. Now, we were told, Muslim extremism had blossomed into terrorism. We were reminded that Islamic extremists claimed they were carrying out the injunction in the Qur'an: "All must be converted to Islam, even by means of force."

The War on Terror was unlike any other waged by America and its allies; it was a conflict that had no boundaries—a war against a concept. The grand strategy seemed to strike out with maximum force at anyone who shook hands with a terrorist. This appealed to the Marines around me; it adhered to our beloved KISS principle—keep it simple, stupid—and played to our strengths: killing people and breaking things. First we'd stomped Afghanistan, hunting down the Taliban and al-Qaeda; now Iraq would become the next battlefield in the "war on terror." The justification for attacking this country was, initially, the contention that Iraq was hiding weapons of mass destruction. We were told it was a war to "liberate an oppressed people." We didn't care; we just wanted everyone to shut up and start the show. The professional warrior has an almost lunatic ambivalence about concepts like war and patriotism. Patriotism to a Marine is like body odor; we've all got it, but we're too polite to mention it. We don't feel a patriotic surge from events like 9/11; we joined because of some innate inner sense that the world is always in danger, and we knew we were just the people to protect the world from its problems.

While civilians talk about patriotism, Marines talk about sex, drinking, stupid things done while drinking, stupid things done while not drinking, and sex. As for war, we don't waste much effort thinking about the why; we've all got our opinions, but the how takes up enough of our time, and when someone is shooting at you, the how is all you need to worry about. We all want to go to war and hope we never do. Even if you don't believe in the cause you're fighting for, you believe in the Marines to the right and left of you, and you fight for them, to keep them alive, to get them home. It's that simple.

At the time this was all shaping up, I was a Marine Second Lieutenant just out of Officer Candidates School (OCS) and The Basic School (TBS), a nine-month training program that is required for all officers. They called my type a "butter bar," meaning we were as malleable as we were inexperienced. I was about to hit the fleet, and my first duty station was in the middle of the desert somewhere between Las Vegas and Los Angeles. My marathon drive across America consisted of two days of caffeine-high, music-blaring, high-speed driving from Virginia Beach to an out-of-the-way place called Twentynine Palms, California, to check in to my unit. That place got its name because at one time there were about Twentynine palms that were able to survive out there. Now there was a swath of burned-out hippie desert rats who built little shacks in the middle of the sand and called it home. In the middle of it, meth shacks and Joshua trees stood out in the stretch of desert, but little else. With my service alpha uniform on, a World War II–looking, olive-drab tailored suit, I finally reached the Marine base. After the junior Marine at the gate saluted and waved me through, I followed my map to the unit's location. When I arrived at the unit, an airplane hangar, I checked my hair and my light coat of makeup in the rearview mirror to make sure I was squared away before stepping out of the car into the heat. I looked as squared away as I could be, considering. Damn, the place was hot. My foot made it out of the door and was instantly covered with powdery sand. The place was like stepping onto Mars. Conveniently located in the middle of nowhere—halfway to hell, if you ask most Marines—Twentynine Palms is possibly the worst place on earth to get stationed. I dusted off my polished shoes, and I was determined to like every grain of this damned place.

With medical records, check-in papers, and orders in hand, I walked into the unit where I would remain for the next three years until I either opted out of the Corps or rotated to another location. Even though it was November, the air was like something out of a blast furnace, with a dry heat dehydrating you faster than you could drink. Dust devils swirled in the distance against a landscape of sand dunes and barren mountains. It was quite beautiful when I could see past the tight squint of my eyelids against the brightness. I walked up the ladder well to the second deck to greet my new chain of command. Marines stared at me as I came in. After some brief procedures with administration, I was told the Commanding Officer (CO) was waiting to meet me. Marching into his office, I announced, "Second Lieutenant Jane Blair, checking in as ordered, sir." I stopped directly in front of his desk at the position of attention, and I stared into the distance behind him.

"At ease, Lieutenant." The CO, Lieutenant Colonel Scott Mykleby, sat in his chair and scrutinized me. His blue Nordic eyes punctuated his ruddy complexion. He had one of those faces that as a whole still looked young beneath his otherwise middle-aged features. His fingers tapped his desk, and he leaned back in his chair. His flaxen hair made him look out of place against the dull colors of his office. Pictures of his other aviation units, his awards, and military paraphernalia decorated the walls. I looked at him from the corner of my eye to avoid turning my head. After some preliminary questions, he jumped to the point.

"You need to get settled into the area as quickly as possible. Take the time you need to get your affairs squared away. But, as you've probably heard, there's a rumor of war going around, and I need to have you ready." He promptly dismissed me. Walking out of his office, my pulse still slightly elevated and sweat pouring off my face, I saw the Sergeant Major and Executive Officer (XO) curiously peering out of their offices. As I passed the XO's hatch, he called out, "Hey, Lieutenant, not so fast." Major Cepeda, the XO, was an attractive Hispanic officer in his late thirties whose eyes cut through any bullshit he detected.

"So the new boot is on deck." He smirked at me. He had dealt with a lot of butter bars before. Like all newly minted Second Lieutenants, I was affectionately also known as "the boot." I wasn't happy about this.

"I heard you're from Manhattan?" he continued.

"Yes, sir."

"What part?"

"71st and 1st."

"I'm from 104th and 1st."

"A New Yorker, too, sir?"

"No shit, of course I am! You're quick on the uptake. Welcome aboard, Lieutenant. So tell me about yourself." He lifted his cup and sipped coffee while waiting for me to say something "bootish" again.

"Well, sir, I was stationed at . . ."

"No, no, no. I can read your bio. Tell me about *yourself*. What makes the Lieutenant tick?"

"I went to school in New . . ."

"I read that in your biography, Lieutenant. What else?"

"Sir, I was an artist . . ."

"An artist . . . well, well, we can put you to good use here. So what else?"

"I like to write."

"Even better. I've got a great writing project to get you started on. It's called a Jagman. It's got your name written all over it."

"Yes, sir."

A Jagman (Judge Advocate General Manual) was a notoriously tedious investigative report that documents a suspected crime. All lieutenants ended up working on it because these minor investigations required a lot of technical justification and bureaucratic writing. It was a perfect task to pass off to a junior officer. Despite this assignment, the XO seemed like an interesting man to work for, and his easygoing attitude meshed well with his sarcastic style.

Before I could experience the usual harassments that are part and parcel of being the boot, I began to get strong indications from the senior officers that we would be deployed. No one was interested in meeting the new officer. My arrival was quickly overshadowed by the talk of war spreading all over the base. All we knew is we were going to invade Iraq.

My new unit was an Unmanned Aerial Vehicle (UAV) Squadron. We were one of two UAV units in the Corps, and most Marines hadn't even heard of us. UAVs were up-and-coming military technology that some leaders embraced and others shunned. Our aircraft was the Pioneer, a pilotless drone that flew ahead of friendly forces in order to provide reconnaissance. During the Gulf War, UAVs were first employed by the Marine Corps during combat operations, and they were used to locate, survey, and facilitate destruction of targets by artillery, air, or naval gunfire assets. Iraqis during the earlier Gulf War called Desert Storm had often surrendered to the sound of the UAV alone because they knew artillery or air strikes could hit them within minutes.

Our Pioneer RQ-2B was the sole UAV asset in the Marine Corps and would be critical for combat operations. We would be providing tactical reconnaissance and imagery for all of the deployed Marine Forces. UAVs were an anomaly partially because they were aerial reconnaissance and would be pushed far ahead of the infantry during real-world operations. Even though the unit used to be part of the ground combat element a couple years ago, Marine Corps planners decided to switch it to the wing, or air combat element. The Marine planners did this so that the UAVs could be controlled like an air asset and therefore would require pilots to command the squadron. Pilots would know how to operate the UAVs in airspace and how to ensure there wasn't a midair collision with other aircraft. That said, during combat operations and training, the ground combat elements would assign missions to the UAV squadron.

Therefore my UAV unit was part of the 3rd Marine Air Wing, which in turn was an element of the I Marine Expeditionary Force (I MEF). I MEF was one of three MEFs in the Marine Corps. The Marine Corps operated on the structure of threes: I MEF was on the West Coast, II MEF on the East Coast, and III MEF was located in Okinawa, Japan. I MEF, known fondly as the "Imperial MEF," not only included 3rd Marine Aircraft Wing (MAW), but also a ground element called 1st Marine Division. The 1st Marine Division included infantry, artillery, armored units, and support units. The 11th Marines Artillery Regiment was the artillery unit part of this division, and my husband's unit was 3rd Battalion, 11th Marines. Both my husband's artillery unit and my unit were part of I MEF and both would support 1st Marine Division's operations in Iraq. My husband, Peter, was an artillery officer and had checked into his unit a couple weeks before me. We bought a house and got married all within the first month of arriving.

★   ★   ★

Two hours later, after meeting the officers and checking in, I walked down the hall to meet the Marines. The moment new officers meet their Marines for the first time is as defining a moment as teachers stepping in front of their first classes. Having spent time in the enlisted ranks just a year ago, it was particularly strange to think about how this role reversal would take place. Rather than looking to the example of a leader, I would *be* the leader. I was placed in the collections section by the CO. Since I was not the senior officer in the section, I would be more of a deputy rather than their direct leader until one of the other officers left. When I walked in the shop to meet the Marines, I was surprised by how senior they were.

The collections section was composed of thirteen Marines: two officers, Lieutenant Tony Debucher and Lieutenant Lisa Bishop; one SNOIC, Gunnery Sergeant Roberts; six imagery analysts; and three collections analysts. Rather than making some kind of impressive entrance, I walked into the room, as if by accident, to find myself facing all the Marines. I had to say something, quick.

"Good morning, everyone."

The Marines rose instantly and said loudly and almost in unison, "Good morning, ma'am."

I stood there in awe. Despite my lackluster performance, the Marines all did exactly as they were supposed to, all because of the insignia of rank I now wore on my uniform. I smiled inside and then introduced myself.

★   ★   ★

After a couple weeks spent getting to know the Marines in my unit, the deployment order didn't seem to be coming after all. Ready to go, waiting for the word, monotony became the enemy. The Marines' personal gear had been packed, and without computers, televisions, video games, and the infinite electronica of their generation, they went into withdrawal—and like all junkies, they got mean. Marines getting deployed picked fights with those who weren't deploying. Marines with black eyes walked around like they had won a trophy for manliness. It was like a dress rehearsal for the actual fight that lay ahead. The truth is, we had no idea what was going to happen over there. Most of us tried not to think about it. Fear was useless. If they said go, we were going, and there wasn't a thing to do about it. So, like all good Marines, we made fun of each other in the meantime.

Trading vaccination stories was how we passed the time while we waited. We had just gotten our series of anthrax shots; an AIDS test; a urinalysis; and tuberculosis, flu, tetanus, hepatitis A and B, and smallpox shots. The smallpox shot was the worst. An oozing, pus-infected wound at the injection site was a normal reaction.

The Sergeant Major was first in line for his smallpox shot, not because he was eager to get it, but because he wanted to set the example for his Marines. He was tall, wide-shouldered, and tan from years in the sun. The squareness of his jaw was almost a caricature, and his angular features looked like they had been sculpted through years of disciplined work. He looked like he belonged in Texas during the Wild West days, and his prior drill instructor training was reflected in his John Wayne coolness. His strange, slow, deliberate gait gave Marines enough warning to knock off anything they might be doing that could get them into trouble. Was his walk the result of a war injury or an affectation? No one knew. As unsympathetic as he could appear at times, he would take a bullet for any one of his Marines. His steely gaze stunned the Marines, and he stood confident, commanding their attention with his baritone bellow.

"I'm going first, because I'm going to get this shit over with! The rest of you, fall in line!" The Marines quickly formed a long line that stretched the length of half a football field. The corpsman made several punctures on his arm, and he walked away smiling. Marines followed his example behind him.

Some of us, including me, had gotten sick after getting our shots. Most of us were nauseated, had stomach cramps, headaches, or felt generally unwell. It was more than physical sickness; we were sick of waiting. We sat through endless pre-deployment classes on every subject from chemical attacks to alcohol abuse to sexually transmitted diseases. Getting gassed was our big fear. None of us wanted to die with vomit streaming out of our mouths, blood blisters swelling on our skin, slowly asphyxiating while defecating in our mission-oriented protective posture (MOPP) suits. We had medical briefs that showed us the worst of it. An auditorium full of Marines winced as we looked at photo after photo of faces and bodies of mutilated humans, as if out of a horror movie, with boils and unrecognizable, bloody features. Smallpox attacks, anthrax, sarin gas bombs, nerve agents like VX, mustard gas, and chemicals that cooked your blood on contact were just some of the various ways we could suffer slow, painful deaths if we didn't wear our MOPP suits properly.

We went through brief after brief until we had run the gamut of topics preparing us for war. With talk of war on every news program and magazine, we had been saddled up for it for months. Now it was already January 2003. Every day we wondered if it was our day to be called. Units had already begun to leave for Iraq, but no one knew exactly when the day would come. Most of our base in Twentynine Palms had left.

The Twentynine Palms base was a unique place to the Marine Corps. Despite its reputation as being the worst place to be stationed, it was the best place for training. This was the only place in the Marine Corps where units on base were deliberately arranged into Regimental Combat Teams (RCTs). This meant that all the units in the same location on the base would be deployed together, and when they trained, they could train together and plan operations as if they were forward deployed to a location outside the continental United States (CONUS). It was an elegant design, as the units received the maximum time training together.* My unit, VMU-1, was a fixed wing, medium-lift, UAV squadron known as the "watchdogs." During combat operations, my unit would be in direct support to our RCT known as RCT 7.

★ ★ ★

As units began deploying, the base was emptying fast. Normally, deployment meant leaving a wife or girlfriend behind. But as a female Marine, it meant leaving my husband—but not behind. Peter had been called the week before. After months of expectation, his was the first unit called from our Twentynine Palms base, and in two hours he was gone. The deployment of his unit was a wake-up call to all of us. I had stayed up all night before he left. Then he was gone, just like that. We had been eating dinner in the new house we'd bought two weeks before. It was in one of those sprawling new developments, a picture-perfect four-bedroom home surrounded by pristine desert lined with Joshua trees. Inside, our boxes were half-opened—I wasn't sure if I should unpack or repack the boxes. So there they remained, littering the house, in a state of both coming and going. Our seabags lay neatly stacked by the door, waiting to be

---

*The units that comprised this RCT, or RCT 7, included: 3/11 Artillery Battalion, 7th Marine Infantry Regiment, 3rd Battalion, 4th Marine Infantry Battalion, AAVs, tanks, assorted support units, and various units of the wing, such as my unit, VMU-1.

picked up. We lit a fire that night and were sitting quietly on the couch when Peter turned to me and said, "I feel like this is the first day we've gotten to relax; we finally finished everything we need to do. Now, we can finally enjoy the place!"

"Yes, finally."

We had just finished dinner when the phone rang. Peter reluctantly answered it. After a quick exchange of words, he hung up, looking troubled.

"What's wrong?"

"My unit is having an all-hands formation back at the base. It's probably only a recall drill for accountability. We're supposed to bring our gear to stage it just in case we get the call to go."

"Are you sure it's just a drill?"

"They didn't say."

"Do you want me to come?"

"You might as well, just in case."

It wasn't a drill. They were actually leaving. My heart hit the deck. His CO had gotten the call just an hour prior, and there was an extra plane available to transport troops to Kuwait. They asked the base which units were ready to leave, and Peter's unit, the artillery unit that would support all of 7th Marines, made the list. Within five hours of that call, they were boarding the white buses to the airfield. Hundreds of Marines gathered in the darkness, and stacks of identical seabags were staged and loaded into the buses. It was bitterly cold outside as families and friends hugged and kissed their Marines. What could they say? What last words or touch could fill the unknown? I couldn't believe it was happening. I didn't believe we were going to go until it was happening. I stood there in my thin sweater by Peter's side. I chose to freeze rather than leave. I watched my husband go off to war as a disciplined Marine would, outwardly stoic, inwardly crumbling. As a wife, holding back tears, I wondered when the man I loved would return to me. Before he stepped on the bus, he handed me a small, sealed manila envelope.

"If I die," he said, "open it." He kissed me good-bye one last time and left.

I drove home alone in the darkness of the desert. At home, I turned the key in the doorknob and walked into a dark, quiet place. I stared at the spot where Peter's seabag had been, in a house we had barely known, and at a picture of a husband who was gone. The fire had all but died out, but the faintest hint of smoldering embers remained. The sealed letter he had given me I placed in my seabag. Walking to the bathroom, I brushed my teeth, washed my face, grabbed a snack, and then spent the entire night in bed pretending I was asleep.

★   ★   ★

After Peter left, the base emptied out. Unit after unit packed up and got on planes heading to Kuwait. Only the spouses remained, mostly women, of course. Some ladies, usually the junior enlisted wives, already had earned the notorious title "Westpac widow." Westpac referred to the fact that they were spouses of Marines from the western Pacific region, in bases like Camp Pendleton and Twentynine Palms. And widows, well, that just meant they acted like their husbands were dead. As soon as their husbands had deployed, these Westpac widows threw off their wedding rings and hit the bars, finding any available men in the area who were not deployed. Some became six-month whores, even changing the lights on their porches to red or blue, indicating that they were available for company; others shacked up with another dude, but in any case, were available for service. Most of the ladies remained steadfast, however, and for them, deployment was difficult. They maintained the household alone, often with several children, and did all the work, usually without help of friends or family since they were hundreds or thousands of miles away from their hometowns. So, like all things, there were good and bad spouses. Whores and Madonnas.

Despite this, I developed an affinity for the wives of the Marines who had left. I'm not the most ladylike of chicks, but I found a way of bonding with some of the wives. The officers' base housing complex, Ocotillo Heights (where most of them lived) was known as the "Ocotillo Baby Factory." It was set up like a typical American development. Each family had their own duplex with a garage, backyard, and grill. The military was fairly generous with benefits because it made families feel more secure and that, in turn, meant higher rates of retention of officers and enlisted personnel. I always speculated that this policy seems to have worked because the reenlistment rate was much higher for Marines with families than without. The military provided all kinds of facilities for the families—day care, a community center, pools, parks, free health care, and recreation centers. Hence, the drive for these young wives appeared to be to have a million children. It seemed to me as though they were all in a competition—some had two, some had four, but they all almost always seemed to be pregnant. They pushed their baby carriages down the street in pretty spring dresses, looking like something out of *Pleasantville*.

I was the only officer's wife who didn't have, nor was carrying, a baby. In the past, all the wives shared stories of their children and lived for their newly created young families. I tried to relate, but I didn't feel I had much in common with them. Peter's departure changed things. We now shared the anxiety of seeing our husbands off to war. Because of that, I called the Key Volunteers Network (wives who kept other wives informed about the deployed Marines) daily. No news. We were told not to expect any. Our husbands arrived safely in Kuwait, that much we knew. But they were too far out in the middle of nowhere. All I could really do was to try not to think about the fact that I had been married just a month ago.

Peter and I had been married without a ceremony or reception, in a drive-through chapel in Las Vegas. We hadn't planned it that way. But it was only a two-hour drive from our base in Twentynine Palms. Las Vegas was the type of place my husband and I hated. To two native New Yorkers, the seediness and desperation of Las Vegas made it a less-than-desirable place to get married. But we were pretty desperate, and it had the advantage of proximity.

The big wedding we planned for May 2003 had to be canceled. We agreed we should marry immediately to secure benefits for one another and to ensure that if it did come to combat and something happened to one of us, we'd managed to have at least a short time together as husband and wife. When we received word that we were leaving for sure, we chose the cheapest way to go. We planned to have a big wedding when we returned, so we didn't want our impromptu wedding to dampen the memories of our "real" celebration. So in late December 2002, a day before our scheduled flight to visit our families, we drove to Las Vegas and stood in the twenty-four-hour marriage-license center just before midnight with bikers, strippers, and teenage runaways and paid $50 for the right to have our dedicated, monogamous relationship legally recognized by the state of Nevada and, by extension, the United States—and, most important, by the Marine Corps. We intended to get up early and hunt for the cheapest little chapel in Vegas. We wanted the ceremony to be as forgettable as possible, a mere legal formality. Such was not to be.

Driving back to the hotel, we saw a drive-through chapel that was still open. It was perfect, and we promptly agreed to pull in and do the deed. We paid our $40, and I filled out the information card the minister uses for the ceremony. After a few minutes of either frenzied rehearsal or a quick round of drinks, a female minister appeared in the window. She asked, "Do ya wanna Elvis impersonator?"

We declined. She looked taken aback when we also said no to the photo, corsage, and all the frivolous extras they try to overcharge you for in order to make the event more "memorable." No, we said, we just want the ceremony. She smelled like cheap gin.

After disappearing for a moment, she began. She actually had quite a way with words, and I got a little misty. Not that I was going to cry, but like most men and nearly all Marines, Peter can't even deal with the thought of female tears, so he began to look for an opportunity to lighten the mood. It came sooner than I expected. I admit my handwriting is difficult to read, and to a minister who seemed less than sober, my first name, Jane, became Jan. As she blundered merrily along, Peter saw his opportunity and exploited the situation. The minister said, "Now Peter, I want you to repeat after me. I, Peter . . ."

He responded, "I, Peter . . ."

"Take you, Jan . . ."

"Take you, Jan . . ."

Maybe I shouldn't have hit Peter as we said our vows. The minister looked concerned as I immediately sent a left hook flying at Peter's face. He took it square on the jaw and was a bit dazed but still managed to start laughing, which got me laughing, too, even though my nerves had caused me to hit him much harder than I had planned. The minister looked puzzled and almost stopped—but with freaks in Vegas being as common as jaywalkers in New York, she drove on with her job, and soon we pulled away as man and wife.

★   ★   ★

All the anxieties of my husband going to war were compounded by the knowledge that I'd be leading my Marines in a combat mission as well. It was a strange dichotomy but so was being a wife and a Marine. I knew I couldn't get distracted worrying about him because my Marines depended on me. Somehow, I was scared out of my mind and entirely confident at the same time. It had been two weeks since my husband called from his unit's stopover in Germany. I knew he probably couldn't call again, but I never guessed it would be so hard. How do you get by not knowing when your husband will return? How do you say good-bye to someone going to war? See you later? See you in a while? Never will I see you again? I couldn't even take comfort in knowing that I would be safe at home myself, watching the news on television. Soon, I would be gone, too.

The quiet of my new home filled me with the reminder that I would be deployed. When I tried to read, my mind was haunted by the silence. On television, the news programs continually reported on the deployment of troops and the run-up to war. The media seemed almost too confident about the military's abilities. Reporters and pundits seemed to severely underestimate Iraqi forces, minimizing the fact that there would likely be casualties on our side as well. There was nothing I could take comfort in and no one who would understand. I just had to suck up my feelings and not complain.

There was so much to take care of before I left. I sent all my mail and bills to my mother, who promised that she would be vigilant about paying everything on time. I put all our valuables, including our wallets, in a safe deposit box. I canceled the cable, the electricity, and everything else. I got so tense in the days leading up to deployment that I locked myself out of my house twice and had to call the locksmith. I had never felt so alone.

★   ★   ★

Back at the base, my life was devoted to my work with the unit and to training for war. My Marines were turning out to be a most interesting group of individuals: Corporal Warseck, a gangly six-foot, five-inch Marine, was a self-professed Celtic warrior in the Society for Creative Anachronism; Sergeant Young, a dark-green Marine (what Marines called African American Marines) with short curly hair and a muscular build, talked with an Indiana twang and baked pies and cakes for the section every week. He loved to cook and to sing—and to sing while he wasn't cooking, too—and it wasn't uncommon to hear him break out into some '80s tune in the middle of the office.

Sergeant Leppan had been on the firing range and had just come back to the unit. He was the dark horse and had gotten into a serious altercation with his past lieutenant because the Sergeant's ex-wife practically assaulted this officer; instead of the ex-wife taking the heat, the Sergeant took the brunt of the punishment. Despite this, he was an intense, talkative Marine who was intent on educating the section on the enemy order of battle we would likely encounter in Iraq. I'd watch him educating the younger Marines on the numbers, composition, and strength of an enemy force. He showed them pictures of everything we would likely encounter and made them memorize what these units, such as an enemy tank force, would look like if you were looking down at them from a bird's-eye view thousands of feet above. Corporal Parker, an athletically built female with dark brown hair secured perfectly in a bun, was a foundation of the section. Her presence alone was both sincere and stern. She wouldn't take anyone's bullshit, and they all knew it. Corporal Parker gave the impression of sweetness, but she was the only Marine who didn't flinch when she mentioned her time going through survival, evasion, resistance, and escape (SERE), a reenactment of prison camp that's described as being so real you forget the instructors are on your side. Techniques of breaking in Marines employed in SERE training were intended to prepare U.S. military for evading capture, if possible, and surviving in enemy territory or coping with what they might be subjected to as a POW if the enemy employed brutal "enhanced interrogation." How to escape from captivity was another part of this extremely rigorous and, indeed, painful and frightening training. Some men were permanently scarred from this experience. But Corporal Parker insisted it wasn't that bad.

To complete the picture, Corporal Nail, tall, thin, youthful-looking, and very good-natured, seemed to be the most ordinary member of the group—until he removed his shirt, at which point it became clear that his tattoo-covered body probably meant his normalcy was a veil. Sergeant Davila had just checked in, so I didn't know much about him yet. Sergeant Beaty was the old man of the group, as bald as he was talkative. Sergeant Venaleck, on the other hand, was as pale as he was serious and adjusted his glasses carefully as he scrutinized the visuals that he would later show the rest of the Marines in preparation for their imagery training. It was obvious that he was the quiet leader who would ensure the well-being of all the other Marines.

As for the officers in the section, there was First Lieutenant Lisa Bishop, a thin, wispy young woman whose idea of fun was tandem surfing in Los Angeles. She entered competitions with her husband where she would get on his shoulders while they were catching a wave in Malibu. She was sweet but quiet and dead set on getting out of the Corps once her contract was up.

"This place is just not for me. You'll see, women just don't get treated the same," she told me.

The senior officer was Tony Debucher, also a First Lieutenant. From the start, he clearly didn't want me there. After I talked to him for about fifteen minutes, giving him a motivating speech about my background and how I could be an asset to the section, he just shook his head and said, "I'm going to put you down in the supply section because we don't need any help up here. Besides, I don't know where you came from. I wasn't expecting you to arrive; you just popped up on our radar about a week before you checked in. I think two officers is enough. If the CO wants you back up here, we'll discuss it then."

I clenched my jaw and tried to control my rising pulse as rage radiated down my spine. But then I took a breath and felt sorry for him. The fact that Debucher wasn't standing up for me made me think he was one of those unfortunate souls who had forgotten that after mission accomplishment comes troop welfare, and he wasn't taking care of me, one of his Marines. By the grace of God, this misbegotten breed is a minority, but the fickle finger of fate had put one across the desk from me, smiling like he was doing me a favor by putting me away in a warehouse, away from his eye. I couldn't raise too many objections, and I took it because I was only a butter bar and he was a First Lieutenant. So I sucked it up and hoped that the harmony of my universe would eventually reassert itself.

In the meantime, I studied the maps, camps, roads, and Iraqi language and culture—anything to increase my odds of surviving over there. The next day, First Lieutenant Debucher gave a brief to the squadron about what our unit could expect once we got to Iraq. He basically pointed to the map and gave a casual snapshot of the area without details. It was the worst brief I had ever heard. I couldn't hold it in anymore, and I told him so.

"I could have helped you prep for that brief if you needed background information, Debucher."

"Nah, that's all they need to hear, no need to get technical," he said.

"That was the most incomplete situation report I've heard, and you know I have the background with that area."

"Who do you think you are? I told you to just stay down in supply. I know what I'm doing, and they don't need all that cultural shit and regurgitation of enemy positions. No one here even understands that shit. Just stay in your box."

★   ★   ★

Camp Coyote, Ali Al Salem Air Base, Al Jaber Air Base, Camp Commando—all seven thousand Marines from my higher headquarters were already at these Kuwaiti camps. Every day, I heard in the media that what I was being told was restricted or classified. I knew I probably wouldn't be able to tell anyone back home where I was or what I was doing.

All I knew was that I was one of two female officers in my unit. The unit had a total of twelve females being deployed—the rest were in some stage of pregnancy. The twelve of us knew we would be some of the only women going into combat. We had apparently already caused a big controversy. They had told us we still might not be able to go because we would be working exclusively with 1st Marine Division and its regiments, all ground combat units, all male. Females weren't allowed in ground element units that were regimental level or below, as those units would be in direct combat. Despite this rule, my unit would be moving as a ground maneuver force and would therefore be doing a combat mission, extremely taboo for female Marines. Women weren't supposed to be in combat in the Marine Corps, by order of Congress. Still, my CO had gone to bat for us. He called the other female officer, Lieutenant Bishop, and me into his office.

"Congress says you can't go with us. That's what the Generals told me. I told the Generals who were trying to pull you that we would not be mission capable without the females."

"What did they say, sir?"

"They understood that we had a very unique unit and hadn't planned for females to be part of the ground war. They said I could take you as far as Kuwait but no farther. I explained to them once again that without the females in the unit, the squadron couldn't function. But the fight doesn't look good, ladies. But chances are this is an argument that I am going to lose, ladies. Our female flight surgeon has been pulled already and given a new job. Still, I'm going to do everything in my power to take you guys with me all the way. I know you all want to be in the fight as much as the rest of us."

As we were leaving the CO's office, he called me back.

"Hey, Jane . . ."

"Yes sir?"

"You're back up in the collections section. I want you up there, and I want you to get our Marines savvy with cultural knowledge of the region. I know you used to live over there."

★　★　★

I'd never even thought about the fact that I was female until some backwater, hillbilly Marine decided not to salute me because he "didn't salute female officers." That's when I proceeded to chew some ass, telling him he was living in the wrong century. If he thought I should be wearing a veil and cooking dinner at home, why wasn't he living in Afghanistan? While I perceived myself as a six-foot, four-inch hard ass, I was in actuality a petite five-foot, four-inch female. But as a Marine, I've got no qualms about living up to the standard that all Marines must. I didn't agree with what Lisa Bishop had said to me. The females were treated the same as men for the most part, as long as they were Marines before they were anything else.

I didn't join the Marine Corps for money, for a career, or for machismo. I wanted that abstract, intangible quality that Marines seem to magically possess. That quality, a mixture of a warrior mentality, courage, and leadership, doesn't have a word in the English language except "Marine." I know it sounds corny, but I was an idealist. I liked the core values—Marines strive to be unsurpassed, to be the world's finest. They are motivated by challenge. Boot camp and OCS were welcome challenges for me, and I trained before I went to both. I was always an athlete, and I wanted to train to be among the best. In boot camp, the drill instructors hated me for it, because they wanted recruits to fit in; in OCS they rewarded me for it, and I excelled. After seeing more than 50 percent of the females dropped from my officer class, we knew that those who remained belonged there. When I earned my commission, I was not skirting by; I did my best to excel. I never wanted to be mediocre. One of my classmates at OCS said it succinctly. When being questioned by the battalion CO as to why he joined the Corps, he brazenly said, "I heard they were looking for the best."

And he was. We all were. Marine Corps officers are some of the best and brightest people I have ever met. To surround yourself with such excellence is part of what makes the Corps so great. We men and women were not only the future of America, we were also its protectors. We crafted the destiny of America in the sense that if we failed, our nation failed. So we never failed. Failure was not an option.

When I first joined in 1999, things had been different for me. I finished my college degree a couple years earlier and had studied the philosophy of science at the State University of New York. I had a cozy job in human resources at a Fortune 500 company and a great 150-year-old farmhouse in Pennsylvania. At twenty-six, I had a nice life with plenty of friends and a good career ahead of me. It was a perfectly comfortable existence. One day, I was at work and I read an article about how the 24th Marine Expeditionary Unit (MEU) had helped earthquake victims in Turkey. I realized that I wasn't happy with my comfortable life. My life had been all about *me*, and there was a lot more to life than me and more to life than finding perfect comfort.

My parents had raised me in both New York City and Miami Beach. My father had been a criminal defense attorney and my mother a postmodern painter. I never knew anyone in the military when I was growing up. I never even knew what the military did. Instead, my parents took me to lavish parties attended by the rich and famous, where people like Andy

Warhol and Prince were the norm. To say the least, my childhood wasn't normal. On some days, my father would take me into the jails to show me what it was like to be a criminal. I would watch his trials in court and learn about the rights of the accused. My mother taught me how to be an artist by showing me the beauty of the world. She taught me how to transform the things I saw and bring them to life on canvas. My life had been idyllic until I was fifteen, when I got into a disfiguring accident by falling off a bicycle along the side of a hill while my family and I were vacationing in Puerto Rico. After plastic and reconstructive surgery, I learned for a short while what it was like to be ugly and disfigured and briefly unable to speak. But, thankfully, I was young and I recovered. During high school, I got accepted to an exclusive magnet arts school, where I studied visual art. My parents and my experiences transformed me into an adult before I had a chance to be a girl. Somehow along the way, even with the liberal arts background in which I grew up, I felt a little too safe and a little too privileged.

After high school I decided to travel rather than go straight to college. I had always been an adventurer. At age ten, I biked fifty miles from Miami Beach to Fort Lauderdale and back without ever telling my parents. As a teenager, I participated on the toughest Outward Bound programs, climbed glaciers at the Gore Range in Colorado, and spent a summer on archaeological digs exploring Anasazi ruins in the Southwest. And at eighteen, I spent a year and a half after high school living in a Greek Orthodox monastery in Sinai, Egypt, traveling, hiking, and adventuring solo across the Middle East during the Gulf War. I planned twenty-five-mile day treks across the Negev and slept in Bedouin camps for weeks, living in the desert alone as a solitary traveler. Then, one day, when I was in the Middle East, I called home. My father had a softball-sized tumor in his lung. He was in the operating room when I called. I got on the next plane I could find and spent the next months in the intensive care unit of a hospital. Within a year, my father slipped into a coma and died of lymphoma. My father's yearlong struggle in the intensive care unit battling cancer removed any frivolities that remained in my life. My father's death made me realize safety was just an illusion. No one was going to protect me anymore.

I joined the Corps because I recognized that I was weak and that my life to date had consisted of nothing more than an effort to make myself as comfortable and as safe as possible. I wanted to become unsafe, and I wanted to be uncomfortable. I wanted to do something real, something that mattered to more people than just me. I wanted to stand in the cold and the rain for a purpose and burn the weakness from my body and from my soul. I knew that if I did this, at the end of my life I would be able to look back and know that I had truly lived it. And I knew that if I didn't do this, at the end of my life I would look back and wonder if I had even been alive. So I joined the Corps and burned away the layer of cotton gauze that I wrapped around myself as I walked through this life, that cushion of comfort and complacency that buffered me from the world. By doing so, I brought myself closer to reality, and I saw the things that were not beautiful about the world but that needed to change.

★   ★   ★

Waiting to find out if I would go to Iraq, I was suddenly confronted with the realization that my decision to join the military was not some painted canvas that I could wash over with gesso, but a decision that I was committed to and that I couldn't escape. It was something so real in its immediacy that the only out that I was given was the knowledge that I couldn't be concerned about life or death. Death was a possibility. Admittedly, I had some serious reservations about it. I had already heard about some problems with women in combat during the Gulf War. There had been urban legends about a female Army Captain going into the fetal position when taking fire. I didn't know if it was true, but I questioned its logic. Just because one woman did it didn't mean we all would. Others told stories of women who would freak out if they broke a nail or who would break down and cry uncontrollably under stress. I had never met a female Marine who acted this way. The stupidity of this line of reasoning was perfectly illustrated after the war by my husband, who told me about a male officer, a grunt First Lieutenant, who curled into a ball on a roof in Baghdad and shrieked, "Are they gone? Are they gone?" after receiving small arms fire from Fedayeen guerrillas. It seems there are certain people, male and female, who fold in extreme situations. Soon, I would find out for myself. I tried not to be negative about it for my CO's sake. He had fought for us to go. I wasn't going to let him down.

   Lieutenant Colonel Scott Mykleby, our CO, was a seasoned combat veteran who had been the lead Cobra pilot in the Scott O'Grady rescue. I learned this from the pictures that lined his office walls and from speaking to him about his combat experiences. One day in his office, he told me that in 1995, Captain O'Grady had been shot down in his F-16 while attempting to evade surface-to-air missiles over Bosnia. After O'Grady crashed, no one knew if he was dead or alive until he activated his beacon signal just before dawn after being on the ground for several days. Upon receiving the signal, a rescue team formed a Tactical Recovery of Aircraft and Personnel (TRAP) mission to extract him during daylight hours. Since he had already been on the ground at that point for six days, time was of the essence. While leading a Cobra team as part of the rescue mission effort, Lieutenant Colonel Mykleby established contact with O'Grady and secured his location so helicopters could extract him.

Extremely confident, poised, and intelligent, Lieutenant Colonel Mykleby was just the type of CO we needed to lead us in combat. And, when it came down to it, he had no reservations about sending us, because he knew how to train us, physically and mentally, to be ready. Of course, I had no idea what to expect, outside of the images I'd seen in old war movies. I fully accepted the idea that I would be taking fire and ordering Marines to return fire. After all, I had signed the contract, said the oath, and taken the commission.

But the other females of my unit had been given a new fear—that of being in combat. At OCS and TBS, we had gone through the same training as the males, learning the basics of being an infantry platoon commander. While at OCS, our training was largely segregated, but our second course, TBS, was integrated training. We led platoons, sometimes companies, of our male and female peers through realistic combat scenarios, even under live fire. We forged our way through advanced navigation courses, presented briefs in front of 250 of our peers and superiors, and tested alongside the men in endurance events that everyone dreaded regardless of gender. The women proved their athletic prowess among some of the fittest young men in America—and in many cases, we matched the competition. Mental preparation was the difference. In sharpness, wit, and knowledge, we were equal to our male peers, but Congress and the powers that be told us we were mentally unprepared to actually go to war. We had often been told that we would never be put in a combat role—that's why we were excluded from all the combat MOSs (Military Occupational Specialty). Naturally, we always felt that, somehow, if we were put in harm's way, it would be by accident. But this war was unlike anything we had seen before, and my unit's mission could be combat driven. The Amazonians, Plato's Thracian woman, Joan of Arc, Israeli soldiers, and the amazing female Soviet soldiers during the Russian invasion of Afghanistan all were examples of women in combat. It is not a new concept, only one that has been driven out of society in the last few centuries. America fosters the idea that the ideal woman is the weak woman. Just look in any *Vogue* at the emaciated but often physically unfit women who are deemed beautiful. Meanwhile, in GQ, equally beautiful men are expected to maintain their physique through weightlifting and exercise. If women were held to that standard of physical fitness, we'd have much different expectations of them. Women would no longer be victims, portrayed as fragile creatures in need of men's care and protection. They would be thin and muscular, capable of any task that fell before them. Hell, just look at the good wife in the Old Testament,

> A wife of noble character who can find? She is worth far more than rubies. Her husband has full confidence in her and lacks nothing of value. She brings him good, not harm, all the days of her life. She selects wool and flax and works with eager hands. She is like the merchant ships, bringing her food from afar. She gets up while it is still dark; she provides food for her family and portions for her servant girls.
>
> She considers a field and buys it; out of her earnings she plants a vineyard. She sets about her work vigorously; her arms are strong for her tasks. She sees that her trading is profitable, and her lamp does not go out at night.

That was the ideal I sought to emulate.

2

THE CALL

*If women are expected to do the same work as men, we must teach
them the same things.*

—Plato

The first time Peter and I met, my face was in the dirt, covered with mud,
and I was crawling under barbed wire with my rifle. I don't know how
he found that appealing, but somehow during The Basic School he was able
to see past the mud on my face. Peter was the smartest man I ever met.
Even though he was a "shave tail" and therefore was coming straight out
of college into the Marine Corps, I remember during a tactical war game
exercise, our training Captain called on him because he looked as if he
wasn't paying attention. In spite of having no prior tactics training, Peter
managed to give a perfect case scenario answer that impressed the teacher
so much that he ended the lesson shortly after that.

"Well, I guess that's about it, I can't add much to that," the Captain said.

During training, Peter earned the highest aptitude score in the entire
school. He was like that: he was always acing tests like the SAT, GRE,
and LSAT without any effort. But he was very humble about it. Very few
people knew he was brilliant. He said his secret to scoring well on the tests
was that he didn't worry about his scores. He just focused on the moment,
and life took care of the rest. Even though Peter was six years younger than
me, he acted like an older man. He'd always read or smoke during breaks
in our training, oblivious to the chatter of our colleagues around us. When
we met, he was a handsome young man of twenty-two, taller than almost
anyone else and solidly built, with a rare gentlemanly quality to him. He
would push other Lieutenants out of the way when they tried to sit next to

me in class, and he would sit next to me instead. When I looked shocked he would say, "Hey, he who hesitates is lost."

Right before he deployed and we were all still in Twentynine Palms, my husband and I attended his unit's "hail and farewell," an informal event that welcomed new officers to the unit and said good-bye to the officers leaving. Typical time spent in any unit was approximately three years, so every couple of months there was a new crop of rotating Marines coming and going. Such events were held in the Officers Club. All the officers and SNCOs in the unit would come for drinks and hors d'oeuvres, and the CO, or the senior officer on deck, and all the new officers would make speeches. Although he normally would have passed this off as a work event, Peter told me to come. We were both counting the days until we would leave for Kuwait and wanted to maximize our time together. I arrived at the club at 1630, and his whole chain of command was filtering in. I went over to a group of his fellow Lieutenants that I recognized, and we began chatting. As usual, I was the only female there. After some socializing, my husband walked in just as we were all being ushered outside.

As we stood outside, the CO of 3rd Artillery, 11th Marines, Lieutenant Colonel Hymes, made a speech about the new Marines who had entered the unit. An artillery unit, 3/11 was part of the 11th Marine Artillery Regiment, which in turn was part of 1st Marine Division. They were one of three artillery battalions from the West Coast that were in support of the infantry for all of 1st Marine Division. Peter's unit was a combat arms unit, meaning that, from the regiment on down, there were only males in it. That meant I was the only female there, since I was the only spouse who was a Marine, as it was a "Marine only" event. As all the Marines gathered for the event, the CO began. "These are your peers who you're going to war with—this is your team," he said. "Take a look at who's around you because that's who's fighting with you."

Then he welcomed a new officer who had come straight from college to the fleet. It was customary for all being hailed or bid farewell to make a speech after the CO's remarks. The fresh, inexperienced Second Lieutenant began, "Thanks for welcoming me aboard. It's great to be here. I wasn't sure what to expect, checking into a new unit, but you've all been very helpful. I'm looking forward to working with you all." The heckling began, along with a dim note of snickering.

"Oh, God! He's already broken the ten-second rule!" one of the First Lieutenants chuckled.

"What's the ten-second rule?"

"If you talk more than ten seconds during the hail you're tagged. A marked man. You've been in the Marine Corps for thirty-five seconds; what could you possibly have to say? Say hello and then shut up so I can go on libo."

"Roger, I'm tracking now."

We laughed as the new Lieutenant continued, "I went to school at Princeton University and graduated summa cum laude, and I'm glad to work with you all; I think this all could be very interesting. I wanted to be in the infantry, but artillery was my second choice, so I can't complain too much." He saw the crowd was not laughing.

"Like I said, it will be great to work with all of you, and I can't wait to go into combat! Oorah!"

Lieutenant Blake, who was standing next to me, shook his head in disbelief at the sheer jackassery of the statement. Lieutenant Blake, whose nickname was "the senator" because of his diplomatic demeanor, was a Harvard graduate. He turned to me and said, "No one in their right mind is glad to go to combat! And why is he giving us his resume? This guy is a boot!"

After the CO hailed all the new Lieutenants, he suddenly turned to my husband and said to the crowd, "It looks like we have another addition to our family."

Peter was stunned—he had been hailed several months ago. But the CO continued, "Lieutenant Blair has brought a new Lieutenant into the battalion as well—Lieutenant Blair actual." I was so shocked he was hailing me that I almost looked around to see who he was talking about. "Lieutenant Blair actual" was the running joke because everyone thought it was funny that my husband married a fellow lieutenant. "Actual" was a term used on the radio in order to identify you as being the "actual" officer using a specific call sign, as opposed to his radio operator. So if you called for Thunder-6 and got an eighteen-year-old kid who was really the CO's driver, you'd say, "Let me talk to your actual," and he'd put 3/11's CO on. "Blair actual" had become my nickname, and everyone in the battalion was learning who I was.

The CO continued, "It's not often we usher a female into our battalion." Everyone laughed, adding to my embarrassment. Artillery, as I mentioned, was a "no females allowed" combat job.

"But Lieutenant Blair is herself part of the UAV squadron and will be flying missions alongside us. And as I understand it, she is going forward as well. So please welcome her to 3/11."

I turned beet red; I hadn't even realized the CO knew who I was. But it was time for my speech. Lieutenant Blake eyed me and whispered, "Ten seconds!"

"Thanks. My unit's going to be following in trace of you all, so just make sure you don't shoot our aircraft down!"

Everyone laughed and then the Sergeant Major quipped, "Ma'am, you're in the wing, so just bring us ice!" Laughter erupted again. Grunts joked about the wing. The wing was soft. In combat, the wing units were usually in the rear operating areas with the ice, gear, and equipment. Technically, my unit was indeed a wing unit. However, we were told we would be in direct support of combat units, meaning we would be moving forward with them. But that was just conjecture; no one but my chain of command knew that we were going to be operating in combat like that. It was a fairly new concept that was partially a result of my CO, Lieutenant Colonel Mykleby, who suggested this tactic when he met with 1st Marine Division leadership. They asked him if they thought the UAVs would be able to push in front of the grunts and support them throughout the fight from forward points. My CO said yes and developed a strategy called "scoot tactics." This would allow the UAVs to provide coverage for all the frontline units, because we would become a highly mobile autonomous unit that would move independently from everyone else. We would race ahead, fly the UAV, provide coverage for the grunts, and then pack up and move again, much in the way a traditional ground reconnaissance unit would operate, minus the UAVs.

Peter's CO continued, giving plaques out to the farewells. I turned to Peter and asked, "Did I sound all right?"

"Babe, you could have said anything and they would have laughed: you're a female in a flight suit!"

★ ★ ★

Peter was gone. These were just memories now. It wasn't long after when the call came from my CO.

"Jane, we're having an awards formation. I've got some other word to pass as well."

One of my Marines had just received an award, long overdue because no one else took the time to document his actions. It was the first award I had given a Marine and my first good deed as an officer that I did for another Marine. All two hundred of us in the squadron came into formation. The Marines formed rows and columns, and the officers took their positions in the back. I stood, silently proud of his achievements, watching as the other officers talked quietly among themselves. The officers all were very buddy-buddy, and I wasn't inside their circle yet. The transition from

Corporal to Second Lieutenant was challenging in an entirely different way, and I wasn't entirely sure I liked it yet. There's a veiled rivalry between the officers and enlisted in the Corps. It's kind of a contest of machismo. Generally speaking, the enlisted think the officers are overeducated, self-absorbed careerists who don't give two shits about the actual job. The officers think the enlisted have chips on their shoulders because they're not in charge. I thought back to when I was a Corporal. I promised myself when I was enlisted that if I became an officer, I would take care of my Marines and wouldn't be one of those officers that they resented.

As the Corporal's ceremony finished, the CO called us into a circle. All two hundred Marines seemed uneasy as they gathered around in a semicircle. We knew what he was going to say. The Marines, as you could see in their faces, loved the CO. He was not one of those officers that the enlisted hated. I, too, was beginning to trust him, and I believed he would take care of us no matter what.

"Marines," he said, "this is the moment. We've got the date. Be prepared to leave tomorrow night at 2200. Take this time to spend with your families, and then come back at 2200 with your heads in the game. We're finally leaving; our call has come!"

"Oorah!" A mass cheer arose from the Marines, but it wasn't the same esprit de corps cheer I was used to hearing. This time, there was something underpinning the joy. It was a strange, bubbling feeling that everyone felt erupting inside them. The bubbling was inside me, too, as my heart raced and I thought, "We're going to war."

★ ★ ★

On the day of departure, I locked my front door for the last time and drove to the base. Marines assembled at the armory where we would pick up our T/O weapon, the weapon that was assigned to us based on our billet. My weapons consisted of an M16A2 service rifle, standard issue for Marines, and a 9mm Beretta pistol, standard for a Marine officer. After the necessary checks for weapons serviceability, I walked into my unit's hangar, a large open bay area filled with seabags stacked high to the hangar bay doors, where spouses were offering their final words of solace and affection before letting go of their loved ones. Many of the Marines stood next to their girlfriends, parents, dogs, and children. My CO arrived with his wife and two children. Having already said good-bye to my husband two weeks before, I was keyed up to leave. I stood quietly in the corner, first talking to some of my Marines, then watching everyone else say good-bye. My CO's eleven-year-old son looked sadly off into the distance. In his family, our departure had hit him the hardest. At his age, he most critically needed his dad—these were the years that would come to define his manhood.

When the hour came for us to leave, around 0130, sorrow filled the CO's son's face as he saw the white buses that would take us on the first part of our long journey. Tears were suppressed as he tried to behave like a man for his dad. I turned away as they shared their last hug—one of those private moments in which our mind memorizes the last traces of a loved one's face. The CO returned momentarily, deeply moved and trying to resist the urge to look back. An officer whispered to him, "Sir, I hope that's the hardest thing you will have to do."

"I don't think it will be," the CO said.

That sentiment summed up all our hesitant thoughts. But as we envisioned the scheme of maneuver, the amassing of forces on the Iraqi side, and pushing through its center in trace of the infantry regiments, something told me it would not be the hardest moment.

★ ★ ★

The Middle East had interested me since I was young. That's why I had taken the trip to the Middle East during the Gulf War after I graduated from high school. From living in a Greek Orthodox monastery in Sinai, Egypt, to exploring the Bedouin culture in the Negev, to helping Kurdish refugees in Iraq, to traveling in Jordan, I had spent more than a year in the Middle East during the Gulf War and the first Palestinian intifada in Jerusalem. In Jerusalem I had seen someone stabbed as Scud missiles raced over our heads toward Tel Aviv. I wondered then if the gas masks we were given would be used. But still, I had no reservations about getting a map and taking a solo trip across Jordan. Bedouins and kind Arabs invited me into their homes and shared whatever they could with their mysterious young American guest. I always wore the full black chador out of respect for their beliefs and in order to travel inconspicuously. We shared stories, and they asked nothing of me in return. The things I saw and experienced during that time were both unbelievable and life changing. I couldn't make up some of the fantastic things that occurred.

I laugh now when I remember crossing the Allenby/Hussein Bridge from Jordan into Israel in 1991. It was a long ordeal because of all the checkpoints and screening. I was still dressed in the chador and took a taxi into Jerusalem. I shared a cab with an older, aristocratic Palestinian businessman from Hebron who had been visiting family in Jordan. "There are stabbings everywhere; you must take extra care," he warned me. He invited me to stay with his family if I were to travel through Hebron. I arrived in the old city of Jerusalem at dusk; it was the most haunting place I had ever seen. The ancient city was deserted. But a Crusade-era wall, lit on all sides, accentuated its height and surrounded the ancient city. The deserted stone alleyways twisted through the city, leaving new travelers disoriented. Maze-like passageways, ascending and descending, led to little wooden doors or emptied into courtyards. Without anyone on the street to guide me, there was no way to know where I was going.

The gate I entered led me through cobblestone streets into a network of stone passageways leading to the nexus of the old city through the Christian quarter. I decided to settle on the first pension that I found. Inside, I learned that the Israeli government had just imposed a curfew because of the Palestinian intifada. A soft-spoken German traveler told me that Ben Yahuda, a popular shopping area in the modern part of town, was open. It was within walking distance and still early yet. Excited from having just arrived in Israel, I decided to walk to the area to get something to eat. However, when I arrived at the crowded square of Ben Yahuda, I realized something was terribly wrong. I looked like an Arab in my chador. In the bustling square filled with mostly modern young Israelis in Western clothing, I drew stares very quickly. Young Israelis in American attire looked at me with disdain. After getting a quick bite to eat, I picked up my bag to leave. As I stood up, my Buck knife fell out. Discreetly, I placed it in my bag and began walking back to my pension. As I reached the end of the square, I heard the squealing tires of a military vehicle rapidly approaching. I rushed to get out of the way. But the armored Israeli military vehicle pulled in front of me. About ten Israeli SWAT-style personnel poured from the vehicle, and I was horrified to see that they were headed in my direction. Suddenly, I had ten machine guns pointed at me. They hand-cuffed me and pushed me inside the armored vehicle. I didn't have time to comprehend what was happening, only that I would likely get thrown in jail. As they drove me to a police station, I sat quietly trying to figure out what law I could have broken. Visions of *Midnight Express* filled my head, and I imagined the rest of my life in an Israeli prison.

When I arrived, my armed escorts led me to a police facility, and an investigator took me into a room to be questioned. I was frisked and then interrogated. They looked at me angrily with disgust. For the first time in my life I knew what it was like to be hated. But I didn't know why. As I removed my chador, my long blond hair cascaded out. It was only then that they saw clearly that I was not Arab. The interrogator looked up with a raised eyebrow. The whole scene derailed for them; the mental screen-play of righteous Israeli soldiers interrogating a possible terrorist evaporated, and an awkward silence settled in the room. They were embarrassed, as if they'd suddenly realized I was human, someone who could live next door to them instead of some dehumanized enemy. Realizing who I was just then—an American—they began backpedaling their hostility. They informed me politely that a woman had seen my knife fall to the ground and had called the police. I told them I kept it because I needed it to protect myself. Figuring I'd make the most of my experience, I tried to convince them to let me keep it.

"I travel alone, sir; it would be foolish of me to be without some form of self-defense."

He pondered it, looked at me, understood my reasoning, and told me if I got questioned again to tell them that he let me keep the knife. He handed me his business card and apologized for the confusion.

"It is illegal to carry such a weapon in this country. You know there is an intifada going on right now, right? We had several stabbings in the past week in the same area. But . . . well, under your circumstances, I can understand. Keep your knife. It's a confusing time for us," he said.

"I understand; thanks for your help."

"Shalom. Welcome to Israel."

But it was an innocent time for me, as I was far more naive and audacious then. At eighteen, I was fearless. Now at thirty, I had the same sense of curiosity, although the caution that accompanies experience prohibited me from the free-spirited daring of earlier days. I felt fear at the prospect of what lay ahead for my Marines, for the consequences of the war, and for me. But I also worried about the world, my family, and, above all, my husband. My promise to myself was that I would stay out of harm's way so that if he ever needed me, I would be there. My letters, I promised, would be positive. The problem was he had no way to write me, because I had no address yet. I was totally alone without him, and the thought that he couldn't even reach me frightened me. Even though it had been a month with no word from him, I tried to believe that at least he was getting my letters. I drew solace from that. These were the things I thought about as we sat on the white buses taking us to March Air Force Base for our flight to Kuwait. I had only hope and the unopened letter he had handed me before he left.

3

MATILDA

Freedom is not free, but the U.S. Marine Corps will pay most of your share.

—Ned Dolan

After an unremarkable but very long flight from California, we arrived at Kuwaiti International Airport at midnight and were immediately bused to a secure area. The dreamlike state that comes from being across the world was beginning to set in. Stadium lights lit the area we were in, leaving everything beyond shrouded in darkness. Huge concrete Jersey barriers, barbed wire, and guard towers would have prevented us from seeing anything anyway. We were issued ammo and rules of engagement (ROE) cards, explaining exactly when we could shoot someone, where we could shoot, and how. Strange sounds of hundreds of Marines loading their magazines broke the silence. As we were shuffled chaotically from one barrier to the next, we were asked to show I.D. and give our basic information to the Army personnel maintaining security. An Army Sergeant gave us our safety brief. The buses we would be taking to our staging area had heavy black curtains—we were told to keep them drawn because of all the ambushes and small arms fire the buses had received in the past. Our feet had barely touched the sand on the deck, and already we were the targets. Kuwait might be a "friendly" country, but some of its inhabitants were no friends of the U.S. military forces.

As we drove, I peeked through the curtains, trying to make out the modern urban sprawl that was Kuwait City. It looked a lot like America except for the trash littering the highway and the occasional early rising shepherd with his flock of sheep. After twenty hours of travel, we finally

31

arrived at base camp at Ali Al Salem, not far from the "highway of death," where Iraqi forces were driven to surrender in three days during the Gulf War. The jet lag would take a few days to pass, we were advised. But I would not sleep that night. None of us would. I watched my first Kuwaiti dawn and wondered how, in fact, I had ended up here. I had never thought it would be me. I didn't have any sense of perspective, as it was still dark and the unfamiliar camp was disorienting. I found a CONEX box, a metal container used to carry supplies in the holds of cargo ships and aircraft, and climbed on top to watch the scattered activity beginning to form around the camp.

Our first day was spent in long-overdue sleep as we settled in. The tent city grew before our eyes. Sewers and water pipes were being installed, and we had to traverse the camp by using one-foot-wide planks to cross massive ditches. Post offices, chow halls, and medical clinics were erected every day as new buses came in carrying hundreds of thousands of new personnel. Endless rows and columns of dusty beige tents stretched into the horizon. Possibly two hundred thousand U.S. military were now in our area of responsibility (AOR), which included Kuwait and surrounding countries.

★   ★   ★

It was February 2003. The combination of anxiety and jet lag took its toll. I had dreams of aerial bombardments, of enemy fire. It didn't help that we were told we were within range of enemy artillery. We were clearly vulnerable. Rumors were out of control. Daily, the situation grew more unpredictable as NATO countries still refused to back the United States. Other camps littered the AOR: Al Jaber, Coyote, Matilda, Camp Commando, Camp Doha, Udari Range, TAA Viking. Some were logistical camps, others training areas, some air bases.

Days in our rear area, the area away from the front line of troops, were spent going from meeting to meeting and chow to chow. We slept a great deal and exercised not at all. We couldn't travel anywhere without our gas masks, weapons, and uniforms, so physical training always involved dragging at least twenty pounds of equipment around without the promise of a shower after. Anything we could do to minimize dirtiness helped. Our camp was a staging area, and all of the forces were expected to be there for only a couple weeks. In a matter of days, my unit would move to the remote areas that housed the ground combat elements of the 1st Marine Division, the sleepy-eyed executioners who would bring hell with them on their drive north. Their central headquarters was called Matilda. Matilda was named after the Aussie national anthem, "Waltzing Matilda," a song adapted from the Solomon Islands during World War II. Australia was the staging grounds for 1st Marine Division's island-hopping campaign, and Australia's legendary status as a liberty paradise continues to the present day. Everyone loved Matilda, I was told.

The first week in Ali Al Salem was mostly a period of orientation and climate adaptation. In the distance was a vast unattractive desert, and somewhere in the northwest horizon, Baghdad. It was a mere 329 miles away, like driving from New York to Boston. A mere eight thousand miles away lay home in California, and there and throughout the world, people were protesting the battle I was about to fight.

As we shuttled on a convoy between camps, we drove on the highways of Kuwait. It was the first time that I felt we were no longer participating in an exercise. The CO had told us as much before we headed out.

"Well, gents, this is not practice anymore. Get your ass in gear and pay attention. I don't have time for you to screw off, fall asleep, or get one of your fellow Marines shot. Are you all ready to go?"

"Absolutely, sir!" said one of the Marines.

"Fuck, yeah!" said another. The CO looked at him, shook his head, and smirked.

★   ★   ★

Every time I left base I prayed. With the possibility of rounds being sent downrange, you've got to say every prayer you remember. It was like Pascal's wager: even though the existence of God is not something readily understood, you must accept it at face value. If you believe, you have everything to gain and nothing to lose. But if you don't believe, you can lose everything. Atheists even uttered God's name, even if it was just a "God help me!" or "Oh, God, what are we doing here?" or even "Goddamn!" The fact was, Marines had just been killed outside the gates, and there were people out there who wanted to kill us. Convoys were taking sniper fire all the time—we had heard the stories and seen the bullet holes on the sides of humvees.

We rode in our convoy over the dismal Kuwaiti desert. The only thing that held our interest, besides the flocks of sheep and shepherds, was the Kuwaiti drivers racing past. We regarded them with suspicion, wondering if one was suddenly going to grab an AK-47 and go to town. The Kuwaitis smiled, honked, and waved as they sped by. Smiles meant nothing, though. Who knew if some smiling Kuwaiti was suddenly going to lob a grenade at us?

★ ★ ★

After placing our weapons in condition 1 by inserting magazines and putting a round in the chamber, ready for any immediate threat, we assumed a defensive posture by staggering the vehicles on both sides of the road, spaced apart at wide intervals. Each vehicle contained an equal share of leaders; that way, if one vehicle were to be engaged, all the key leaders wouldn't be in one spot. The weapons we carried also organized us—those with larger weapons were placed in the back of the vehicles so that they had clear shots toward the threat. I loaded my 9mm and my M16 with full magazines. My M16 was my lifeblood, my security blanket. It is hard to describe to civilians how important a weapon is to a Marine. As early as boot camp, Marines are indoctrinated into the cult of the weapon. Christians wear crosses; Marines carry weapons.

Marines never, ever say "my gun" or "piece." During boot camp, mantras such as "this is my rifle" and other ditties help get it through the recruits' heads that the weapon is the livelihood of the Marine. Throughout boot camp, Officer Candidates School, every training exercise, and real-life operation, Marines carry their weapons. But not like a suitcase, a wallet, or lunch. Carrying a weapon is a precise, learned skill requiring continual awareness and discipline. No good Marine would ever point a weapon at another Marine without intending to shoot. It's called muzzle awareness: you always know where your weapon is pointed. It is a very, very bad thing to "flag" someone—to unknowingly wave your weapon at someone. Marines have specific weapons-carrying positions: tactical carry, alert, and ready. A Marine can look at another Marine and judge his skill just by the way he handles his weapon. Drill training reinforces the importance of understanding and becoming intimately familiar with the size, shape, inside, and outside of the weapon. Marines assemble, disassemble, and learn more mantras about weapons conditions, characteristics, height, weight, recoil, firing distance, and every imaginable aspect of the weapon. Marines learn to fire while prone, sitting, kneeling, standing, and moving. "Every Marine is a rifleman," and all Marines can kill equally well. Ask a Marine what "front sight picture" is and see what he tells you.

Every Marine is an M16A2 service rifle–handling expert and can tell you from memory that the maximum effective range of an M16 service rifle at an area target is 2,624.8 feet, and it can fire eight hundred rounds per minute. The M16A2 service rifle is a lightweight, magazine-fed, air-cooled, gas-operated, shoulder-fired weapon, capable of firing either semiautomatic or three-round bursts. A Marine can probably assemble and disassemble a weapon blindfolded. Marines have cleaned weapons so many times that they know the intimate texture of the ribbed hand guards on the upper receiver and the cold steel power of the trigger. It's almost a sexual thing. That's why Marines are encouraged to give their rifles names like Stacy, Melissa, Monica, Electra, Lisa, or, in my case, Max. Your weapon is the only thing that will be by your side in combat, so you better know it intimately.

★   ★   ★

We set out on our four-vehicle convoy down the highway where American firepower had made scrap of Saddam's army twelve years before. Hundreds of SUVs passed us on the road, mostly containing coalition military. Rumors circulated that coalition forces had rented every SUV in Kuwait, and even private Kuwaiti citizens were offering their vehicles for rent. Shepherds and camel caravans littered the medians and spread out, sprinkled intermittently across the landscape. The shepherds wore traditional red scarves with long, flowing dishdashas as they moved their flocks along leisurely; they were oblivious to the streams of military vehicles carrying loaded weapons. We were ready to fire at any sign of danger. The rules of engagement had grown liberal. If you take shots or are threatened, fire with necessary force, we were told. As somber faces in Cadillacs and young Kuwaiti military passed us, we were at first on edge. The third car, however, contained a family with two children waving in joy at the prospect of seeing Americans. Even the mother smiled as they passed us; her shrouded eyes, lined with kohl, looked back at me curiously. Our eyes met for a moment until their car passed. How different our worlds were. Sergeant Sheeler, on the left flank of the vehicle, held his M16 at the ready, looking like he was ready to kill anything that moved. Another vehicle with a small child passed, and Sergeant Sheeler's body tensed as he moved his hands into position along his rifle. But as the child waved, he, too, relaxed and returned the wave and smiled. Most cars responded similarly, and we were impressed by the hospitable posture most Kuwaitis had taken toward us.

"Ma'am, do you think I should be waving back?"

"I don't see why not. You're probably one of the only Americans they've seen." I wasn't sure that was the right answer—for all I knew, any kid could open up on us with an AK-47. He waved at a boy in another passing car, and the kid smiled back enthusiastically, giving us the peace sign.

"You're right, ma'am. If some American soldier gaffed me off when I was ten, I'd probably remember it for the rest of my life."

It's true what some say about perception being everything. During my previous travels in the Middle East, I had formed many conceptions about Arabs that were hard to shed. I had mixed opinions about Arabs, probably because trying to fit Arabs into a single mold is like trying to lump laid-back Californians with high-strung New Yorkers under the banner of "American." Among the Bedouin in the Negev, in Sinai, and in Jordan, I had found openness, hospitality, and spirits free from hatred. They were the true salt of the earth, wanderers and nomads who made their living without owning more than they could carry with them. Among the Palestinians, I had seen the sadness of an oppressed culture in the throes of despair; some with a fiery passion for justice they felt was due them, some with hate for everyone but their own kind, and some silent, patient victims of their unpredictable state. Fundamentalists, traders, kind families, shrewd salesman, master linguists— Arabs were a diverse people. I had always remembered them as a culture whose one common trait was an unsurpassed hospitality, welcoming even those whom they did not know with tea or a warm greeting. It was hard for me to imagine the Arabs that had become Hussein's followers, the Ba'athists and Fedayeen, full of vehement hate and fundamentalist fury. It was hard for me to see the insurgents who believed the only way to remain true to their faith was to kill all those who weren't Muslim.

During the first intifada in Jerusalem, I saw precursors of this kind of hate. When the streets were closed at night to curtail the violence, I saw a man stabbed and violence erupt between Arab and Jew. I even had Palestinian children throw rocks at me. A group of eight-year-olds shouted at me, "America die! America die!" I had been in Jerusalem when the Scuds were launched overhead, gas masks issued, and war announced in the Gulf. Violence had been a part of life in every Arabic nation I visited, but has their history been much different than the general history of the world? If history had taught us anything, then what was it? In 1991, I helped an NGO in Jordan bring supplies into western Iraq. I saw the Iraqis intern their own people in prison camps. Kurds and Shi'ites sometimes waited for years before being released. They lived behind some barbed-wire gate, guilty of nothing but their ancestry, hoping each day for even food. Some had the dubious benefit of an erratic government lottery system, and every year the lucky few would be released. Others would die, or be gassed, or forced to endure prolonged torture. Saddam was the epitome of a culture gone wrong; his time was coming to an end. The faces of those imprisoned Iraqis I would never forget—waiting silently for their freedom.

★   ★   ★

Camp rules: that's what we were faced with. Angles at which you could wear your boonie cover, Port-O-Potty rules, rules about where you could brush your teeth and where you could walk, saluting rules, weapons-carrying rules—rules on rules, heretofore unsurpassed in Marine Corps history. Just as when junior Marines faced with too much free time resort to picking fights and playing football, certain Marine leaders, when faced with too little to do, fill the void with chickenshit. Some grunt leaders asked their Marines to do things like grow mustaches to avoid being mistaken for Iraqis when they crossed the line, only to later tell them to shave them off because many Iraqis had mustaches. Others kept the Marines occupied filling sandbags, only to empty out the day's labor at night. But the worst were the rules in the camp, which were not posted anywhere and seemed to change daily. I was having some serious anger issues over penny-ante shit. Everywhere we went, there were new rules to follow. We bitched about each new rule because complaining was, at least for now, authorized. There's a common saying in the Corps, "The only time to worry about a Marine is when he stops bitching."

It was probably the junior enlisted who had it the worst. Working parties went on 24/7, and sometimes a Corporal would return after six hours spent building large wooden frames for the tents, only to realize he was "volunteering" on another working party in ten minutes. But the officers didn't have it so great, either. We were shifted from meeting to meeting, camp to camp. We were passing once again over the Kuwaiti highways with weapons drawn, expecting to take fire at any moment. Then there was talk about being gassed. I kept thinking it was only a matter of time before my face was melted off by some chemical attack. We had taken the classes and watched countless videos about the effects of nuclear, biological, or chemical attacks, known as NBC. Skin blistering, eyes burning, convulsions, bubbling blood, burning, melting skin, paralysis, death—pictures of all of it flashed in front of our faces. We lived day to day with the thought that any of these possibilities could be our fate.

4

THE WAR PLAN

We sleep safe in our beds because rough men stand ready in the night to visit violence on those who would do us harm.

—attributed to George Orwell

After Officer Candidates School at Quantico, Virginia, the 250 Lieutenants who made it through went on to the next stage of officer training, relocating a couple miles away to a secluded training area known as The Basic School or TBS. It looks like a college campus, and in many ways it is. They call it "the big suck," "total bullshit," or various other non-euphemistic niceties. For six months we learn to be leaders of Marines. Many of us become close friends in the process: Ruehl, Jimenez, McNair, Bock, and Hembrick—these faces flash before me as if it were yesterday. All officers in the Corps have come through here. There I was, standing with my TBS platoon in a circle, wearing woodland cammies, my face cammied up, freezing my ass off while we listen to one of our instructors lecture about patrolling. Captain Quinn tells us point-blank, "Hesitation kills."

One of the Lieutenants is about to ask for more clarification when Captain Quinn gets an intense look on his face and continues, "Hesitation kills in combat. I knew an officer in Haiti who was on patrol with his Marines, and a mob started gathering around them. Turns out half the mob was Haitian police who were trying to prevent the Marines from witnessing them kill some civilians. It was pretty clear the situation was about to get shitty, and they were outnumbered. The Marine officer, without thinking, opened fire even before he gave the order. It wasn't necessary to do so. The Marines began firing, and the police quickly disengaged and ran. The officer knew if he had hesitated even for a moment, they would have ended up dead. Instead, he saved the civilians as well. You've got to be quick when you're out there, or else you could be dead."

★   ★   ★

If nothing else, prewar camps provided a tremendous sense of camaraderie. I met old friends from my earlier enlisted years in the Corps again; old memories were shared and new stories exchanged. Every day, I would bump into someone I knew directly or was introduced to someone I knew indirectly. Not a meal went by that I wasn't exchanging stories about some Gunny I worked with or Lieutenant I went to TBS with. Sergeants had heard about me from peers. Or a Sergeant I had gone to boot camp with would recall the times we shared. It was amazing how the old-boy network connected everyone. I scanned every group of Marines I encountered to see what friendly face emerged and called out to me in reunion. I looked forward to these chance encounters. It was during the war I met Lieutenants Chontosh, Moulton, and Spencer: three Marines who were vastly different from one another, yet whose actions would shape the war to come. They really couldn't be more different: Chontosh was a crazy leader who was on his Colonel's shit list as quickly as he was later considered for the Medal of Honor. Moulton, on the other hand, a Harvard graduate who seized an opportunity, was a model Lieutenant whose newness to the Corps didn't stop him from playing a critical role in shaping the Iraqis' future. Finally, there was Spencer, a Roman-nosed, prior-enlisted hard-charger who managed to make comedy out of every situation. We were all young officers, learning how to be leaders while simultaneously being leaders of Marines. I was yet to discover the crucial contributions these young Lieutenants had made in the success of the initial ground war in Iraq.

★   ★   ★

Anyone who doesn't believe in cycles hasn't studied science. Moon cycles, trends in battle, patterns in nature—history is cyclical in nature, not linear, no matter what your junior high history teacher might have said. Military intelligence likes to define these patterns as "indications" and "warnings." These would define our battle space. Saddam Hussein was its centerpiece. The dictator builds himself palaces a hundred times the size of Buckingham Palace. Shrines, gilded statues, and family trees tracing his "royal heritage" in plated gold are all reminders of his dominion. Thousands fly flags in his honor, and everywhere walls are covered with larger-than-life murals of the man who forced his will on the people to make him the supreme leader and dictator. We had seen the propaganda Saddam wanted us to see—the burning American flags and crowds of Iraqis chanting anti-American slogans—but I wasn't buying it.

Twenty miles away, back in Matilda area, I was hoping the Generals in charge knew what they were doing. As I left the officer tent, it was approaching dusk, and suddenly a new line of tents lay before me, unfamiliar and obliterating my sense of direction. I gained my bearings after only a few moments of wandering the wrong way. Newly dug ten-foot-deep trenches, apparently for sewer lines, stretched as far as the eye could see. Every row of tents contained a labyrinth of trenches, Porta-Johns, washing stations, and smoke pits for the smokers. This was, sadly, my life at base camp—a surreal adventure where one had to accept the current day as the only one that contained any truth.

★   ★   ★

Mail on deployment was huge. Scratch that. Mail was life. It is the best thing that can happen on a deployment. A little reminder from home can go a long way for a Marine. Letters started coming from friends and family. But there was still nothing from my husband, even though I knew he was less than ten miles away. It was clear that some idiot in the mailroom was routing our letters all the way to the United States and back. The idea made my mind turn to thoughts of slowly and violently killing whoever was responsible. Even after I scribbled gigantic letters all over the front of my letters that said, "In Country: Unit-to-Unit Mail," I doubted Peter was getting mine yet, either. I was close to stealing a humvee and driving out there myself. The only thing that prevented me from walking was that I had no idea where he was.

Many of the Marines shared their letters for the amusement of others. All the officers from my unit gathered together in a tent while mail was being distributed. One of the officers had received a stack of letters from a grade school class in his hometown. We sat around the command center, and he passed one to each of us. Many of them had crayon drawings of Marines and military equipment; some even drew American flags or Iraqis. The XO, Major Cepeda, shared his letter with us: "Hey check out this one, it's great: 'I'm glad I'm writing to a Marine because Marines *rock!*'" We chuckled.

Lieutenant Debucher chimed in, "Oh, that's nothing, you've gotta hear this one: 'Dear Marine, Thank you for defending us from terrorists.

What is it like to be near Saddam? Is war scary? What does it feel like to know that you are going to die?"

"Wow! That's harsh!" the XO said while smoking a cigarette. "I thought these letters were supposed be encouraging! That makes me want to kill myself. Talk about pessimism; is this kid on our side?"

While some world citizens protested, others dumped their German and French wines due to the lack of support for the war by those countries. I was bemused by the fact that because we were liberating the Iraqis, they couldn't be demonized with the usual propaganda, like the "Nips," "Gooks," and "Krauts" of previous wars. Instead of being encouraged to hate the people we'd be fighting, we were encouraged to hate the pacifist Europeans who wouldn't help out this time around. Either way, I knew what most of America did not know: come hell or high water, we were already on our countdown to war.

★ ★ ★

As our as-yet-unknown D-Day approached, we were briefly allowed access to e-mail and phones. Everyone else called home, e-mailed, or somehow contacted their spouses and loved ones, but I had yet to receive even a letter. My heart tightened with a frustration I had never experienced before. My husband, along with me, was one of five thousand Marines parked on the front line—on Saddam's doorstep, in range of Saddam's enemy artillery fans whose range reached into Kuwait. We had known from the intelligence briefs we received that the threat was already there. If Saddam wanted to attack us, he could reach us. The stress was eating me alive.

My one consolation was the female hooch—the large, white Bedouin tent where all the units on Ali Al Salem corralled their female officers and SNCOs since there were only thirteen of us. We slept there and joined our units during the day. Because this was just a staging camp, it was a temporary fix. Few of us would actually stay here. Some of the females were pilots, others logisticians, one was with public affairs, and others were with different air wing support units.

We would spend our evenings complaining and laughing about the idiocy and adventures of the day. Sergeant Major Bowen, the senior enlisted in the tent and the Sergeant Major for our sister squadron from the East Coast, was one of my favorites. She was a statuesque woman, resembling a female bodybuilder, the type who didn't take crap from anyone. Her voice boomed, and her no-nonsense attitude made it clear she was a Sergeant Major. When she walked in the room, you knew she was there, as though she emanated some kind of superwoman rays. I was pretty sure she could take down someone with one punch. We would start the battle together, then move our separate ways farther north. She came roaring in the tent, "All right, ladies, mama's home. Tell me, what's the word?"

Among the other Marines in base camp—all 6,000 of them, 5,947 of whom were male—our tent was referred to as "the palace." This was the running joke among the males. Since the chow tent was only a couple tents down, lines would form at dawn as hundreds of individuals waited for morning chow. The line extended past the front of our tent, and we would often hear comments.

"That's the female officer hooch," one Marine would say.

"I don't know what it is about those officers, man, but the higher the rank, the higher they go up on my scale."

"It's the uniforms, I'm telling you, there's nothing like a woman who outranks you in uniform."

"It's just like Jack Nicholson said in that movie, man . . ."

"Stop, dude! Don't say it! I'll fucking explode if you say that shit, son."

We were essentially the only females they would see for months—or for however long we were here. Some of the Marines had visions of us prancing around in Victoria's Secret underwear while primping ourselves. Farther north, Peter was catching Marines watching females through binoculars, giggling like Beavis, he would later tell me. The reality was we never really undressed past our physical training gear. We got showers about every three days. We didn't shave our legs or armpits during the duration of the operation. What was very clear to us was that none of us—not even the single women—had any intention of hooking up with any of them, under any circumstances. Most of us were married, and some of us were dual-spouse military. Those of us who suffered the stress of the wife/Marine dichotomy found that the only way to survive was to assume Dr. Jekyll and Mr. Hyde personalities, bottle it up, and focus on the job.

One of our tent mates, a female Gunnery Sergeant named Diane Raber, was being sent home. The stress had gotten to her. Her husband was with her, in a forward unit, and she said her good-byes to him before she returned home.

"I would rather one of us were at home," she told us, "but I can't do my job knowing he's in harm's way."

A lot of Marines didn't understand what we were going through. But Gunnery Sergeant Raber's husband did. He would often visit us to see how we were holding up. We were glad for his visits, as there were other females also at the breaking point. Many of us were being put in combat roles we hadn't expected, and a few were not comfortable with the idea. We talked about that among ourselves, but we never let our male counterparts know.

Just then, the Sergeant Major burst into the tent and belted out, "Listen up, ladies, don't go outside the tent right now!"

"What's going on?"

"The British just moved into the tents across the way."

"So, what's the problem with that?"

"Well, the Brits took over the hygiene area also. They're all stripped down in the open and are scrubbing down their junk in front of everyone!"

"Holy shit, that's disgusting!"

"Yeah, and these aren't the Royal Marines, they're the fat, nasty wingers. Ladies, trust me, you don't want to go out there."

The Brits had hijacked the area where we brushed our teeth and did our hair in the morning. And there was no stopping them. Crossing past the Brits' tent area, we were always met with the unexpected sight of a naked, grown man lathering up his private parts with soap and water, without shame or discretion. We were horrified. The Brits smiled at us. They seemed to have a different definition of privacy than we did.

★ ★ ★

Naked Brits were the least of my problems—I was having some issues with my own unit. The senior collections officer, First Lieutenant Debucher, seemed to have hijacked all the work. Not only had I missed meeting after meeting because he lied to me and told me there was nothing going on, but he belittled me in front of the other officers. It was clear to me that Debucher wished I had not come. He was very popular with all the other officers. He'd tell one joke after another and have them all laughing. I got the impression that he was not entirely on board with the idea of women in combat, since I often overheard him talking about women as though they were all crazed, emotional things. As for my Marines, I hadn't seen them for days. After a day or two, it was clear that I was being deliberately left out of the loop. When I would ask Debucher what was happening, he would simply say, "There's nothing to concern yourself with." Lisa didn't seem to mind this as much as me. I wasn't sure what to do about the situation, but I knew I had to do something. That same day, the Gunnery Sergeant from my section came by. He was a well-intentioned Marine, soft-spoken and friendly.

"Ma'am. I came to find you and pass you some word."

"Who sent you?"

"Well, I'm actually coming on my own, because I know . . . well, it seemed that you weren't being included in the meetings."

"Gunny, I realize you're trying to help," I told him, "but let me fight this battle. Thanks for looking out, but I need to go find out for myself."

I was furious. My blood boiled at the thought that Lieutenant Debucher was doing this to me again. Not only was it belittling to have a subordinate passing word, but to be deliberately left out of the loop because of some idiot's ego was infuriating. I was certainly not going to fight a war with another Lieutenant who was my boss but whom I couldn't trust. I marched over to the male officers' tent and asked to speak to the Lieutenant. Only Captain Hamill, one of the flight commanders, was there.

"He's not here, Lieutenant Blair."

"Do you know where he went, sir?"

"He went to a division collections meeting. Shouldn't *you* be there?"

"If I knew about it, I would be, sir." I had no choice but to go to the XO, the next in my chain of command, but he had gone, too. I was waiting by the officers' tent when the CO approached me.

"What's going on, Jane?"

"Sir, I'm waiting for the XO."

"He won't be back until tonight. Jane, what's going on? I'm getting that 'look.'"

"Sir, I don't want to go above the chain of command."

"There's nothing the XO and I wouldn't discuss, so you might as well tell me."

I reluctantly spoke.

"Sir, I know I'm new to the squadron, but I don't really feel like one of the officers yet. I'm not getting any word and have been left out of almost everything. I don't even know where my Marines are because the Lieutenant senior to me won't tell me. I feel like I'm deliberately being kept out of the loop. Sir, I don't want to say that it's because I'm a female, but it's happening to Lisa, too."

The CO looked down and thought about it for a minute.

"Let me talk to the Lieutenant and the XO and see what I find out. In the meantime, you are an officer in this squadron, and there is no reason for you to be left out. However, I fully expect you to be at our meetings here every night. If you come by and spend some time with the officers, they will get to know you, and you won't feel left out anymore. Come and play cards with us and get to know some of them. If anyone leaves you out of the loop, it will have to be in front of all of us. No one can hide in the daylight. Put that in your leadership book, Jane."

Although the CO never told me if the Lieutenant had intentionally left me out of the loop, I showed up at the male officers' tent as he had suggested. Lisa refused to go, though. I went by myself to play cards. While playing, the men passed the word. The CO was right. All the officers in each section ran through their tasking list for the day. I noticed Debucher ignored me, pretending I wasn't there. Despite this, I had gotten word from the top, and no one could interfere with that. I did this every night. Because of the change, I also got to know what the Marines in my section were doing and was finally participating in the upcoming missions with them. Things were starting to get better, but I still couldn't help feeling like there was some premeditated animosity against me, for what reason I couldn't guess.

★   ★   ★

That morning, most of the officers and Staff NCOs made their way to division headquarters for operations and intelligence briefings. Once again, our convoy left the barbed-wire perimeter, and our eyes met with the tower and road guards manning their .50-caliber machine guns. Our trip led us only five kilometers away to another city of tents, lined with hundreds of Porta-Johns, vehicles, and generators, a sandy desert filled with barbed-wired forests and CONEX box fortresses.

We had arrived at 1st Marine Division—home of about eight thousand ground-pounding, hard-charging, devil-crushing grunt Marines. There was no mistaking that you were in grand central Marine country. This nucleus was once again fondly known as "Matilda" and was the heart of Marine Corps operations. It was an all-male center, with a couple females, such as me, peripherally attached to the whole. We had come for our G-2 and G-3 intelligence and operations meeting to this part of the tactical assembly area because we were in direct support of them, as one of their primary imagery, surveillance, and reconnaissance assets. We would be providing the division and all its subordinate units with critical intelligence that would help save Marines' lives and help leaders make decisions on the battlefield. Our UAV squadron, although technically part of the wing, would operate like a ground unit, following in trace of the grunts. We were flyers, but we supported the ground combat element.

Several cages stood in front of the division command post—a series of geodesic dome tents surrounded by barbed wire and antennae. The 1st

Marine Division had come up with the bright idea to set up chickens at the perimeter of camps to test for indications of NBC weapons. The grunts would take chickens and pigeons with them to the front line. When they saw poor Henny Penny fall, they would set the alert for an NBC attack. The code word for such an attack was "Gas! Gas! Gas!" Those were the three most frightening words I could ever imagine hearing.

One of the chicken cages was labeled "Geraldine." She looked ill fed, like she was the sole survivor of a nuclear apocalypse. Based on her appearance, I wasn't sure she was going to make it to the start of the war. An obscene number of antennas surrounded the tents, known fondly as "ant hills." Huge satellite dishes flanked the entrance like sentinels. In order to enter, you first had to pass the scrutiny of the Marine who checked badges for proper clearances—an overmuscled Gunnery Sergeant who took his job very seriously. Once cleared, you pushed your way through layers of tent openings that was reminiscent of crawling back into the womb and almost as pleasant—multiple Velcro flaps swallowed you in this tent universe. After pushing through, you arrived inside a laptop corridor heaven, where rows of laptops spread across the span of the largest tent area, with so many top brass passing by it could blind you. After pushing your way past the Lieutenant Colonel corridor, I swerved to avoid Majors who sneered because we were walking on their turf. These tents composed the command posts—various nodes of command and control. Inside were epicenters of operation. The S-3, or operations center, filled one wing of the tent, the S-2, Intelligence/All Source Fusion Center, the other. The tunnel-like tents converged in the center into a large circular tent, which was the CG's briefing area, or watch officer area. Flat-screen televisions lined the front wall of the tent, with a giant projector screen in the center. CNN and FOX News flashed on various screens. It was the first time since being deployed that I had seen a television. The news was all about us. I wanted to stay and watch, but I was in the way of the continual train of officers passing by.

The division's G-2 intelligence was commanded by a Lieutenant Colonel, an impressive and well-spoken officer who introduced himself, then guided us through the entire I MEF intelligence picture. The MEF was the main effort of the Marine Corps' assault on Iraq. The Marines sitting there were a composite of the leadership structure, from infantry battalion COs to operations officers and an assortment of field-grade Majors, Lieutenants Colonel, and Colonels, and the company-grade Captains and SNCOs. Most looked hardened, with faces that were worn with sweat and weather. It was rare to see these men smile; they had a steel-hard bearing and were about as nice as a rattlesnake. Some passed around dip tobacco, grabbed a wad, and shoved it in their mouths. A lot of them turned their water bottles into spit cups and had a talent for getting all that shit into the tiny opening without spilling the black tobacco juice. The Lieutenant Colonel promptly started the meeting and mapped out the entire enemy battle space picture. Then he guided us through the MEF scheme of maneuver—the Marine Corps plan of action for executing the war. Next, he mapped out the Division's plan. Since we were in direct support of the division, this would be our lifeblood. Finally, each RCT intelligence officer spoke.

From what I had heard, the overall plan for 1st Marine Division for the first ninety-six hours was this: 7th Marines was the IMEF main effort. On order, air strikes would be launched throughout Iraq to soften the targets for ground forces to breach the border to seize seven key objectives. The main effort of the attack would assault Basra, destroying the Iraqi 51st Mechanized Division and seizing the Zubayr Pumping Station Complex, otherwise known as the "Crown Jewel" Objective. The crown jewel was the strategic oil pumping station that effectively controlled the gas oil separation plants (GOSPs) in southern Iraq. These GOSPs were essentially the lion's share of wealth in Iraq. Without them, the Iraqis lost their main source of income from their petroleum production. Next on the plan, the MSRs or main roads would be guarded to allow follow-on forces to move through secured areas.

As for the Army's role, the Army's 3rd Infantry Division and 101st Airborne would secure the MSRs from An Nasiriyah to Baghdad and push their way through Baghdad to seize the city.

RCT-7, my brother unit, would breach near Safwan, and Force Recon would seize Safwan Hill, secure MSRs for follow-on forces, and push its way through Az Zubar to gain control of Al Basra and the crown jewel. Both my husband and I were part of RCT-7; therefore, both our units would play a key role in the overall mission's success.

RCT-5 would breach west and push its way through the GOSP area to gain control of the reserve and eliminate enemy threats in the area. It would then push north and rejoin tanks and armored forces (traveling north through Route Edith, the main effort attack area) to secure Highway 8 for follow-on forces, including Alamo Bridge and the Ramalayah area. This operation would be known later as Operation Gambit.

RCT-1 and Task Force Tarawa, 2nd Marine Expeditionary Brigade consisting of RCT-2 and the elements of 2nd Marine Air Wing (MAW), would push farther north to secure areas and the main roads for follow-on forces. They would do a relief in place to turn over their position with the Army in An Nasiriyah in order to maintain control of the area.

THE WAR PLAN 49

The British would seize control of Al Faw and Umm Qasr and relieve I MEF forces in place and provide security when it pushed north.

The Lieutenant Colonel explained that he wanted us to remain flexible after that; once objectives were captured, a more solidified plan would arise for the push toward Baghdad. The reason was that anything could happen. If RCT-7 were to receive heavy resistance or an NBC attack, RCT-5 would have to reinforce. On the other hand, both RCTs could push through without resistance and would be prepared to move forward.

As far as enemy forces were concerned, we assessed that Saddam had the majority of his forces in Baghdad in concentric rings in order of strength. The Medina and Baghdad armies were the redline trigger forces, and if we crossed that terrain, they could launch an NBC attack. The Fedayeen and Republican Guard remained in the inner circle, a final but intense defense in the heart of Baghdad. It was reminiscent of Sultan Mohammed's forces during the siege of Constantinople in 1453. Like the Ottoman caliph who had an elite fighting force of orphans known as the Janissaries who fought to the death, Saddam had the Fedayeen, meaning the "Men of Sacrifice," also mostly orphans who were trained not to surrender until death, whereupon they would be made martyrs and live in a paradise of virgins. The Republican Guard was a loyal, proud fighting force of more than ten thousand. Although he kept these forces in Baghdad, Saddam's overconfidence made me wonder if he had an ace up his sleeve. Somehow I doubted it.

After explaining to my liaison team what was going on, the Lieutenant Colonel told us we would have a big operational meeting the following day and could rendezvous with different units at that time. Debucher, who had just showed up separately, shot me dirty looks when he came in after the meeting was almost finished and asked me what I was doing there.

"I'm getting the information for our unit to brief back to the CO and the officers."

"Well, only one of us needs to go to these, and since I'm senior, it just needs to be me and Gunny. They don't want a lot of people showing up in these secret briefings," he said.

"There were more than a hundred people here, I don't think they noticed a couple more."

"Well, whatever, why don't you go help our unit with logistics or something. That's where we need help."

Lisa and I were pissed off but together decided we'd have to figure out a plan to address this issue later. Worse than that, when we returned to our camp after the brief, Debucher never passed the information we obtained from Matilda to the CO during that evening's officer meeting.

Since the regiments flanked both sides of 1st Marine Division in Camp Matilda, just a couple klicks in each direction, we decided to pay RCT-7 a visit. As explained earlier, since we were on the forefront of combat, all the tactical assembly areas were arranged into RCTs. RCT-7, RCT-5, and RCT-1 were remote base camps where the elements of the combined regimental task forces were pre-staged before moving forward. They were primitive camps with less equipment and facilities than anywhere else. RCT-7 was a huge tent city surrounded by gun parks, motor transportation lots, where all the vehicles were stored, and a mess of Marine Corps gear. They were all resident Twentynine Palms units—basically, our warrior brothers. It was true grunt land, a temporary home to some of the most vicious, hard-core, well-trained desert fighters you'd never hope to cross paths with.

There were Marines there who hadn't showered in twenty-one days, ate only MREs, and received only one piece of mail in a month and a half of deployment. There were no phones, no liberty trips, no televisions. They had just gotten Porta-Johns; before, they had used a wooden ammo crate placed against the back of a tent within view of passersby. They had all gotten some Kuwaiti virus that infected just about everyone in the vicinity. There was no water to wash their hands. They all knew it would get far worse. They were already burning their shit periodically in fifty-gallon drums using diesel fuel to light the fire.

None of them had seen a General around or a Colonel—the highest-ranking officer and their unit commander. The top-ranking officers stayed mostly in Camp Commando and Al Jaber—the big camps where they allegedly had cold soda and Häagen-Dazs in an air-conditioned chow hall. If in response to this a Marine complained and said, "That's bullshit!" that Marine would quickly be "lifed out" by the company Gunny, meaning his life would flash in front of him as the Gunny reminded him first, that he was not being gassed, second, that in Chosin they walked 125 miles in subzero temperatures, and third, that in World War II they never got to change their boots and everyone got trench foot. So who gave a shit if there was Häagen-Dazs, because that shit just made you fat, weak, and ineffective in battle. The grunts had a perverse pride in the hardships they endured, even as they cursed the Marines in the rear areas living the high life with actual showers and fresh food. Some of them may have longed for creature comforts secretly, but if you even suggested to a Marine from RCT-7 that he might enjoy a transfer to the wing or to a logistical support unit such as Combat Service Support Battalion (CSSB), he'd punch you in the throat. Marines are harsh critics of those who do not measure up to their degree of severity. These men were able to cast aside pride, fear, and possessions as mere objects, indulgences for the weak. The privation made them hard, and it made them mean. Some of the Lieutenants speculated that this might be deliberate, that the RCTs were thrown out into the middle of this featureless desert with crap food and barely enough water in order to get them good and pissed off and ready to kill. If that was the plan, it worked.

It was a basic rule set by former Marine Corps Commandant Krulak that the junior-ranking Marines ate before everyone else, and the officers ate last. The grunts expected only a last good meal before setting foot in Iraq or, more important, a call home. Things were not terrible, though, as the Company Gunny was quick to point out at any opportunity. It is, of course, the esprit de corps of the Marines themselves that makes things tolerable. Someone once asked what it was that made the Spartans such fearsome and deadly warriors. The answer: contempt for pleasure. At some level, most Marines understand this. Pleasure is a crutch.

As Lieutenant Bishop and I walked around grunt land, we instantly drew stares from everyone.

"Hey, Lisa," I said.

"Yeah?"

"Do I have something on my face?"

"No."

"Well, those Marines are staring at me like I do."

"I don't know what to tell you; maybe they know you."

"Doubtful."

"They probably just wish they did."

Lisa's husband was co-located in the tactical assembly area. She was as eager to see him as I was to see my husband. I suspected 3rd Artillery, 11th Marines—my husband's unit—was here as well. As I walked farther into grunt land, I kept getting stares. Most Marines stare at females because, let's face it, there weren't a lot of us. On the periphery of my vision, another Marine was staring hard. I was about to lock on him when suddenly I recognized Lieutenant Jimenez, a fellow TBS classmate.

"Lieutenant Blair!"

"Hey, Jimenez! What's up?" We slapped each other's backs heartily. He was a platoon commander for one of the infantry units here.

"It's great to see you. I couldn't believe my eyes. I see two females—you've got to understand, no one here has seen a female for a month or two—and suddenly I realized it was you!"

"Is that why we're getting these stares?"

"Oh yeah—we're all thinking, 'Females still do exist!' It's a real morale booster for them."

We chatted a while, then talked intelligence and planning. Jimenez pulled out a map. I was astounded by how little he had heard.

"So," he said, "most of Division is right along here, and our regiment is five kilometers forward of them. We had to secure this area with about two hundred Marines and that huge berm you see out there."

"Yeah, I saw it. It's pretty hard to miss. You guys are doing a good job securing the perimeter."

"So tell me since you're in the know, how many units are on the front line before us?"

I smirked at him.

He asked again, "There are other units in front of us, right?"

"Well, you see that berm over there?" I pointed one hundred meters ahead.

"Yes?"

"That would be the front line."

"Oh shit! I see. . . . No wonder we're pulling so much security!"

"Yeah, you're basically the front line for the whole operation. The Army's hiding out southwest of here. Camp Udaryi or something."

"Jesus Christ! I had no idea! No one tells us shit over here."

"Don't worry. You guys have a lot of good backup!" We both laughed. Negative thoughts were death out here. There had already been suicide attempts and one actual suicide. You had to keep a lighthearted, worry-free attitude or you were bound to lose it. I said good-bye and along the way ran into other people I knew from Twentynine Palms. After several chats, I walked across the tent camp to find my husband's unit.*

I learned that less than a half mile away was the home of 3/11 Artillery Battalion—"the king of battle." Their battalion slogan reads, "God fights on the side with the best artillery, God fights with 3rd Battalion." It was a rip-off of a Napoleonic slogan, edited for 3/11. This battalion, part of 11th Marine Regiment, was the major fighting force of the Marine Corps, often inflicting the most battle damage of any asset, all due to the M198 155mm howitzer. This was my husband's unit, and after more than a month with no news of him, I was about to see him. Suddenly, alarms went off behind me, vehicles began honking their horns, and everyone began donning and clearing their gas masks. Then the voice alarm came: "Gas! Gas! Gas!"

My heart started racing. Was this a drill or for real? I slid my gas mask over my head and continued on to the 3/11 tents in the distance. It took forever, and I could hear my heart beating fast and my lungs pull harder

---

*First Lieutenant Jimenez was later killed in a firefight in the Al Anbar Province while on his second deployment to Iraq.

to get more air. It was difficult to get used to wearing the mask, no matter how many times I put it on. I walked quickly toward the tent area. You weren't supposed to be out in the open during a gas alarm in case there were incoming rounds from Iraq. The tents were now right in front of me. I felt winded and hot. I had no idea how we would fight with our gas masks on. My face was already dripping with sweat, and the mask was full of steamy air.

I walked over to Peter's camp area. The place was deserted. I opened one of the tents. There was gear, but no one was around. My stomach began to clench. I was starting to feel as if there was no way of ever reaching Peter again, yet the guidon that held the small rectangular-shaped flag with unit symbol and number on it marked the fact that the site had not been abandoned.

A warrant officer appeared, but I couldn't see his face with his mask on. I asked him, with a muffled gas mask voice, "Where's 3/11?"

"Which battery?"

"Mike."

"They're out in the field." The field was an expression used when a unit was deployed or training.

"The field? Where's the field out here?"

"They're about twenty klicks out, rehearsing for D-Day."

"When are they due back?"

"Oh, within the hour. They should all be rolling back soon."

My time was limited, as we were due to leave before the hour's end. We had to get back before dark. My heart sank, but it was clear the Captain who was with us would just have to wait—as the saying goes, it's easier to ask forgiveness than permission. As I waited with little patience, I saw the unmistakable form of towed howitzers rolling back into the position. A heavy fog mixed with upswept sand devoured visibility, and I could only make out the head of the convoy. My plan was to walk to the convoy, and there I would see my husband in his MOPP suit, and somehow we would recognize each other.

Walking half a mile to the now-stopped convoy, I saw the Marines had dismounted and formed a circle around the CO, but no one looked familiar. One of the perimeter guards stopped me.

"3/11?" I pointed to the group of Marines.

"No, ma'am. 5/11. 3/11 will be back in a couple of hours."

I walked back to the battalion area, and to my chagrin, the Captain of my convoy motioned for me to hurry over because we had to leave. I quickly walked back into my husband's tent, left an apple, a note, and a coveted bag of Tootsie Rolls I had been saving for his Marines. As we pulled away, I heard the alarm for all-clear on the gas masks. It was just a drill. As I looked back, I could see in the dusty mist a chain of howitzers rolling in, back from the field. I missed him by minutes. With the shape of this battle, I didn't know if I would ever see him again. As I got in the humvee, I held my emotions in check so that the Marines who were with us would not know my disappointment.

5

COUNTDOWN

Make up your mind to act decidedly and take the consequences. No good is ever done in this world by hesitation.

—Thomas Huxley

Baghdad was collapsing in on itself. Defense ministers were ousted, dissension formed within the upper echelon, the Ba'ath party was being torn in two, power was shut off, and the police force stopped getting paid, all resulting in rampant robberies and prostitution.

Iraqi forces pushed toward the historical Al Faw peninsula—a place where they had seen both the Iran-Iraq War and the Gulf War originate. Judging from the number of forces that had been seen moving in that direction, I assumed they believed we would concentrate our attack from that area. During the Iran-Iraq War, the head of the Shatt al-Arab river fed into this area, and a dispute over who had lawful rights to this key terrain provided the final push to war between Iraq and Iran. During the Gulf War it shared similar importance. We sat looking north at some intimidating enemy threats: GHN-45s, Ababial-100s, Astro-11, and D-30s. This enemy equipment was all long-range artillery equipment, and most of it was positioned toward Kuwait and within range of us, should Saddam decide to launch a preemptive strike. We all hoped our air strikes would destroy these before the ground war was launched. Unless Saddam had something up his sleeve, we were confident we would tear through the border with minimal losses.

Since my unit was a collections asset, we would be following 1st Marine Division's advance to Baghdad. Yet we would be scanning the terrain and skies ahead, seeing exactly what would be in front of them. Mostly, I feared for my husband and all the brave boys of 7th Marines who would be taking out Chemical Ali and the 51st Mechanized Division. "Chemical Ali" was so named because he was in charge of the chemical weapons that had been used against the Iranians as well as the Kurds and other dissident Iraqis during previous Iraqi wars. If we destroyed Chemical Ali as well as the 51st Mech Division, the chances of Saddam deploying chemicals against us was minimal.

The word came down that we would be doing a site survey of our location near division in Kuwait. This would be our tactical assembly area, from which we would fly before and during the war. Our location was about five miles south of Camp Matilda, where most of 1st Marine Division, including my husband's unit, was located. On the following day, we packed up our cozy existence with the air wing units and moved to a new remote location where there was nothing but the Kuwaiti sand, our tents, and a small berm around our perimeter. Our luxuries all had been shed, and the privilege of real food was gone. It was MREs from here on out.

Our new location was a mere thirty kilometers from the border of Iraq and well within range of enemy weapons systems. Our fifty vehicles pulled into the barren desert spot at 1800, just as the sun was setting, and the CO started the clock for assembling camp.

"You have four hours. Go."

We did it in two.

★   ★   ★

Less than a few hours after assembling our tents, we experienced our first real sandstorm in Kuwait, and it hit us hard as we attempted to fight our way to the chow tent. Everything was being blown away around us—several tents had capsized and were about to be carried away by the wind. I was entirely covered with sand and dirt. Inside the chow hall, Marines held down the wooden poles in order to keep the tent from flying away. The chow hall was nothing more than a larger tent that served T-rations— basically larger versions of MREs—preprepared food out of containers. Our breakfast was reminiscent of the Mad Hatter's tea party, minus the tea and scones, as we shifted our seats, held the tables to keep them from collapsing, and grabbed food and light objects that were flying away. There was sand in all our food. But at the time we didn't know that this would be the best chow we would have in months.

★   ★   ★

Despite the weather, I walked up one of the sand berms and briefed the collections update in the command operations center. Lieutenant Debucher had backed off a little and hadn't made much of an appearance in the work area yet since we had relocated. I was grateful for the break and the ability to work. Since we would be supporting 5th Marines for the initial seventy-two hours of the war, we were focused on the strategic oil well areas in the south, including the five gas and oil separation plants (GOSPs) and the Ramyalah oil fields. We would look for indications and warnings of activity at or near the oil wells to determine if the Iraqis would defend, sabotage, or ignore the area. This had the President's attention: GOSP destruction could lead to an unprecedented environmental disaster that would not only cripple a significant part of the oil industry, but devastate the surrounding area. If this important Iraqi infrastructure were to be destroyed or severely damaged, the entire operation was for naught. Coalition forces were counting on using the oil production to help pay for the rebuilding of Iraq's infrastructure. (Apart from the deterioration of virtually every element of Iraq's infrastructure during Saddam's regime, from roads to water and sewage treatment facilities, the war would inevitably entail more damage and degradation.) Everyone's eyes were on us.

By 1300 at midday, we had still little chance of flying our UAV. The weather was teasing us. However, the "sled test," which entailed launching a special red sled on the hydraulic launcher truck to see how far it travels, was successful—it flew well past the cutoff point. There was a great cheer from the squadron members who watched. We could have our first bird up later in the afternoon. To be conservative, because the winds were still at 25 knots and there was rain in the forecast, Lieutenant Colonel Mykleby made the call to wait until the weather cleared to fly.

★   ★   ★

The flight was not scheduled until 2000, well past sunset. Since we were now in direct support of the ground combat element, specifically 1st Marine Division, I had to continuously coordinate with 7th Marine Regiment and 5th Marine Regiment. To my luck, this meant going back to Matilda, which was where Peter's unit was located. Without hesitation I looked at my watch and organized a group of Marines to head out to RCT-7. We drove east out of the berm area where my unit was, until we found the main highway road and hit mile marker 17. From that mile marker, we took a left and went off-roading again in the desert until the large tent camp of thousands of Marines rose up in the horizon.

★   ★   ★

Wind from yesterday's sandstorm had devastated Matilda and RCT-7 as well. The weather in northern Kuwait was phenomenal. I had never seen such consistently bad weather for such long stretches. I guess there's a reason why northern Kuwait was devoid of life. Apart from the few Bedouins who eked out their miserable existence there, only the lizards dared brave the lousy weather. These lizards, varying from electric chartreuse to hazard yellow, looked like they had been created by a nuclear blast. Occasionally, a three-foot-long monstrosity would dart out of a sand cave and scare the bejesus out of me. The insidious wind that continually whipped the dirty sand around gave way to rainstorms that caked the sand on everything, making it into mud. Sand in teeth, in food, in eyes, in everything made living in this place dismal. The shift in temperature was also extreme—at night it would go down to the 40s, and during the day it would reach 80° Fahrenheit. So while being shelled with sand from the Shemal or Sharqi winds blowing from both directions, you'd have to strip off all your warming layers during the day. It wasn't a fun process, especially since that included removing flak vest, Kevlar helmet, gas mask, pistol holster, and other sundry articles. I cursed the weather every day and did push-ups and sit-ups in the sand. My thinking was that everything else sucked, so I might as well get some exercise while getting my face pelted.

Corporal Parker and Sergeant Vivas came with me to take our humvees to RCT-7. Corporal Parker, the SERE School survivor, was one of my Marines—a nineteen-year-old female analyst who possessed the humvee license required to drive the vehicle. She wasn't driving the vehicle, though. Sergeant Vivas asked to drive instead. I never heard Parker complain about anything. She made steel look soft. Sergeant Vivas was my driver. As we tore through the open desert, I looked over to see that he had a grin on his face.

"What's going on, Sergeant Vivas? Why are you so . . . happy?"

"I've never driven a humvee before, but this is the most fun I've had so far out here!" We both laughed. Stateside, our asses would have been in a sling for driving a tactical vehicle without a license, but out here standards had been relaxed out of operational necessity. He tore through the open desert, Matilda still in the distance. We flew over the berms and smashed back into the ground until we reached the camp.

"You think it's going to rain, ma'am?" Corporal Parker asked.

"There's not a cloud in the sky," I said.

"You want some charms, ma'am?" Sergeant Vivas asked me. Charms were hard candies that came in most of the MREs.

"Sure."

"Don't do it, ma'am!" said Corporal Parker. Too late. I had popped one in my mouth.

"Why?"

"Everyone knows charms are bad luck."

"What's the worst that can happen? Look where we're at."

"It usually rains, and then we can't fly our birds," Parker said.

"It's not going to rain," Sergeant Vivas said.

We parked near RCT-7's command post, which consisted of a series of DRASH (deployable rapid assembly shelter) tents and antennas. Recall that the DRASH tent was the womb-like tent that resembled some kind of animal tentacles. The three Marines and I walked into the S-2, where I met Captain Neetles, the regimental S-2A. He was the second in command of the section, and we would be reporting our information to him and his boss, the Lieutenant Colonel who had briefed us a couple days ago about the intelligence and operations plans. Neetles was one of those way-over-the-top geniuses, the kind that just look like they should be in intelligence. Of course he wore glasses and had wild hair, even though it was cut short like a Marine. Just as I was getting ready to shake his hand, we were hit with a gas drill again.

"Gas! Gas! Gas!" announced the loudspeakers situated around the camp.

"They like doing this around here," I told my Marines after I had donned and cleared my gas mask. My voice emitter on my gas mask allowed me to sound off.

"Jane, we got the Op Order," Captain Neetles said.

"What did you say, sir?" It was hard to hear with the gas masks.

"*The air assault will start any day. We got the order to go!*" he shouted.

My Marines and I spent the next hour comparing our maps, plotting out the suspected positions of enemy units in Iraq, and inputting the data on the computer. After confirming that our understanding of the enemy picture looked like what 7th Marines had on their maps, I left my Marines updating our maps while I wandered off toward my husband's position, which was less than two hundred meters away.

On the way, I saw an SUV with "TV" duct taped to its side. Next to it was a CNN van, surrounded by news reporters polishing their enormous amount of gear. The embedded media was both reassuring and frightening. On one hand, it was good to see that they would be recording us on video along the way. On the other hand, it was very frustrating to know that they traveled among us with so many luxuries we were not given. Our greatest pleasure was the sleep we got in the warmth of our sleeping bags, never knowing when, if ever, we would go home again. It seemed unfair that the media would be broadcasting our miseries. While we were all dodging bullets, peace-loving slackers were sitting on their plush couches in their cozy living rooms eating pizza and drinking beer. The media would report our actions—but they would never understand our mind-set. Civilians would watch us on television, but they would only understand what the media wanted them to see. It would be just one distant car chase for them, like watching O.J. flee the LAPD. A CNN reporter turned and smiled at me. I nodded back.

"Goddamned civilians!" I heard another Marine whisper to his buddy as they walked by the media.

★ ★ ★

In the distance, the howitzers of 3rd Artillery Battalion, 11th Marines remained staged in the gun park—a good indicator that Peter might actually be here this time. The gas mask drill had ended, and I was glad to remove my mask yet again. There was no way of getting used to them; it's like being underwater breathing in a diving mask. There's always a feeling that there's not enough air and you're going to suffocate. As I walked over to the officers' tent, a familiar face greeted me—Lieutenant Ty Yount, Mike Battery's XO.

"Well, look who it is!" he said, smiling. "We were wondering where the hell you were! I guess you're looking for your husband?"

"Absolutely. Where are you hiding him?"

"He's around here somewhere; he seems to have just disappeared!" He opened up the tent flap and shouted into the tent, "Female on deck!" so the Marines wouldn't be caught with their pants down. As he said that, my husband appeared, standing outside the tent in the distance, looking at me in disbelief. He walked over quickly. We had often talked about this moment and whether we would see each other, but now it was real. It seemed like forever had passed since he had left, even though it had been just a short time. As we embraced, another gas mask drill sounded.

"I don't think this one is a drill," the XO said.

"What do you mean?" We all spent the next minute donning and clearing our masks and were sitting inside the tent. A group of officers and SNCOs sat on the floor around the tent. They had no chairs or cots, so they used MRE cases as furniture.

"Well, the drills always go at 1000 to 1200—it's 1400 right now."

"I've got an itch right on the side of my face," a Staff Sergeant said.

"Sucks to be you."

"What happens if you throw up in the mask?"

"You'll die!" said the XO.

"That would fuckin' suck! After living through poisonous gas, you die in your own vomit." Four SNCOs sat in the back of the room playing poker with their gas masks on.

"That's very Dada," Peter said, pointing at the poker game. The photographer embedded with Mike Battery snapped a photo; a week later it was page 5 of the *Marine Corps Times*. After the photographer left, we sat down for a long time waiting for the all-clear to sound. But it did not come when it usually did. Peter and I sat down and looked at each other in disbelief. The XO shook his head, and he looked as if he was laughing.

"That's God's way of punishing you!" he said. We all laughed, but with the gas masks on, it sounded like we were suffocating, which made us laugh harder.

He continued, "See, we all can't see our wives, so now as punishment, all you can do is stare at each other in your gas masks."

"Fuck, I can't breathe now," the Staff Sergeant complained. The Gunnery Sergeant made Darth Vader breathing voices with his gas mask. Everyone sounded like Darth Vader.

★   ★   ★

At last the drill ended. As it turned out, some PFC had gotten on the command radio and called the gas mask drill. Without any clear indication of an attack and without authorization, he decided that a gas attack was imminent. He fouled up and panicked. They had mistaken it for real until the PFC 'fessed up his error. No sooner had the drill ended than Peter grabbed me and walked me over to the motor pool where they kept the vehicles. Peter had a plan, and it evidently involved borrowing one of the humvees. Peter asked one of his Corporals if the soft-back humvee was being used.

"It's all yours, sir. But the CO told me to tell everyone to wear flak and Kevlar helmet."

"Roger." Peter motioned for me to get in the vehicle.

"Shouldn't we get our gear?"

"What the hell for?"

Peter started up the humvee, and we took off like Bonnie and Clyde into the desert, but this time it was in Kuwait, fifteen miles from the Iraqi border. When we had gotten away from the camp, we parked in the middle of a barren wilderness. Only the huge electric lines swung in the distance, connecting to giant steel electric towers, the wires pendulously leading to the border of Iraq.

"This is crazy. Won't you get into trouble for this?"

"Yeah, but do I care?"

"You know this is the northernmost point of U.S. troops?"

"Yeah, we're the front line!" Peter looked so different. They had all shaved their heads in his unit and tried to grow mustaches. Peter couldn't grow one, so he had just a hint of stubble beneath his nose. We sat in the vehicle quietly. We let the silence say what we didn't want to say out loud and were happy just to look at one another. Peter took my hand, and we both understood. We locked in an embrace and, despite our dirtiness, reclaimed the understanding between us, which was ours alone.

★　★　★

We drove back to the motor pool, and the Marines all eyed us suspiciously.

"Don't worry about them," Peter said.

"They're going to talk."

"I'll just tell them I owe them five hundred points."

"What do you mean?"

"We've got this game we play—anyone who says 'That's bullshit!' about all the stupid things we do or the rules we have to follow gets points. At the end, we're going to have a party and trade in points for dollars to go toward our after-war celebration. So next time they see me, I'm going to say, 'Yeah, it's bullshit, give me five hundred points.' Then they'll all know they got justice."

"So who has the most points?"

"Well, up to this point, my Corporal did for complaining about not having a shower and for getting a two-day trip down to the Air Force Base. But I'm pretty sure I'm way ahead on points now."

"How much is a point worth?"

"About a dollar!" We soon stopped laughing, though.

"They say the order to cross the line of departure is going to come in a few days," I said.

"They've been saying that for four freakin' weeks now."

"It's true this time—I think we are going for sure. I saw the message when I was in the command operations center. So I won't see you for a while."

"We'll be fine. You'll see, I'll find you out there."

"Promise?"

"Yes, I promise."

What I felt at that moment is hard to describe: joy mixed with some notion that we both soon could be gassed, lying in a dark ditch somewhere. No longer caring who saw us, we locked in a final embrace, and I left my husband to his battles while I headed back to mine.

My visit ended too soon. Before I knew it, I was off again on my convoy, heading back to my unit's position. As we pulled away down the sandy trail, a hailstorm erupted from the sky, followed by an ungodly heavy rain. I had a smirk I couldn't hide, and I said to Corporal Parker and Sergeant Vivas, "I guess I shouldn't have had the charms!"

Back at the flight line, it was 1930. We arrived just as the rain ended. At 2000, the UAV went sailing into the great beyond and, to our happiness, did not crash. It was our first successful flight for Operation Enduring Freedom.

6

DREAD SILENCE REPOSES

War is the unfolding of miscalculations.

—Barbara W. Tuchman

Back in America, while we were spinning up for combat, things progressed in the typical fashion: Americans watched television, ate as much as they liked, and enjoyed their leisure time. But there were those who were different, those affected by their soldier, Marine, or Airman's absence. Wives, mothers, fathers, brothers all watched television with apprehension, finding themselves sometimes absorbed in CNN or FOX and other times pretending those networks didn't exist. They waited nervously by the mailbox, hoping the word they received from their loved ones did not speak of war. Some hung yellow ribbons and displayed flags; others hung "War is not the answer" signs. It had always been the same during war—World War II, Korea, Peloponnesus, and the Crusades. Any war that forced loved ones to wait for the return of their hero was an age-old tale. War seemed to always be part of our collective human existence. Peter says humanity has four basic pastimes: war, sex, money, and politics. It is hard to believe, after studying history, how war has ever made a difference. After all, war continues in every culture and doesn't appear to permanently resolve anything. One day, America is handing out Stinger missiles for the Afghanis to fight off the Russians; the next day we are being shot at by Taliban Afghans with RPGs. Perhaps war is just an essential aspect of human existence, a necessary evil of sorts. Perhaps war kept us alive and free by challenging ideologies that would have otherwise threatened civilization as a whole.

I couldn't answer those questions; all I knew was that war was at our doorstep. Our world had no stability. To think that humanity exists in a state of stability was just an illusion anyway. After all, it is said that humanity is just three meals and twenty-four hours away from barbarism. I guess I never believed it would be me at war. After reading book upon book on the subject, I never understood the courage and resolve it took to go to war. I didn't see how someone could voluntarily do an amphibious assault on a beach like Normandy or Iwo Jima. Why would anyone voluntarily get shot at? Would we be gassed en masse with a heavy dose of VX or sarin, or would we take shrapnel from a grenade or RPGs? I wasn't ready to die yet.

It wasn't like I didn't know what I had signed up for. They made sure the concept was engraved into your skull before you left basic training. Hell, I lived out the contract in boot camp, Officer Candidates School (OCS), and The Basic School (TBS). Just in case I had any doubts about what I was doing—I had plenty of rehearsals. The fact that we were always training for combat was implicit: it was one of those things Marines knew but never spoke about. Of course we wanted to go to combat, because that is exactly what it said in our contract. But of course we were too macho to go around talking about how much we hated it out here. Instead, we were gung ho.

★   ★   ★

Operation Southern Focus began just as Operation Southern Watch ended. This covert switch was only known in classified realms at the time. The demise of the twelve-year air campaign meant that all air assets were not only flying for a different mission, but we all had different engagement criteria. Previously in the "no-fly zone" during Operation Southern Focus, we couldn't attack ground targets since the rules of engagement specified that NATO aircraft could only go after Iraqi military planes or helicopters flying into that zone. With the change now to Operation Southern Focus, any enemy targets that presented themselves as hostile threats toward coalition forces could be engaged.

Since now we were on our own in the middle of the desert, and the air wing units that usually provided support to us were in the southern part of Kuwait, we would be flying in support for 1st Marine Division, meaning RCT-1, RCT-5, and RCT-7. Our first combat mission for the squadron was in support of Operation Southern Focus. It was 28 February 2003. According to the Warning Order, we were only four days from D-Day, but we had just learned it would be pushed back ten days. Our mission was primarily route reconnaissance. We would look for road trafficability—what roads could be used by enemy and friendly forces—and alternate routes to An Nasiriyah, which was considered a strategic choke point. We all were concerned about An Nasiriyah. We felt An Nasiriyah would be the "trigger line," the area which, when crossed by coalition forces, would set off the main effort of Saddam's forces. It would initiate an NBC attack, or destruction of a major dam that would have catastrophic effects on the area (including flooding all the roads), or launching of unconventional warfare. This point was, terrain-wise, Saddam's center of gravity.

I took my seat next to two of my Sergeants, Venaleck and Leppan, both imagery analysts, and one of my Corporals, named Warseck. The imagery analysts were trained to look at extremely fine details—they could literally make out differences in models of vehicles with their extensive training. Their job was to watch the high-resolution video monitor and interpret what we were viewing. The collections analyst's job was to provide an enemy situational update and keep track of enemy movement and changes. He would also copy down SALUTE and SPOT reports on pieces of bright yellow paper called "yellow canaries" that would aid in rapidly passing valuable intelligence to forward units. SALUTE and SPOT reports were basically quick reports that documented enemy size, activity, location, unit presence, time, and equipment. I'd type them up on "chat," a military chat room that allowed me to talk to the intelligence sections in every unit, to let all the units that were monitoring chat know where the enemy units were located, and they in turn let all the frontline units know where the threats we saw were. If we lost chat, we could call back using our tactical phones. My job was not only to supervise the collections section when I was collections mission officer, but also to maintain a high level of understanding of the entire strategic intelligence picture. After the mission, I would summarize the information collected and distribute it to all the key players in the campaign. It was an important job: we had the ability to save a lot of Marines' lives and kill a lot of enemies as long as we watched the video carefully.

While Lieutenant Debucher's hostility toward me was obvious, my Marines were, on the whole, exceptional—they not only passed screening of their criminal, moral, physical, and financial records, but they also all tested at the top of the charts for the military. Their extensive schooling placed them in an elite class—they were not standard issue. But, like all smart Marines, what they lacked in problems, they made up in quirky personalities. Each one was a masterpiece of strange. What made it worse for me was that they all liked Debucher: in fact, a lot of people did. He was always telling jokes and never gave the Marines a hard time, so his easygoing attitude tricked people into believing he was also good at his job. To make matters worse, I never saw him do any actual work, which made it that much more difficult for me out there. I wondered if I was the only one who noticed.

We all put on our headsets. Called the internal communications system (ICS), these radio links were how we communicated with the pilots and the other remote personnel during the flight. The CO's voice came on, and we all listened attentively.

"Well, Marines, this is it—our first combat mission. It's red ink time. If you don't know what that means—well, you can log this in as combat mission time. This is a historic moment; our squadron is no longer training. Good luck, Marines!"

Outside, the flight line was lit up like Christmas with sixty different colored chemlights lighting up the darkness. It was surprisingly haunting. Above, the stars were their colorless mirror images—countless stars stretched across the clear sky, puncturing the darkness. "Freddy," or bird 011, was sitting on the launcher truck, ready for takeoff. I stepped out of the humvee to watch the takeoff. It was my first time watching, surprisingly. Before long, the engine broke the silence with a swift, explosive hum. Staff Sergeant Moore, one of the air maintenance chiefs, stood next to me in the darkness, waiting for the launch.

"First flight over the border," I said.

"This is your first night flight, isn't it, ma'am?" he said.

"It is, Staff Sergeant."

"Well, you better stand back, the bird makes a lot of noise."

As he said it, "Freddy" took off in an exhilarating motion, cutting the air like an arrow heading for its mark. Its loud motor roared as it sped off into the distance, and as the sound grew fainter, the UAV was lost to our eyes in the night sky.

"That was a textbook takeoff!" Staff Sergeant Moore observed.

"Damn, that looked near perfect with my untrained eyes," I replied. "Hopefully this'll set the tone for the entire op."

In the ground control station (GCS), S-3 Marines, including the internal and external pilot, flew the bird, monitoring its altitude and path along the checkpoints. The external pilot executed the initial takeoff and the loitering around the camp until the UAV acquired a signal and was passed to the control of the internal pilot. We flew up to eight thousand feet and soon would cross the Iraqi border. At that altitude, it would be hard for the enemy to hear the bird passing overhead. Once we lowered to six thousand feet, the bird could be heard by the average person.

Surreal lunar images were displayed on the monitor inside the combat operations center (COC). Most of the Marines in the squadron who weren't working piled into the COC to watch this first flight. We were all stoked. Here we were, looking at imagery we had seen in pictures and from other collections sources. Now, we were seeing it firsthand. For the moment, we were the tip of the spear. In this tent, we shared the knowledge that no one knew what was going on in Iraq but us.

Sergeant Leppan, looking very intense, zoomed in on some black dots on the screen. The night vision equipment in the bird could see heat-emitting images as well as the terrain features of the cooling landscape below. Because it was night, this is the camera we would use. During the day, we could alternate between our infrared camera and our regular one.

"What's that?" I asked.

"Well, ma'am, it looks like a flock of sheep." He was a little miffed at my ignorance, but he smiled.

"Oh, so what's that?" I asked, indicating a fast-moving dot encircling the sheep. I thought for sure I had spotted something noteworthy.

"That would be the crazed sheepdog who's barking at the UAV!" We laughed. I couldn't figure out how my imagery analysts could distinguish one thing from another at the height we were flying. But they did.

The UAV crept slowly north into the lines that marked the border between the two countries. The CO came on the ICS again.

"Marines . . . well, this is the moment. We're in Iraq." We all cheered, but inside we were nervous. A strange disquieting feeling came over me. We had just passed into a world we had only read about—the mythic world of Iraq. We were not reading about it anymore. We were making history.

The terrain in Iraq from six thousand feet didn't look very different from Kuwait. We were seeing very little save the numerous revetments, or tank ditches, which were sprinkled throughout our route. Just when I thought we weren't going to see anything, we finally came upon the gas oil separation plants, part of Division Objective 3. Down below, we saw men hurriedly throwing boxes into the backs of parked pickup trucks when they heard the bird. Motorcycles, possibly the command vehicles, raced around to each vehicle, passing word. Within forty-five minutes, they were gone. No more than three hundred meters away was a flaming oil trench, the kind that was used during the Gulf War and the Iran-Iraq War to prevent aircrafts from reaching a strategic target. They dug large trenches around the area and filled them with crude oil. They would then ignite them, forming both an igneous pit and an obscurant for oncoming forces. All we could see was a line of burning oil and the heat waves produced by the infrared imagery. Then, suddenly, we saw static on the screen. Apparently the signal from the bird to the radio link was occasionally lost. However, the bird had a preprogrammed route and would follow the route back if a signal was not reestablished. We waited for the image to come back.

"Goddamn it! Where the hell is the bird?" The mission commander, Captain Hamill cursed, yelling in the headset.

"She'll be comin' round the mountain, sir, just watch," Sergeant Young, another imagery analyst, said. He started humming "She'll Be Coming 'Round the Mountain." He was always smiling and singing. I couldn't understand how he was always so cheerful. He was from Indiana but sounded like he was from Georgia. Sergeant Young was quite different from the average Marine. Back in garrison, his singing was welcome; out here, Sergeant Leppan was getting annoyed.

We had lost our first aircraft—I had no doubt. She wasn't "coming around the mountain," I told Sergeant Young. Two hours had passed, and there was no response. If it didn't acquire a signal, even though it would come back in the vicinity, it would eventually crash from lack of fuel. Several of the squadron members left. I walked over to the GCS.

"I'm guessing we should write this one off," I said to Captain Hamill, who was now reading a technical manual, trying to figure out a solution to our problem.

"This is not good. It should have returned an hour ago."

Sergeant Young chimed in, "Looks like we're going to have to go into Iraq with a couple vehicles and a .50 cal and pick up her remains!"

"Yeah, great freakin' plan! We'll just tell the Iraqi forces on the border that we need to pick up our aircraft."

"It's the gremlin watchdogs," said Sergeant Leppan.

"The what?" I asked.

"Ma'am, they're the little hand-sized demons that jump on top of the UAV and rewire it for a little while so they can take it wherever they want. Then they return it to us after they're finished playing around."

"I see . . . interesting theory, Sergeant Leppan." Our watchdog squadron patch looked like a gremlin demon with wings. At the moment, Sergeant Leppan looked crazed.

Leppan was another interesting Marine. He would draw pictures of Victoria's Secret models kissing and pass them around the shop.

"Look ma'am!" he'd say and show me one.

"Jesus, Sergeant, don't show me that shit." The drawing itself was pretty good. In addition to his love for drawing women, he was also a pagan and wore a pentagram around his neck. He did not lack creativity, though, and in my opinion, his strategic imagery training at a joint imagery center had made him one of the best analysts we had.

By now it was around midnight and the mission commander, Captain Hamill, was writing this off as a combat loss. As we starting packing things away, we thought we heard our sister squadron's bird returning home.

"Is that their UAV?"

"They're not flying right now—my God . . ."

"It's Freddy!" The external pilot was jumping up and down, waving his cover, or what civilians call a hat, in the air. Many squadron members near the flight line started cheering.

"She's come home! How crazy is that, she's back!" one Marine yelled.

"Miracles never cease to happen," Sergeant Young added emphatically.

The external pilot regained his composure and guided the UAV back in safely to the ground.

"See ma'am, she came around the mountain." Sergeant Young smiled.

★　★　★

On the following day came the first real mishap. We were sitting in the collections humvee, which was parked adjacent to the launcher truck. As the Marines launched the bird, we could hear its propeller heading straight for us. It was called a soft launch; in other words, the bird did not get enough lift to take off. But it did take off—just not upward. Instead, all 450 pounds of it flew straight toward us. We all ran and hit the deck. We heard a crash next to us, but before we could react, debris and the still-spinning engine flew at us. We felt wood splinters and metal shards. The engine, still turning, lay right outside the humvee, near Sergeant Young's feet. We looked at each other and shook our heads in disbelief. As it turned out, the launcher truck's pneumatic belt had snapped, leading to a class B mishap. There were no flights for the remainder of the day.

Capitalizing on our half day off, several of the officers, including me, took a trip down to the legendary "Camp Doha," the nerve center of the whole operation. Doha, unlike the forgotten camp where we were living, had all the amenities of a regular base in the States, including a PX, and the usual assortment of fast food franchises. Marines spoke of it in tones usually reserved for places like heaven or strip clubs. The whole collections section, at my request, had given me lists of PX items to bring back, including a Kentucky Fried Chicken order.

At Doha, you needed the permission of a colonel-level rank or above to enter the camp. We had come prepared. When we arrived, we showed security our approval papers, passed through tight checkpoints, and quickly oriented ourselves to the huge base. After taking care of some logistical concerns, we headed over to the PX. The indoor mall rose up like some kind of holy shrine. You could almost hear the choir of angels singing Handel. Dozens of franchises lined the inside of the immense food court, a mecca of grease, corpulence, and the consumerism that makes America great. Until then, I hadn't realized how starved I really was. We were all eating about one MRE each day—a mere 1,200 calories. I was experiencing a little shock, because I was so overwhelmed by the choices. I stood there, stunned, unable to make any decisions whatsoever. We had only been here a little more than a month, but Doha's food court was vastly different from anything we had seen. As I scanned the huge indoor mall filled with personnel from every branch of the military services, I saw a familiar face. It was Lieutenant Ryan Ruehl, one of my classmates from OCS and TBS, who now was the forward observer for Baker Company, 1st Battalion, 7th Marines, part of RCT-7.

"What the hell are you doing here?" Lieutenant Ruehl asked, smiling. "What's going on?"

"Oh, God," he said. "You don't even know what I've been going through. I'm attached to the unit from hell."

"What do you mean?" We walked over to the food court and grabbed some chow from one of the stands.

"Well, the company I'm attached to is run by a Major who thinks he's so hardcore that he's set up all these extreme rules for us. We can't sleep in anything but the green shell of our sleeping bag, so every night we shiver the whole night through. We can't go anywhere, even to the head, without asking a 'combat buddy' to come with us. The guy's gone crazy. He thinks we'll get soft. He's so bat-shit insane that he's gotten all these letters from his own wife, and they're sitting on his rack, unopened! He thinks reading them is going to remind him of home, and he'll lose it. I mean, morale in the unit is at an all-time low. We've had so many Marines close to the edge that we had to take away all their ammo, and now we're in condition 4. I mean, if we can't even be trusted to put magazines in our weapons in a combat zone, what's he going to do when we have to shoot our weapons?"

"That's crazy! Condition 4 in this environment? Someone should leave a Martha Stewart magazine on his rack as payback."

"Oh, God! He'd lose it. He'd probably hold a formation in the sandstorm until someone came forward and 'fessed up. You know, the worst part of it is, my Marines and I live in tents right across from Alpha Company, and they've got a normal CO—they all can eat the candy they brought, watch DVDs, and listen to music. They're in good spirits and train just as hard as we do. My Marines see that, and they hate the CO even more."

"We're not allowed to take our boots off when we go to sleep," he continued. "We only get to take them off, one at a time, for fifteen minutes a day. We're not allowed to wear our boonie covers. We get up at 0500 and don't stop working until 2200. The Marines are going absolutely fucking ape shit."

"What do you mean?"

"Dude, we had a Lance Corporal get medivacked to Germany because he and his buddy decided it would be a good idea to have a play knife fight with their actual K-Bars. Things were going fine until one guy grabbed the other's blade, and the second guy pulled the knife out of his fist. He severed the kid's tendons."

"Jesus, dude." I shook my head in disbelief.

"That's not all. Some of the Marines are getting trench foot from wearing their boots all the time. The XO mentioned it to the CO, ya know, to drop the hint that maybe these guys should air their feet out, and all he said was, 'Marines in World War II endured trench foot for five years.'"

"What the hell is going on over there?"

Ruehl just shook his head. "He wants us to be the physically hardest company in theater. He wants us to be able to endure any hardship and blah, blah, fucking blah. He's driving those Marines fucking insane. I walked by the enlisted tent last night and heard all this noise, so I poked my head in and saw the most horrible thing I've ever seen in my life."

"What, man?"

"They'd laid all their flashlights along the walkway with alternating red and blue lenses, like a whatever the fuck you call it. . . ."

"A catwalk?"

"Yeah, exactly. They were having a goddamn fashion show. And these two Marines were walking down the catwalk, buck-ass naked, smearing MRE cheese all over their chests, and everyone was cheering them on."

"Dude, that's crazy."

"Oh, I know. I just hope he knows what he's freakin' doing."

"I'm sorry you've got to live like that," I said. "But if it makes you feel better, even at the wing things aren't that great—the Air Force has prohibited the Marines from using any of their facilities. So we're already living on MREs."

"I really don't care about missing this trash myself—I mean, if I go the whole deployment without taking a shower, then that's just the way things are—it's the junior enlisted I'm worried about," he said, with circles under his eyes and misery carved across his face.

We said good-bye, and I made a stop at KFC to get a family meal for my section. After linking back up with my convoy, I could smell the aroma of the fast food. "This will be the last time for a long time," I thought. But my Marines would be happy, at least for one meal.

We arrived back at the flight line just as a group of Marines, including some of my section, piled onto the back of the seven-ton truck.

"Where are you going, Marines?"

"We had a second mishap, ma'am. Not too bad, but they've canceled the flights for the day."

"All right, but I need all of the section to stay here for a brief."

Sergeant Leppan and Sergeant Young jumped out of the truck.

"What's going on, ma'am?" Sergeant Young said.

"We've got a briefing with Colonel Sanders to discuss his secret recipe."

"Roger! I'll quickly round up everyone!"

It only took a couple minutes until all ten of the collections Marines were huddled around two bags in the back of the humvee. I've never seen a group of Marines get so excited. It reminded me of kids drooling over Halloween candy until I looked in their eyes—then it was more like teenagers with a porno magazine stolen from Dad's garage. We closed the flap so no one else could see. Sharing was for suckers. The eager bunch unveiled the goods.

"This is going to be the best brief I ever had!" Sergeant Young said, while Sergeant Leppan followed with, "This is better than Christmas!" As we all dug in, everyone was quieter than I'd ever heard them before. It didn't occur to me at the time how pathetic it was to get so excited about such a small thing. The XO, Major Cepeda, poked his head in, but he was still out of range to see what was going on.

"Hey, Lieutenant, I need to go over tomorrow's mission details with you once you finish your meeting," Major Cepeda said.

"Roger that, sir," I said, trying not to let him witness our depravity.

After he left, we all laughed at our plates stacked high with food. All the Marines looked toward me, and I said, "This is like the Last Supper."

Sergeant Beaty, a hardworking Marine nicknamed "Mule" because he always volunteered for the bad jobs, said, "Thank you very much, ma'am—we all appreciate this very much."

I replied, "Don't thank me just yet. Save your thanks for if I do something that really means something."

"Well, thanks anyway!" they all said. It was the little things that really seemed to make a difference in their lives. I let them all finish their meal and walked out. But I saw Sergeant Beaty leave shortly after me, and he was standing in the distance, looking fairly somber. He was the oldest in the section, even older than Lieutenant Debucher and me, and he had been through a rough divorce before we deployed. I walked over to him.

"What's going on, Sergeant Beaty?"

"Well, ma'am, it's nothing important."

"Yes, it is."

"Well, I don't know if my ex-wife will write me, and I left things jacked up, especially with my kid. No one has written, and I'm tired of doing all the bitch work in the shop."

"We all aren't getting letters—the mail system here is really screwed up," I said. "Hang in there, and maybe we can get you a call back to the States. As for the bitch work, I'll put a stop to that."

"Things were so different in the Gulf War," he said.

"How do you mean?"

"America seemed to give a damn about us then; now they pretend we're not here. I know they don't support the war, but that doesn't mean they can't support us. I remember AT&T had phone booths set up everywhere, and we got free calls back home. Mail came from strangers. People sent furniture, food, or whatever else they could to troops they didn't even know. Chow was brought to us from franchise restaurants—we always had pizza and soda. We all felt like America gave a damn, and because of that, we were happy. But now, all we see is sandstorms and sand-filled tents. There's occasional mail, no calls, no newspapers, cold showers, and sometimes only MREs. Someone's forgotten us out here, ma'am."

He was right—it did feel like America had forgotten us. What little news filtered in to us had left us all disheartened. We heard of the protests for peace and all the talk against the war. We understood. No one likes war, and we didn't like being here ourselves. But we knew our duty was to protect and defend America and its way of life without hesitation. Somehow in the protests, the American people had forgotten about more than two hundred thousand of us who sat here, endangering our lives for them.

The yellow ribbon magnets on the back of their SUVs didn't help us. We didn't even exist for most of these people until the fact was rubbed in their noses on cable television. To Marines, civilians seem selfish and soft as they waddle their pampered, fat behinds through shopping malls, whining about the heat in 65° weather. It becomes hard for us to remember why we signed up to protect them, to provide them with the blanket of freedom they wrap themselves in.

7

UNCERTAINTY AND HUMAN FACTORS

If you entrench yourself behind strong fortifications, you compel the enemy to seek a solution elsewhere.

—Karl von Clausewitz

The Marine on watch stretched his tired arms up to the night sky. I watched him, cold and uncertain, his eyes glazed over the horizon. Walking his post restlessly, he studied every movement in the blackened desert. His challenges and passwords were mantras in his mind. I could hear him at a distance repeating ditties to keep himself awake. Just like me, he waited for the word—the final call on his mission, when we would all cross the line of departure into Iraq. As I watched him in the distance, the voice of Peter filled my mind, and scattered snapshots of our short time together passed dreamlike through my thoughts. He is what I fight for; he is the reason for my return. I know the Marine on watch sees me, but he doesn't turn to look. He knows from glancing at me from the corner of his eye that I'm not the enemy.

★ ★ ★

We had been deployed for less than two months. One of the Marines had already received his "Dear John" letter with the divorce contract included. While the United Nations was still deciding our fate, I was resting in my tent on my sleeping bag. I finished reading a book and checked my watch. 1000. I had already read almost all of the fifteen books I brought with me. If I saw my husband again, I'd have to get him to exchange some books. Just then, I saw a large object scurry across Lieutenant Bishop's sleeping bag, coming to a rest on top of her. A huge rat sat on top of her sleeping bag, and as she moved slightly, it went scurrying away. She lifted her head and looked at me.

"Was that was I thought it was?" she asked.

"If you were thinking it was a huge rat, then yes it was."

"Jesus! This place is disgusting."

It was almost time for my mission back at the flight line a couple miles away. After shaking off copious amounts of sand from everything I picked up, I assembled my twenty-five to thirty pounds of mandatory gear. Walking to the flight line was easier than getting a humvee. I'd have to round up an enlisted NCO who could drive it, pulling them from whatever they were doing for hours. Not worth it.

I scaled the berm that surrounded the camp and put my weapon into condition 2, which meant inserting a magazine without putting a round in the chamber. Outside the bermed-in area, the weapons condition became either condition 2 or 1, depending on how high headquarters felt the threat was that day. Condition 1 meant you were ready to kill. The Marines on guard duty in an entrenched position on the corner of the berm acknowledged me. A mile in the distance was the hastily constructed airfield; surrounding it, the launch truck, antennas, and tents could be made out in the distance. Beyond that, huge Kuwaiti electric towers flanked the road that led to Iraq. Our makeshift airfield was only about a half mile from the highway—not too safe, considering any of the Kuwaiti vehicles that passed by on the highway could easily drive over loaded with insurgents and explosives. From the berm area to the airfield, I walked across the empty desert about another half a klick; it was a long distance to walk back to the camp area where we slept. It was nice to be out walking alone. Moments alone were hard to find out here.

Days passed like this: lonely, uneventful, and full of anxiety about what was to come. Early one morning, I walked to the tent in the bermed area where they kept the vehicles. I was supposed to go in a convoy heading to a meeting in Al Jaber, one of the big, joint air bases. There was no one in sight except for the three enlisted guys who were driving the officers there.

"What do we do, ma'am? Do you want us to get the vehicles?" they asked me. It was already 0715, and we were supposed to leave at 0720. Like a good officer, I made a command decision and said, "Bring the vehicles around and be prepared to leave no later than 0800."

At exactly 0730, Captain Long, one of the S-3 officers who was the convoy leader came around and said, "Hey, Lieutenant, where the hell are the drivers?"

"They are getting the vehicles, sir," I replied.

"Did you tell them to be here at 0800?"

"Yes, I did. There was no one else around, so I made the call."

"You need to learn your role," he said. "I'm in charge, and we needed to leave by 0730."

"There was no one here on time," I responded. "We wouldn't have been able to leave by that time, even if the drivers were still here, because they didn't have the vehicles."

"Before you make a decision again, Lieutenant, you need to ask the people who are in charge." I would have made the point that it's difficult to be in charge when you're not physically there, not to mention lazy as hell, but I decided it might not have gone over in the professional spirit I intended.

Captain Long walked away, cursing my name and mumbling something about Lieutenants. But our flight surgeon, Lieutenant Commander Dave Lambert, had heard the whole thing and approached me. Doc was one of those square-jawed, handsome, doctor types.

"Jane, don't ever let anyone talk to you like that again. You were in the right."

"I know I was right, Doc, but he gets all flipped about it."

"I know you're the junior officer in the squadron. But he still shouldn't be talking to you like that. Men need to be cursed back at. Throw a couple of 'fucks' and 'shits' in there next time, and he'll fucking shut up quick, because he's wrong, and he's just trying to intimidate you. It's like the apes that puff out their chests to look more intimidating. They're posturing. Just put the fucker in his place. He wasn't around in time to let the drivers know, and you did the right thing."

"So you're saying if I raised my voice and cursed at him he'd respect me?"

"Fucking A. That's how men are. Simple. You'd fucking intimidate him, and that's what he needs. He'd never talk to you like that again, I guarantee you."

"OK, Doc, but if I get brought in front of the CO for disrespect toward a senior officer, I'm going to blame you!" I said jokingly.

"I outrank most of them anyway; I've got your back. I don't want to go to this shitty meeting anyway," Doc Lambert said.

He was right. Docs are very perceptive in the battlefield environment because they are not in the chain of command, and they are not Marines— they are officers in the U.S. Navy. Their ability to see from a different perspective often yields good, honest advice. Such was the case with Doc Lambert.

The three vehicles arrived at 0745. Inside, I felt satisfaction knowing that we would have been waiting another half hour had the Captain given them the order when he arrived. As we pulled away from the secured perimeter, we made our weapons condition 1. Doc Lambert sat across from me in our humvee.

"I don't think females should be in combat," he told me in a matter-of-fact fashion. He loved Socratic dialogue and pushing people's buttons. I wondered if he also loved getting his nose broken.

"I don't think so, either, but here I am. It's not like I had a choice."

"Choice or no choice, most of the females I've seen out here are emotional basket cases. You should hear some of the things I do. Women are too emotional. They're not conditioned for this type of environment."

"Women are a lot more vocal in their feelings then men are; that's all. Men express anger, women cry. Same emotion. You think the men are conditioned for this? Wait until the bullets start flying and see how many of your fearless boys wet themselves."

★   ★   ★

After the dust had settled the following afternoon, I lay down on my sand bag, studying the history of Iraq and Saddam Hussein. My head was filled with thoughts of getting ambushed, rushing into enemy fire, being gassed and dying a horrible death, and shoving a knife into a man's neck. I thought about my Marines, the other soldiers in this campaign, and the Iraqis themselves who would be the victims of the future war. I thought about what the Iraqi soldiers' mind-set was. I imagined being a sacrificial martyr—sarin gas leaking into my MOPP suit, the suit itself manufactured by the lowest bidder. Then I imagined the Marines being victorious and tearing through Iraq. My mind drifted to stories of Hue City, the Chosin Reservoir, Iwo Jima, Belleau Wood—I remembered the spirit of the Marines through their worst and best moments. I thought of all the possibilities. For a moment, I was confident this was going to be a piece of cake.

Grabbing an MRE out of my pack, I began preparing a lunch of "pasta with alfredo sauce," affectionately called "pasta with a money shot" by many Marines. I added peanut butter—mixing different combinations of ingredients was the key to surviving long-term MRE consumption. Just as I had heated up my lunch, Lieutenant Guardini, the other female in our tent, came barreling in with her gas mask on screaming, "Gas! Gas! Gas!"

Lieutenant Bishop and I didn't see what the panic was about, since we were used to the drills by now. Outside we heard a conspicuous explosion in the distance, and then we heard the loudspeakers come on, issuing the same warning.

"This is not a drill!" Lieutenant Guardini said emphatically. I grabbed my mask out of its holder and held my breath as I threw it on. They taught us that we had nine seconds to don and clear before the gas started affecting us. Shock took hold of me, and fear drifted back in. Feelings of horror and panic surfaced as I thought, "This is it. Now it all begins."

I felt crippled and vulnerable. I waited with terror-stricken eyes and a rapid pulse, expecting the first bombs to impact. We had nowhere to run because the bunkers had not been dug yet. A feeling of nausea overcame me. I looked around at the dusty tent and closed my eyes. As I listened to my breathing, I regained my calm. Outside, voices on a loudspeaker resounded, "Stay in your tents, stay in your tents for accountability."

"What the hell's going on?" Lieutenant Bishop said. Our roommate disappeared through the flaps of the tent to get accountability of her troops. Our Marines were all at the flight line, so we could do nothing except wait. Then, through the tent's entrance flaps, in tumbled three female junior enlisted Marines and one Navy corpsman. One of the Marines was an NBC chief, and the other two were radio operators.

Lieutenant Bishop and I loaded our magazines into our pistols, not knowing what kind of threat we were under. My heart was racing so fast it made me sick. But on the outside, I appeared eerily calm. The females who had just entered were huddled in the corner. I told them, "Hey, Marines, sit down and relax as best as you can. We don't know if this is even real or not. Chances are, it's just a false alarm."

One of the females was starting to hyperventilate with her mask on. She was ready to rip the mask off her face and started to cry.

"What's going on out there, ma'am?" One of the junior Marines asked me.

Rule number one of being an officer: never let on that you don't know what the hell's going on, because the Marines will never have confidence in you again.

"The NBC sensors were probably tripped accidentally," I said. "I can guarantee you if this was really serious, they would be doing more than counting heads out there to get accountability."

She seemed to accept that, but you could tell that she was seriously freaking out. Her noncommissioned officer was trying to reassure her. As we waited, I thought back to *Battle Leadership* by Captain Adolf Von Schell, a book we read in The Basic School. The book read like an after-action report about lessons learned in combat by a German officer in World War I. One thing that stood out was the idea that an officer should never act nervous in front of his troops. At one point he describes taking shelter from an artillery barrage in a farmhouse with his company. Once he got his men indoors, his mind began to fill with horrific images of the house being hit by an artillery round, collapsing around them, and trapping them as the building burned to the ground. Unwilling to appear indecisive or scared, he didn't want to take his men back out. He compromised by sitting in the doorway in a kitchen chair. Overcome by exhaustion, he involuntarily dozed off, which is not perhaps ideal during an attack. But falling asleep had an unintended positive consequence: when his men saw him napping casually in the doorway, they assumed he must have known something that they didn't and that they were perfectly safe. It calmed his men immeasurably.

With a long-dead German infantry officer in mind, I walked to the table we constructed of MRE boxes and sat on the box I used as a chair.

"Hey, Lisa . . . let's finish our card game." Lisa, confident that this was a drill, walked over, and we started a new game of gin rummy. Ridiculously, we sat there playing cards in our gas masks. After a few minutes, I could see from the corner of my eye that the girl had calmed down considerably and was chatting with the other women. After about another half hour, the loudspeaker said, "All clear, unmask, unmask."

The female Marines thanked us and left. As it turned out, the false gas alert happened when one of the perimeter "snipers," the chemical sensors that lined the perimeter, was accidentally triggered. By the time the false alarm was over, it was already one hour into our chow hours, and we heard every Marine on camp making a mad dash for the new chow tent. When we opened the flap, we saw a line of about five hundred Marines waiting.

"Jesus, they don't miss a beat do they, Lisa?" I joked.

"No, they don't, and that's why we're going to kick Saddam's ass."

8

RED INK

Only the dead have seen the last of war. —Plato

With our importance in providing reconnaissance and surveillance to the Marine Corps, my CO could not afford another mishap. We already had two UAVs go down because of weather-related complications. Lieutenant Colonel Mykleby, an aggressive but sensible individual, never substituted his drive for common sense. Sometime in mid-March, he brought the whole squadron together to give us an update on the situation, as he often did. As we were gathered around him, the CO explained to us that President Bush gave a speech warning that Iraq had forty-eight hours to stand down. With only a moment's notice, we were told to be ready to pull out of Kuwait and breach the border into Iraq. It was called a "stand to," which basically meant that we should be prepared to leave. We would be going to Iraq any day. The CO scratched his hair before he spoke, "I'm bringing you all back," he said to us as we stood there. "As long as you stick by me and do what I tell you, I'm bringing you all back with me."

Without a doubt, we were on our way to war. My dusty sleeping bag was thrown into my larger Alice pack, and I stuffed the rest of my gear into my seabag. The thought of leaving this godforsaken dust camp was a relief anyway. No use prolonging the inevitable. I moved my gear up to the flight line and set my things beside my vehicle. The order was given that we would be conducting twenty-four-hour continuous operations. As our final countdown began, all the MEF units began their push to the northern border to their tactical assembly areas.

Our last missions before troops were launched were the most essential. Whatever enemy order of battle we would find could potentially shift battlefield plans and positions for us. We were done with our rehearsal—what we found now, we would destroy. Our area of operations was Division Objectives centered on the gas oil separation plants (GOSPs). Our sister squadron covered the rest of Division Objectives, including the "crown jewel"—the central nervous system of the GOSPs.

As I walked into the collections tent, Sergeant Leppan and Sergeant Venaleck, two of the imagery analysts, were on the first twelve hours of missions, and I would be the officer in charge. My struggle with Lieutenant Debucher was ongoing, but during this critical mission, he had gotten stuck back at base camp and, because of an elevated threat level, was not allowed to come to the flight line. We were told whoever was here now would stay for the next twenty-four hours. By then, the first coalition air strikes were expected to begin.

"Well, this is it," I said complacently.

"Yes, ma'am. It doesn't get any more real than this," said Sergeant Leppan.

Our operations center was filled with everyone from our squadron who wanted to see what was about to unfold. The CO, OpsO, and Sergeant Major took turns sitting in with the XO as mission commander.

Our bird was launched, and we flew over the GOSPs. I sat at a computer in a type of military chat room that allowed me to talk to the intelligence sections in every unit—not just MEF, but to all coalition force networks. I could instantly reach anyone from Division, of whom we were in direct support, to the grunts on the front line, to the leaders of the MEF, all the way up to the Central Command (CENTCOM) leader and Coalition Forces Land Component Command (CFLCC), who was the leader of the entire operation. Both of these commands, after the President, controlled every decision out here.

As our first mission began that day, on 19 March 2003, Dusty, or bird 07, pushed north over the Iraqi border. Iraq still seemed like an illusion, an unknown world of enemy forces that I had just seen through black-and-white aerial images. After about an hour and a half of loitering over the GOSP area, the bird pushed farther north.

With everyone watching, from the President on down, suddenly my small section began getting a lot of attention. Apparently, the Predators and other strategic imagery collection platforms couldn't be employed fast enough to provide on-the-spot coverage of the vital GOSP area. Soon, we learned we were the single point of collections in that area. Our section of Marines was under a lot of pressure. While the imagery Sergeants took turns interpreting what the bird was seeing from a real-time live feed, the analysts were collecting information on the enemy and friendly positions and the order of battle. They plotted the things we saw on a wall-sized map inside the tent. Like an elaborate game of Go, the blue symbols marked coalition positions or "friendlies," and red enemy symbols marked a carefully orchestrated series of actions—together, they marked territory that would continually change as the battle space evolved over time.

Looking over at the Sergeants who stared diligently at their plasma screens, I saw what the bird saw, high over Iraq, scanning the terrain the Marines would soon pass through. The analysts perhaps did not realize how key they were to the success of both launching the war and creating the overall enemy picture for the entire MEF. Force reconnaissance had traditionally done this for the infantry, but now the distances were much larger. Force reconnaissance was still located along the border, making its way onto Safwan Hill, where they would capture this key piece of terrain in order to deny the enemy use of the one commanding view in southern Iraq.

Sergeant Leppan called out the enemy order of battle for one of the Corporals to copy down. The Corporal quickly scribbled a SALUTE report on canary yellow paper and updated his map. He then handed me the sheet of paper. The SALUTE described the movement of an enemy artillery battery we had been looking for.

"It looks like they are shifting positions," Sergeant Leppan said, adding, "They know something's about to happen."

We decided to fly our bird north to an area we had not imaged before. We found another D-30 position, but this time, the Iraqi soldiers had a different response, one that we had heard about from the Gulf War. We saw all the personnel run from the equipment like before, but instead of shooting, they began waving white cloths in the air. They all waved their hands, obviously trying to surrender. As the flight continued, all the other units we saw did exactly the same, and for the first time I had the confidence that this war, when it started, would see a lot of enemy units capitulating. I breathed a sigh of relief, believing for the first time that it might be possible to roll through the country with little opposition.

My last flight ended at midnight, and I wandered away from the tents slightly wired but mostly ready to crash. The air was bitterly cold. I had not prepared to sleep in my bag tonight; I had already packed it in my vehicle. Cursing my lack of planning, I tried to nestle myself in a fetal position next to a generator, only to lie there for a better part of an hour freezing to death. As I surveyed the camp for a warm place to hibernate for the night, another gas drill came. They had told us there would be no more drills, but the nuclear, biological, and chemical detectors would trigger at almost anything. As I donned and cleared my mask, I found a small area near a gap in the tent that provided some heat. My mind drifted and entered an unknown limbo between awake and asleep.

When I woke, my face was covered in sweat, and my breathing was shallow. In the darkness, I was sure I had been buried alive. It took me a moment to realize that I still had my gas mask on. I sucked in half breaths. As I gasped for air, I removed the mask, looked at my watch, and saw it was an hour until dawn, about 0630, the morning of 20 March.

★   ★   ★

Winston Churchill once said that there is nothing so wonderful as to be shot at and missed. He understood. The first flicker of light had not yet come. Thousands of Marines and soldiers readied themselves for this moment. All who have gone to war have asked themselves what decisions brought them there. Why were they in that place at that time, risking their lives? To know that life hangs on the edge of not years, but a precise moment, makes those minutes more memorable, more valuable. To know one is standing in the middle of a killing field between life and death invigorates the mind and body. Combat awakens one to true life, a life above the somnambulant half-life of the fat and happy civilian. It awakens the instinct, the wild thing inside. Whatever was going through Saddam's mind up to the deadline was probably reinforced by the fifteen-hundred-pound JDAMs (joint direct attack munitions) smart bombs that were crashing into his palaces just about now. There was some serious softening of targets taking place, and as I walked to the communications vehicles, I heard the BBC give a live report from Baghdad. Air strikes had begun on some formidable targets to eliminate the chance of Iraqi forces doing major damage to coalition forces. Strolling over to the collections area, I peeked inside to see how Lieutenant Debucher's shift was going. Only two Sergeants were there.

"Where's your fearless leader?" I asked.

"You mean the Lieutenant?"

"Yes."

"Oh, he left a couple hours ago."

"What do you mean he *left*?"

"The Lieutenant went to rack out."

"Roger. . . . I guess this is my mission now." I didn't mind being in the mix, but I was somewhat surprised at the lack of zeal from others.

Debucher hadn't even woken me up. Meanwhile, my heart was pounding with adrenaline. Damn, our country had just entered a war. How can you sleep when you're in it?

Quickly, I assembled my contacts, which included several calls to Division G-2. Staff Sergeant Barrios, a Marine I had known when I was prior enlisted, was our liaison for the day. We quickly brought everyone up on chat, establishing an Internet chat room with all the key units, and soon communications was up and running.

"1st Marine Division, what do you want us to look out for this flight?" I asked.

"UAVs, you will be in direct support of RCT-5, effective immediately. We will pass all information to them from this net or secondary by radio or TAC phone. RCT-5 is moving to their position by breach point 2. We need you to fly Route Edith and then push down to the GOSPs in order to determine if the order of battle has shifted or if there are indications of unusual activity near the GOSPs. Report all findings, including negative reports."

On the side of the chat I read all the agencies that were monitoring: Division = Blue Diamond, RCT-5 = Grizzly, 11th Marines = Cannon cockers, MEF = MEF, CFLCC, CENTCOM. Holy shit, this was the moment. Closing my eyes, I took a deep breath. I traced out a route in my head and planned the best way to go. I knew this area well by now. After bringing the information over to the operations center, the mission commander and I hashed out a route of advance. Route Edith was the western approach, on which 1st Tanks Reinforced would push up toward the main service route—Route 8—past the GOSPs. They would remain there and guard that key terrain until other units caught up to them. Route 8 connected Baghdad to Al Basra, the two largest cities in Iraq. We had flown it as a dress rehearsal the day before and had seen nothing. On our first flyover through the area, we had determined there were a number of untrafficable areas that Division had not planned for. These choke points of quarries and mines would have severely impeded movement. The 5th Marines were ecstatic that we had already preflighted their route. These were all new tactics—although Pioneers had been involved in the Gulf War and Bosnia, it had never been to this extent and with upgraded technology. We were bringing a new dimension to the battle space.

By now, the whole tent was filled with personnel. Even high-ranking personnel from MEF had come over to check out what we were doing.

As we flew over Route Edith, things were different. No longer were there empty boneyards of tanks left from the Gulf War. Now the route contained tanks and armored vehicles hiding in revetments, moving personnel, and artillery pieces shifting positions. The ground was alive with activity. As we got to checkpoint 7, we suddenly came upon two tank companies stretched across the horizon, a total of twenty plus tanks. I reported: "S—20+, A—On line in staggered formation, L—RQU134 980, U—UNK, T—1830z, E—poss tank companies."

"Are they hot?" Division asked—in other words, were they real and not decoys? The infrared camera made the tanks that were warm look black.

"Yes." RCT-5 would have to roll through this area soon enough. Then, without warning, the screen suddenly flashed the words, "*Lightning, Lightning, Lightning.*"

"What the hell does that mean?" I asked. I turned around, but no one seemed to know. A couple of Marines shrugged.

"It looks important," a Marine echoed back.

"No shit, Lance Corporal; she wasn't asking your opinion," one of my Sergeants shouted out, squaring the Marine away.

Although no one knew what it meant, I had enough sense to know that I needed to find out. "What does 'lightning' mean?" I asked MEF on the chat.

No response. So I put the general question out to the whole chat room.

"Does anyone know what 'lightning' means and why MEF isn't responding?"

Division answered right away, "It means Scuds are inbound and they are heading straight toward your general position!"

Fuck.

Cold flames ran up my back as I shouted, "Gear up!" Word spread like wildfire, and soon everyone's collective asses were fired up and running in every direction: we didn't have a bunker. Some decided to shout "Gas! Gas! Gas!" and mass confusion and terror filled our camp. We were all severely fucked. The CO walked over briskly. "Jane, what's going on?"

"Scuds are inbound to our pos, sir!" I said frantically.

"Did you call a gas alert?"

"No sir, that just kind of happened."

"Jesus, you can't shout like that, Jane. The Marines are going to freak out and say the sky is falling and starting crying out to Jesus. You know how panic spreads."

"Sorry about that, sir. But there are Scuds in . . ."

"Find out where they are going first."

I felt like a spaz. Way to go, Jane, fuck up your first combat experience. Just then, we heard the Patriot batteries next to us fire off a few volleys to intercept the Scuds. They seemed to be right above us. We heard loud booms and then silence. The chat flashed back with some words.

"What are they saying now, Jane?" My CO asked.

"Sir, MEF reports Scuds have been intercepted by Patriot missiles."

"Well, no shit."

I felt a little ashamed that in my first combat experience I had become so flustered. I had always been such a calm, collected person. And it is a leader's responsibility, no matter how chaotic the situation, to remain at ease at all times. Otherwise, the Marines will react even more strongly. Clearly, I hadn't learned that lesson. Before my heart rate had returned to normal, another lightning alert came through.

"Lightning. Scuds inbound at grid RQU130 782. Launch Grid RQU 156 984."

My Marines quickly calculated.

"Launch site is from Al Faw Peninsula and impact site is . . . Camp Commando, MEF Headquarters. . . ."

"They're very inaccurate, so are they sure those are Scuds? That's the port; they could be Seersuckers." Seersuckers, or "Silkworms," were portside surface-to-surface missiles primarily used as antiship missiles. As we were debating the veracity of my claim, another message came.

"There was an explosion at Camp Commando."

Before we could react, someone called out another gas alert. We donned and cleared again. It was hard to tell what was real at this point, and the Scuds could be armed with chemical munitions. This shit was getting out of control fast.

"Rounds down, over." We heard the neighboring Patriot battery once again launch to intercept the Scuds. I tore off my gas mask, eager to read the messages on the computer.

"One impact in Camp Commando, one in tactical assembly area Viking, no assessed casualties," MEF said.

"All clear." It had been a long two minutes of waiting. I could tell my CO was still monitoring me to make sure I didn't flip the panic switch again.

TAA Viking was close by. That was a pre-staging area for the infantry troops who just needed the word from higher to breach the berm and cross over into Iraq. I tried the MEF G-2 cell again: "MEF—how copy?"

"We're up—sorry for the delay—we all ran into the bunker, everyone in the COC is OK. The explosion was near the guard post, about a half kilometer away. Got to go again—lgting—lightaening- lgting!" The words were misspelled, but the meaning was clear.

"Jesus, bunker down," I said to everyone, this time more pissed off than panicked. Patriot missiles filled the sky, and it sounded like a war above us. Once again we waited until I saw the words, "Rounds down, impacted at 0 of 4 targets, Scuds intercepted by Patriots."

"Oorah, Patriots!"

By this time, I was beginning to accept that if God willed it and the Scuds flew at us, there was nothing I could do anyway. So I eased into an un-settled calm. This same alerts came in intermittently and went on throughout the day, but fortunately, the Patriot batteries seemed to be knocking them down. What a freaking day. This was it—combat. Day one down.

9

TIME ON TARGET

The problem in defense is how far you can go without destroying from within what you are trying to defend from without.

—Dwight D. Eisenhower

Feign weakness at your strength: that is one principle we learned in The Basic School. The enemy will be fooled into believing they had discovered a gap in the defense, and they will seize the advantage and attack at that spot. This was the coalition defense that sat along the Kuwait border. We were told that CENTCOM planners had deliberately pretended to amass troops on the Turkish border so that Saddam would leave his strongest forces in the north. As it turned out, Turkey refused to admit U.S. forces. Our ground forces still held steady on the Kuwaiti border. It wasn't yet time to cross over. But as night fell, things began to speed up again.

Back on my camp, all attention was on what we were going to see. Our mission, once again, was to check the status of the crucial gas oil separation plants (GOSPs). Sergeant Venaleck and Sergeant Leppan sat with me, watching the screen. There was still no sign of Lieutenant Debucher. I wasn't complaining. We had not been to this area since the previous night's mission. The eerie beauty of the GOSPs as viewed from our infrared camera most definitely did not resemble the view from the ground. For us, the haunting auras of each oil well fire burned softly like an incandescent candle. They were, for us, glowing beacons of hope for the Iraqi people and for us, as this particular area held all the future wealth for the country. We counted the familiar GOSPs and moved down to GOSP 6. As we moved into position, Sergeant Venaleck said, in his dispassionate way, "Ma'am, I think there's something wrong with GOSP 6."

"What do you mean, Sergeant?" I fought to look and I saw a massive fire emanating from the oil well. "What does that look like to you?"

"It looks like they've blown GOSP 6."

"Are you sure, Sergeant?" If they had blown the GOSPs, MEF wouldn't make it in time to prevent destruction, since their assault was planned for 0600 the following day, nearly twelve hours from now.

"Ma'am, that's what it looks like."

My heart started beating faster. I got on the chat and typed, "MEF & Div—GOSP 6 appears to be on fire and appears to be damaged."

MEF answered immediately: "Are you saying the GOSP has been blown?"

"My analysts are confirming that, standby. . . ."

Suddenly, there was a flurry of responses. MEF came back on: "All nets, MEF has priority on this. This is MEF, please confirm that there is deliberate damage to GOSPs." Ever meticulous, Sergeant Venaleck thoroughly scanned the picture and compared it to prior imagery. As the camera panned around, other damaged oil wells were now visible. Before we could answer, we started getting questions from the highest channels on the chat.

"This is the CFLCC-CENTCOM—confirm damage to GOSP area."

The CO came over to monitor the chat. I explained the situation to him: "Sir, the analysts clearly see damage to both the GOSPs and oil wells. The CFLCC wants confirmation, but we can't be 100 percent on this."

"Nothing is ever 100 percent. Scan the rest of the area and just tell them your best analysis."

"Mission Commander, let's get a thorough look at this whole GOSP area before giving a final answer." I asked CFLCC if we could have a couple minutes to finalize our analysis. Everyone waited patiently. As the UAV passed GOSP 2S, we saw deliberate abandonment and overpressuring of the oil tanks. Several of the giant oil tanks were bubbling over with oil and leaking everywhere. Next to the processing plant, several more oil wells had been blown.

"Sergeant Venaleck, please confirm or deny whether the GOSPs have been blown or not. Is there any way to do that?"

"Not 100 percent. But they appear damaged."

"You realize what's at stake here, right? If we say yes, they may take action. Not to put pressure on you, but if you assess that they have been tampered with, then that's what we have to go with."

"I have an idea, ma'am. Let's look at the POL site next to GOSP 6. If the oil tank is destroyed, then the GOSP has been blown." We averted the bird back to GOSP 6. The oil tanks appeared intact.

"Ma'am, GOSP 6 is intact."

"Thank God."

"Unfortunately, ma'am, we counted seven oil wells that had been damaged, and the only way that can happen is by deliberate tampering."

"Roger." I typed on the chat, "GOSP 6 is intact."

MEF answered, "Do you realize you almost launched MEF twelve hours early???"

"MEF," I wrote again, "That's not all: GOSP 6 is intact, but there are at least seven oil wells that have deliberately been blown in the vicinity." There was an eerie several-minute pause on chat. We scanned the GOSP area further and saw huge eruptions of fire thrusting out in bursts from the damaged oil wells. MEF finally came back on chat.

"Are you certain?"

"As certain as we can be; there is an unmistakable difference in what we are seeing right now." As I replied, we watched in horror as a pipeline erupted in flames, the flames racing the course of pipes.

"We are confirming that there is severe damage to several oil wells and along the pipe system. Part of the pipeline system is now bursting and erupting in flame."

The next thing we knew, MEF responded, "We just confirmed with CFLCC; air strikes will begin in an hour, and ground attack has been moved up to 2300."

I held my breath for a moment and collected myself. I turned to Sergeant Venaleck and said, "Hey, Sergeant Venaleck."

"Yes, ma'am?"

"I think we just launched the ground war."

★ ★ ★

Whether we were the ones who kicked off the ground war or not, there was no turning back. We were going to war, whether it be at 2300 or 0900, and that was that. Our future lay now in the training we had rehearsed and in the quick assuredness of our actions. It was Thursday, 20 March, and we had begun what we now knew as "Operation Iraqi Freedom."

Deep within the Iraqi sky, our UAV struggled through oil-saturated air. In front of the GOSP area, several oil trenches had been lit to try to obscure aerial observation of Iraqi ground troops, a tactic they had also employed during the Gulf War. After the imagery analysts had exploited and annotated the collected imagery on the oil wells, we passed it off to MEF. Our bird was struggling in the sky, and we waited to find something on the

Iraqi ground. I just walked in to the tent area where Debucher had been working with the Marines. He had actually stayed up throughout the night, and now, his head bobbing up and down, he was about to fall asleep. Even though it was my turn at the mission, he said, "Jane, I've got this. Don't worry about it; you're just crowding the area. Why don't you get some rest so you can be fresh for the drive up to Iraq tomorrow."

"I just woke up." I said.

"Well . . . we don't need you . . . here." Debucher nodded off again.

"Debucher, you're falling asleep. Let me have a go so you can put your head down for a while."

"I'm not tired." He nodded off again. Just then, the CO came by and saw what sad shape Debucher was in.

"Tony, you need to get some sleep now. You're done for today." Debucher wandered off reluctantly but cracked a few jokes to the crew before he left.

About half an hour after Debucher left, we began routing the bird back south when a sudden hot flash flew across the screen. Hot objects then exploded on the ground. There were hot spots all across the screen. Things were being destroyed everywhere.

"They did kick off the attack early," Sergeant Leppan remarked.

"That was fast." At that moment, we again had a command loss, meaning the bird had temporarily lost its signal connection. It would reroute itself on its own and go into autopilot on a preprogrammed course. Usually this was not a problem. However, Division came on chat again and wrote, "200 Tomahawk Land Attack Missile inbound at your last position."

"Jesus, they're dropping bombs right over our bird's head." Sergeant Young said.

"They're going to hit our bird!" another Marine said. At that moment, our bird came into view. All we could see on the camera were large explosions in the distance. We all looked in awe.

"Are you up, UAVs?" Division asked.

"Yes, but you almost killed our bird."

We moved east to the Ramalayah oil fields, where friendly forces soon would be in place. We moved around, searching for enemy order of battle, but everything seemed to have moved position before we could target it again. Finally we scanned to the west, and there, sitting in revetments, was a manned 59-1 battery of enemy artillery.

"Hey, we found something!"

"Geronimo!" said Sergeant Young.

"Sergeant Young, go get the CO and OpsO!"

Everyone piled into the room again and watched the screen as we positioned the bird to get a good visual of the entire battery. When the CO came in, he immediately called for Captain Hamill. Captain Graham Hamill was a Cobra pilot on his B billet, meaning he was in a nonflying billet. He was one of those always-pissed-off officers who never seemed to smile. That usually meant that they were competent. He worked as one of the mission commanders and was one of our most experienced forward air controllers.

"Graham," the CO said, "we need to conduct an adjust-fire mission."

"Roger that, sir."

Although UAVs had been originally designed to spot targets and conduct adjust-fire missions, there was no SOP on how this was done. Because of this, this type of mission was new, and in the uncertain environment of war, most leaders were skeptical about doing it for real.

But it not only was working, but it worked well. We could better adjust fire on targets because our viewpoint from above was ideal. To me, the idea of hunter and killer teams—with us as the hunters and artillery as the killers—was very reflective of the way I liked to operate. After we convinced Division to give us direct communications to the fire direction center, Major Sharp got on the chat from 11th Marines, my husband's higher headquarters unit.

"We need the center grid of the battery."

"Center grid = RQU280 320."

"Roger that, standby." Captain Hamill calculated the azimuth from the screen to the distance and angle from the gun line.

"Two minutes to TOT."

"Shot over," 11th Marines said. Eleventh Marines fired a volley of artillery rounds at the target.

"Shot out," I typed, acknowledging that the rounds were inbound to the target.

Suddenly, our camera on the UAV jumped out of position. We had just gotten a new one with a high-resolution color image, and the Marines were still training on it. It had a strange glitch where it would jump out of position.

"Goddamn it!" Sergeant Leppan was pissed off. It was a race for time to get the camera focused back to the target range.

"We'll get it back in time, just relax," the Major Cepeda said calmly over the ICS. Then, just in time, the camera settled back. We saw an impact about five hundred meters short of the area.

Captain Hamill adjusted his fire and said, "Right 400, down 200."

In about two minutes, we saw rounds impact the right side of the battery in a circle of powdery death.

"Damn, we almost got it! Tell them 'left 100, up 50,' fire for effect."

"Roger," I said.

Cascading rings of artillery soon enveloped the right side of the target, then the bottom, and then finally almost on target.

"Tell them 'repeat.'" I said.

I finally got to type the forbidden word of military communications, "repeat," which meant only one thing: you were about to rain death and destruction. At last, the target was saturated with perfect ringlets of rounds impacting every few seconds. They hit dead on.

For the first time we cheered, and then I typed, "End of Mission, record as target, BDA—Battery destroyed, poss FDC destroyed."

Reports came in of cheers across various command centers, and we heard that we had destroyed the first significant enemy equipment. Our squadron had done something it hadn't done before—we had conducted our first combat mission and used UAVs and artillery to destroy a target. To me, this validated what I had learned in school about reconnaissance pull—in other words, operations no longer made plans, but determined how to act based on intelligence reconnaissance. As ground forces began to breach the border between Kuwait and Iraq, we were destroying targets ahead of them. The more enemy units we spotted, the more targets we could give to air and artillery assets. Mostly, it was a desperate struggle to save as many lives as possible. I thought about all the forces that would be passing through the gauntlet, among them my husband. I knew we had to do all we could to protect those behind us.

As the bird returned to base, on the screen we saw enormous explosions in the distant horizon. They were different than before. Fiery objects seemed to be catapulting across the horizon in a projectile motion. We traced the objects back to their origin. Before us was a perfect regiment of artillery. The awesome aerial sight of seventy-two 155mm M198 howitzers lobbing rounds to a target somewhere in Iraq is one I will never forget. And somewhere below was my husband, who was part of this regiment. I wished the fire would continue—not just so the targets would be destroyed, but so that I knew he was still safe before crossing into Iraq.

★   ★   ★

At that precise moment on the Iraqi-Kuwaiti border, the first volley of artillery was fired in the Battle of Basra, thus beginning the ground assault in

Operation Iraqi Freedom. In the "echo area," the percussive zone on the artillery firing line, Marines were bleeding from their ears and noses. Marines of RCT-7 had begun its highly orchestrated attack to seize the Crown Jewel Objective. Farther to the west, RCT-5 already began its assault into Iraq to seize the oil facilities to prevent their destruction. Unbeknownst to Peter, I had seen the Iraqis begin to sabotage this vital piece of Iraqi infrastructure, but he did not know why they were firing so prematurely. The Marines all complained but were at the same time relieved that they had pushed off eight hours ahead of schedule.

Six klicks—otherwise known as kilometers—to the south of the 11th Marines, the earth smelled of a blend of cordite and smoldering decay that had drifted into our area from forty kilometers ahead. In the distance, we could hear the echo of the regimental fires launching artillery at targets and the distance boom of the air strikes dropping ordnance. The stir of war was everywhere. After several nights of intermittent sleep, I succumbed to a state of hyperalertness, where I was just wired on an adrenaline high. It was some strange state of existence in which I merely completed each task in front of me. There was nothing external, no distractions. The once-incessant thoughts of my husband had been replaced by a strange state of indifference. Pleasure and happiness were so far removed that I operated as though my old life had never existed. There was too much on my mind for it to even wander to soft images of his face and his touch. I remained focused, like some feral animal in search of food. Instinct, adrenaline, and existential nothingness. My feelings just switched off, and I felt nothing.

My biggest fear was not getting shot, but concern that our operation would not run smoothly. We had just been given the order that we would be moving to Iraq in the next twenty-four hours. Judging from the trouble I had already seen in the way the operation had been run, I had little faith in the overall plan. It struck me as strange that I had heard only the first ninety-six hours briefed in detail. The rest of the plan was an amorphous "what if." No one I knew had seen a commander's intent, the long-range strategic plan of what our end result was supposed to be. Other than ending up at Baghdad, gaining control of key terrain throughout the area of operation, and liberating the country, we weren't sure what we were supposed to do afterward. As it turns out, for my unit personally, the Generals on up forgot that there were thirteen females in our unit, and it looked like we were going into Iraq in a very untraditional way: we would be jumping from one location to another, sometimes ahead of combat units, in order to provide coverage for the infantry units.

It seemed to me that we were severely underestimating the enemy. I had no idea what would happen next, but with all the terrorist threats, possibilities of guerrilla tactics, and insurgent attacks, I had serious reservations. In fact, I was downright terrified that we had a severe lack of planning for the long-term outcome of this thing. What would happen after we occupied the country? Would Walmart and McDonald's miraculously appear? Or were they hoping that the people of Iraq would be motivated to restart their world anew on their own? I saw and heard of no plan for reconstruction. I wondered if there was one. I could only imagine that this would be an ugly, asymmetric war that would take months, if not years, to accomplish.

Coalition forces were moving into Iraq and had seized some of the objectives. My husband was with 7th Marines in support of the objectives to secure Basra. I had just read the report that came through that the crown jewel was now secured. Although 5th Marines had already reached the GOSPs, we had learned of the first casualty—Second Lieutenant Childers. I had known who he was—he had gone through The Basic School the same time I did. Why did I feel responsible? I thought back to how we could have scanned the area better for enemy positions. Even though it was absurd to think I had anything to do with it, I felt guilty—but, even more, angry that our first brother had fallen.

10

ON THE SHORE, DIMLY SEEN

The die is cast. —Julius Caesar, upon crossing the Rubicon

We are leaving tomorrow morning," said Lieutenant Colonel Mykleby. It was 21 March; only twenty-four hours after the war had begun. We had received a Warning Order to redeploy to a forward operating base called Jalibah Airbase, an abandoned Iraqi airfield about two hundred kilometers northwest of our current position.

"Too late to turn back," I thought to myself. From my perspective of watching the flights, the northernmost point of the forward line of troops was Ramalayah—a good eighty kilometers southeast of Jalibah.

I figured that they knew what they were doing, as the Army had secured that area already. We had just learned that 2nd Tanks, part of RCT-2, had pushed their way up Route Edith and had secured Highway 8. We flew over them on the bird we had up, which would probably be our last bird up in Kuwait. I watched as the friendly tanks parked themselves alone and unafraid on the newly secured highway. Farther up on the shore near the Alamo Bridge were the Amtracs (armored tracked vehicles). They sat alone on the edge of the battle space, buttoned up along the bank of the river. It was a strangely lonely sight, surreal and quietly horrible. I peered down at the frontline troops in an almost dreamlike state. This sight was almost something I felt I was never meant to witness. For a moment I imagined how the military had once hired psychics to telepathically remote view themselves into situations and report back information. This is how it seemed for us now. Below, a lone Marine walked outside his vehicle, and the whole of Iraq stretched before him.

And briefly, I thought, he looked up and saw that there were others—us—watching and protecting him.

After circling the friendly positions for a while, we moved north, again past the front line. We crossed the Alamo Bridge and the Euphrates, which irrigated an area that was surprisingly fertile compared to the rest of Iraq. Directly across the bridge we followed the tree line and found the enemy armor position. Less than three kilometers away were several T-52s (Russian-made tanks), BMPs (Russian fighting vehicles), and a battery of 59-1s enemy artillery pointed directly at the friendly position across the bridge. We could see on our maps and from the blue force tracker device that showed us where all the friendly and enemy forces were. The friendlies were us, and well, the enemies—anyone not us.

"Holy shit!" said one of the imagery analysts. I quickly called Division on the tactical phone.

"Division, do you know there are about seven tanks and a battery of enemy artillery staring across the shore at your boys, just across Alamo Bridge?"

"No, we didn't."

"Can we call for fire on them?"

"Standby." I waited patiently.

"Danger close. 5/11 Artillery said they're too close."

"Too close? They're three kilometers away! I thought danger close was six hundred meters!"

"Standby," Division said again. Minutes later, they came back with a reply.

"Fires said the battle space geometry was wrong. From where friendly artillery is, they could easily light up the friendlies instead."

"Roger." But I kept thinking about those boys in the Amtracs. It seemed so frustrating that in the United States, civilian communication was so far advanced that anyone could pick up a cell phone to speak to someone. I wanted to warn them, at least tell them what was ahead. Our communications system was inefficient; it was difficult most times to even talk to Division, let alone a battalion or company. I perceived this as one of the military's critical vulnerabilities at the time; the length of time to communicate with another unit was just unsatisfactory. The poor kid stood out on the edge, all alone, and no one could warn him.

We circled back to the friendly position. The Amtracs still faced north, still buttoned up.

"Sergeant Leppan, what do you think those boys are thinking right now?"

"Ma'am, they're probably hoping there aren't seven tanks and a battery of artillery pointed at them."

"Then what's the point of us being up here if we can't even tell them?"

"Tell them what, ma'am?"

"That we can protect them. That we have eyes on the target."

We orbited again. There was nothing we could do. Sergeant Leppan looked at me and said, "Ma'am, these are friendlies; do you want us to press ahead?"

"Sorry, yes, Sergeant, let's move to the south." We circled low, and the UAV made a loop in the dark sky. I just hoped the sound of the UAVs was somehow reassuring to the troops below, knowing that a friendly scout was somehow watching out for them. But in this case, the reassurance would have been misleading.

★ ★ ★

Morning came, and we lined up our convoy facing north. We found out that the enemy forces we had seen last night had been abandoned, and so our Amtracs got through without being assaulted. It had taken us only two hours to pack up, and now we were pressing on. The squadron of about 180 Marines was ready to convoy into Iraq. The CO gathered us in a circle to give us one of his trademark last-minute motivational speeches.

"Marines, this is it. We have trained for years to do what we are about to do now. The training is done, and it's time to do this for real. Remember, if you come across Iraqis, and they have a weapon, you don't hesitate—you aim, you fire, and you shoot the son of a bitch down. If the Iraqis drive in front of you, I don't care if it's some red-headed Irish midget wearing a purple suit waving a white flag—if he's preventing the convoy from moving, you run him down. This is not the time for cowardice and not the time to back down; this is a decisive moment in which lives are shaped, in which men are made. You are going to see many things out there, many of which will change the way you think forever. But you will get through this. Marines, I make you this promise: if you stick by me and listen to what I say, we are all going to come back together."

Some of the Marines' faces were windswept; others were covered with sand. Some seemed visibly nervous, some afraid. I studied all their faces as the CO spoke. Would we all make it? And if we did, would these faces be changed by the time we returned? Many of the enlisted members looked so young. Some looked too baby-faced to be fighting, to be at war. Many of them were still teenagers, and their faces still bore the naive overconfidence of adolescence. Most of them seemed like boys, now that I looked around.

It troubled me that some of the senior leaders in the unit seemed frazzled and undone by the rapid pace at which events were progressing. The CO was not that way, and I promised myself that I never would be, either. He exuded confidence. His words had noticeably changed the expressions on many of the Marines' faces. Where there had been fear, there was now a serene assurance. As the formation parted, I left with my eyes set on Iraq, with insouciance I had never before possessed.

The squadron pulled onto the highway, and I watched the kilometer markers dwindle as we approached the border of Iraq. The Kuwaiti desert passed quickly on both sides of the road. I counted down the digits—10, 9, 8 . . .—until we reached Iraq.

★   ★   ★

I had read that during the Gulf War Shi'ites had asked for help overthrowing Saddam. Both Iraqi civilians and military deserters were ready to take up arms against him. George H. W. Bush had even given a speech calling for Iraqis to stage a coup against Saddam. Many civilians took a stand and brought their plans to the American military. But the Americans were not able to commit their forces to seize Iraq since they had only planned for the Kuwaiti operation—expelling Iraqi forces from Kuwait but not driving on to Baghdad. When the Shi'ites needed us the most and rallied for our support, we were forced to withdraw due to lack of planning for this contingency operation.

As soon as we withdrew, Saddam set the example by executing thousands of Shi'ites and Kurds for their uprising. Now, I questioned if the Shi'ites would still welcome us with open arms. People in fear will rally around what is familiar to them, not always what is right.

Another problem I saw was the terrorist nature of the Fedayeen forces and the potential influence they could have. They could easily blend into the civilian population until it was time to ambush us. Just as the Mujahedin had done, they could lie in wait for the front line to pass through and then attack the supply chains. I worried that we didn't have enough forces to meet this threat.

As we moved toward the border, I had no fear when we saw Safwan Hill and the gateway into Iraq. Although I kept my hand on my pistol, the berm area was not the mystic entrance it had seemed from the UAV. A

United Nations watchtower, painted white, stood above, between the border of Iraq and Kuwait, primitive and in ill repair. My thoughts raced through the mosaic of images I had created about Iraq. From overhead, the country had seemed like a shadowy, alien, enemy world. Passing into it, my thoughts emptied into some dynamic mix of possibility. As that mosaic changed, we became part of the chaotic mixture in the battle space known as Iraq.

Safwan, the first border town, was strangely reminiscent of the ancient ruins in Upper Egypt—a crumbling civilization sustained only at the most basic levels. The border area was marked with burning hulks of metal and trash and rubble. Iraq was in ruins. It wasn't just the damage or scattered refuse I had seen littered on the side of the roads in Kuwait: this was a neglected civilization. Unlike Upper Egypt, where the little-changed relationship between man and nature created a primitive charm, Iraq was not quaint. Safwan was a lost world in which the buildings had no character; they were just empty vessels to house sad souls. Vacant, lifeless faces of Iraqis appeared in the distance, staring at our convoy as it moved into Iraq.

We were told not to stop under any circumstances. As we came closer to the Iraqis who watched us, their faces were expressionless. The whole town seemed to have checked out, and only the children seemed to smile. Mothers in head-to-toe black chadors reached out their hands, hoping for handouts from our vehicles. Some children tried to run alongside the vehicles. The men, in dishdashas, stood at a distance, whispering to each other. Only the children made eye contact with us. As I pulled out my Nikon to try to snap some photos, the adults dashed away or covered their faces. It seemed as if we were some bizarre kind of parade.

We quickly passed through Safwan and entered the open highway; coalition forces guarded every intersecting road. The burning pipelines and revetments we had seen from the UAV were all over the sides of the roads. Jalibah was still a good three-hour convoy ahead. I saw the British with Iraqi soldiers in a holding area surrounded by concertina wire—the prisoners, in military uniforms, had their hands tied behind their backs. Their AK-47s had been stripped from them and were lying broken, in a pile, near the guards outside. The prisoners looked defeated and abandoned, as if the war for them had been going on for years. They stared into the distance, waiting for a new life.

★   ★   ★

The entire area leading up to Jalibah was supposed to be secured, but we all knew that you couldn't secure cities like Basra, with more than one million inhabitants, in twenty-four hours. Securing an area was something said when a threat was not visible, not something that meant that we maintained control of the area. Here we were rolling through secured areas, and there wasn't a soul in sight. That didn't settle right in my head, so as we rolled through Iraq, I told my .50 cal gunner beside me to stay vigilant.

My vehicle was fifteenth in the convoy. The driver, Corporal Reynolds, was a Mormon and an air maintenance chief. At twenty-seven, he was mature and should have been a Sergeant or Staff Sergeant, but his particular job did not promote quickly. Corporal Cano was my .50 cal gunner, a gung-ho air maintenance tech from Texas. Our five-ton truck was the "bird truck," and carried five of the eight UAVs we had on hand. It was one of the most mission-critical vehicles we had.

As we cruised through Iraq, we rolled past many of the areas we had imaged with the bird, and it was strange to see that "God's-eye view" transformed into a three-dimensional world. At one intersection, the British were providing security with tanks and Scorpions (light armor reconnaissance vehicles); evidently they had already relieved the Marines who were pushing north. On the side of the road lay more destroyed vehicles and burning hulks. Across the road, I saw more EPWs; a group of about fifty Iraqi soldiers were being led into a circular corral of barbed wire. We sped past the Ramalayah oilfields. We neared Highway 8, the spot where, only twelve short hours ago, we had seen the tanks secure the highway—and where, only a few kilometers north, I had watched those solitary Amtracs sitting on the shore. Things, important things, passed by so quickly.

Every mile or so, we saw the reassuring sight of friendly forces along the sides of the roads. Vehicles, marked with identifying symbols of the units they were in, lined the road. The vehicles we were passing at that moment were marked with familiar tags.

"That's strange," I thought to myself, "why are we passing the artillery?" As we coasted farther north, we saw elements of 7th Marines, our infantry brothers from Twentynine Palms, parked on the side of the road, providing security and pointing north.

"That's weird," remarked Sergeant Corporal Reynolds. "Ma'am, why are we moving past the infantry?"

Finding no better explanation than the one I devised myself, I said, "It's just a remain-behind security element, probably to offer a guard position and safe passage for support convoys such as ourselves."

"Oh, good to go."

We pushed north. By the time it started getting dark, we had reached checkpoint 4 of 5 and were forty kilometers from Jalibah. We had a lot of inexperienced drivers who had never driven with night-vision goggles (NVGs) and blackout conditions. Without NVGs, all you could see was a dimly lit shadow of the convoy; only the sound gave away our position. It was hard to see the vehicle in front of us, and the NVGs distorted the distance between the vehicles, making it seem like we were much closer than we really were. Because of the security posture, we would drive in the dark with 150 meters between the vehicles. Driving north, we began passing tanks with their guns pointing north, then a never-ending series of Amtracs and light armored reconnaissance (LAR) vehicles. These units were the heavy armored units in the Marine Corps—the ones that lead the way in war.

"Ma'am, why are we passing armored convoys? This is about all of MEF!"

"Relax, they're probably reinforcements."

By the time we were only ten kilometers from Jalibah, we were halted in a backlog of military vehicle traffic. We formed a herringbone and waited by the side of the road. I had to piss badly, but there was no place for privacy. I walked about five feet into a reedy area. Looking ahead, I saw a feral dog eating the rotting corpse of a horse. Flies swarmed madly. We couldn't wander more than a couple feet past the vehicles for fear of getting attacked. My eyes scanned the horizon for a place to go to the bathroom. I wandered a couple feet more and in the near distance, by a small stream next to a mud building, laid a decomposing body. Looking closer, I noticed he was Arab, but his dishdasha had been lifted over his face, and his genitals were exposed. I turned away. I looked around to see if the other Marines had noticed, but he was well concealed between the reeds in the water and mud. His arms had been blown off, and his torso was smashed open, his organs scattered about. A cluster of yellow flowers, the first of spring, were crushed beneath the remains of his body. I did not mention the corpse; it was something I didn't want to share with the others.

We continued on our way again, and our vehicles pulled out again along the road. The sky had all but lost its color. It was cold as hell. My mind was getting heavy with exhaustion, and I was jonesing for caffeine. We hadn't eaten or drank all day—I had avoided drinking water simply because I still didn't have a place to pee. It dawned on me that I had to figure out a way to have some privacy, but there was none to be had. I tried rationalizing: if I could survive at least three days without water, I had two days to go, but I still had to piss now. We weren't stopping. We had been driving in our convoy for about four hours straight without stop since our last break. My CO said he wouldn't tolerate extra privileges for the ladies, and I didn't want to be the one to break his rule. It was a real problem. On the verge of pissing myself, I finally told the Corporals not to look in my direction. I cut an empty water bottle in half with my knife. I pulled a poncho out and covered myself, pulled my pants down, and pissed in the plastic bottle. When I finished, I dumped the bottle over the side of the vehicle. My embarrassment was obvious, but the Corporals said nothing to me. They pretended not to notice. There wasn't room for shame out here. We kept driving, and soon my thoughts shifted back to the surroundings. I found it more and more difficult to focus my eyes. Finally, we came to a long halt. As our vehicles remained stopped for what seemed like hours, the motor's hum occasionally lulled me to sleep. I drifted in and out of consciousness. Despite my sheer exhaustion, the bitter cold kept me from falling deeply asleep. Misery was setting in fast. I continued listening on the tactical radio for any messages from the convoy commander.

"This is Watchdog 6," the radio echoed finally. Watchdog 6 was the CO. "We're going to do a tactical halt in this position; we might be here for a while."

Most of us got out and posted security. Since our vehicle's cab had no roof, the three of us were shivering violently, even wearing our MOPP suits and flak jackets. Iraq was cold, even in March. My fingers had long since gone numb.

"Hey, Corporal Cano, get yourself off that gun and get your head down for a little while. I'll provide security—you, too, Corporal Reynolds."

No sooner had I said that than they were bedded down in the vehicle. There was no objection, so they must have been tired. Corporal Reynolds gave me his NVGs to use.

I pointed my M16 out of the cab as I shivered and cursed whatever had put me in this mess. What the hell was I thinking when I joined? Here I was somewhere in Iraq, a big target in a vehicle. I questioned every pattern of thought that had led me to this point. Surely this was the stupidest decision I had made in my life.

I thought back to the day I swore in and gave my oath of enlistment. The recruiting station took me to the military entrance processing station (MEPS) center, where they process all the potential recruits right before they ship them off to their chosen service's basic training. We were escorted into a tiny red room with glass doors. It looked like a church or shrine, except it had service flags flanking a big emblem of the United States. It was very official looking. We sat down in the chapel's chairs and waited.

Finally, a senior military officer came in the room and had us stand up and raise our right hands. He asked us to repeat after him. I listened to the words I echoed back:

> I, state your name, do solemnly swear that I will support and defend the Constitution of the United States against all enemies, foreign and domestic; that I will bear true faith and allegiance to the same; and that I will obey the orders of the President of the United States and the orders of the officers appointed over me, according to regulations and the Uniform Code of Military Justice. So help me God.

It all sounded very grim, but I thought to myself, "I'll never have to do that, but I'll do it if I have to."

When I first joined, I was single and unafraid of anything life put in my way. Ironically, the four years I had spent in the Corps had changed me, and I had grown more cautious. And then, for God's sake, only two months ago I had gotten married! I was a newlywed without my husband. A bride still, on a honeymoon alone in Iraq spent shivering, pointing my M16 downrange, ready to kill anything. Pretty freaking romantic. I thought back on my happy life and wondered if I was really prepared to die. I thought about my life while I sat there trembling. I laughed. "I've got no choice now—to live or die," I thought. "I just have to survive and keep my Marines safe as best I can."

I scanned the perimeter with my NVGs, which made everything that emanated light appear in various shades of green. Unexpectedly, I saw several hundred objects about one hundred meters away. Focusing my NVGs, I couldn't believe what I saw. About one thousand Iraqi EPWs were being escorted across the road. They were cuffed and had bags over their heads. Some were in only their underwear. They were being taken into covered seven-ton trucks. Even though I was starting to hallucinate after nearly forty-eight hours without sleep, it was clear what I was seeing. It blew my mind that the whole time we were sitting here, I hadn't even realized this was going on. After they had escorted about half the prisoners, the Major Cepeda came on the radio.

"Marines, we will be moving shortly. The Corporal of the guard here at the checkpoint says this is the FLOT for the Marines, and he needs to call the CO to get approval for us to pass."

I relayed the information to my Corporals in the truck.

"What? What does that mean?"

"I think the Army is supposed to have it secured after this point, so they're probably doing a changeover."

"Oh, Roger that." In reality, my unit was now the front line. But we didn't know it.

★ ★ ★

We soon got word on the radio, and the vehicles started rolling again. As my vehicle passed the modest-looking checkpoint, it was open road from here until Jalibah airfield. In a semiconscious state, I saw a crescent statue rising out of the ground like some bad hallucination. After more confusion and tumbling in and out of consciousness, we were told the airfield had not yet been cleared of mines but that there was a secured position three kilometers down the road. There, exhausted, we arranged the vehicles in convoy order, posted security, and then tried to sleep.

It was already dawn when I awoke. Across the horizon, sand dune after sand dune stretched as far as the eye could see. The soupy air made me feel cold and sweaty at the same time. The white cement airstrip was the only man-made structure in sight, apart from our convoy. We were the only unit here. If a war was going on, we certainly couldn't see it from here. On the ground, small leafless shrubs decorated the otherwise lifeless area. Closer to the ground, strange orange, radioactive-looking wild squash meandered everywhere, looking like round bomblets.

At midday, the senior leadership met by the CO's vehicle for a briefing. The CO said we would roll north to Qalat Sikar, a northern airstrip and town near Al Kut. Since I had not heard the intelligence picture for two days, I was a bit apprehensive as to whether that area and the route to it were secure. Still, the CO insisted that, despite the fact that we were traveling unescorted and with only security ammo on us, the route would be safe enough. Our plan was to push north as fast as we could and take out any targets that blocked our path, whether civilian or military. The map showed that we would have to pass through An Nasiriyah, a sizeable city we had been told was a serious choke point. Historically, it was a city designed to protect its citizens against insurgent attacks, with a geometric layout of streets. Established by the Ottoman leader Muntafiquah, the sheikh of the Confederation of Arab Tribes, the layout of grid streets protected it from outside attacks.

When I returned to my vehicle after the convoy briefing, one of the communication chiefs was listening to the BBC newscast on a tactical radio.

"Ma'am, check this out." Staff Sergeant Smith called me over. He was a tall, blond, well-respected Marine who had a wife, also a Marine, back in

Twentynine Palms. He and I had bonded quickly and were always sharing stories with one another.

On the BBC news broadcast, we heard reports about An Nasiriyah and how the area was not yet secured. We were within kicking distance of that city. An Army convoy had just been ambushed going through our future route—Marines had not even gone near the city yet.

The BBC lost signal, but we started hearing rumors that the Army convoy was rolling across town on the main highway when the lead vehicle got lost and led them the wrong way. During the ambush, a squad of personnel including a female, PFC Lynch, took heavy fire and was taken prisoner by Iraqis armed with RPGs. The story we heard was that the prisoners were paraded around Baghdad, then tortured and killed. Our convoy was supposed to pass through An Nasiriyah in two hours. A sickness filled me. Where the hell was the infantry? What the fuck were we doing?

A reconnaissance scout vehicle from the checkpoint that we had passed informed us that we were, indeed, entirely on our own. Not only that, but the infantry Lieutenant told us we had passed all the other Marine units and were the forward line to the southwest. Apparently, someone had not realized that "aerial recon" was not the same thing as "ground recon."

We knew now what to expect from Nasiriyah—word spread fast. The insurgents would fight militia-style, using asymmetric warfare. Perhaps Saddam had spoken the truth when he said he was going to lure the troops into the cities and, when they had grown complacent, start a street insurgency that would gradually whittle down our will to fight. What the Generals had once thought was a nice, sterile plan of removing Saddam from power was now crumbling upon them into an ugly, dangerous battle.

11

A DANGEROUS POSITION

We saw the lightning and that was the guns and then we heard the thunder and that was the big guns; and then we heard the rain falling and that was the blood falling; and when we came to get in the crops, it was dead men that we reaped.

—Harriet Tubman

Our plan was to move that afternoon. We only had only a skirmish's worth of ammo; our Marines had only sixty rounds for their M16s and thirty rounds for their pistols. I felt very perturbed. I knew when I heard we would push through Nasiriyah that it would be a difficult situation. We heard on our shortwave radio that there were still civilians everywhere in the city, in the streets alongside the Iraqi forces. It reminded me of what General Krulak called the "three-block war": on one street would be friendlies and observation posts, the next street we would be providing humanitarian assistance, and on the next street, we would be engaged in full-scale battle.

My CO came over and spoke to each officer personally. That's the way he was. He wanted to make sure we were all mentally prepared. He ordered one of the officers in the seven-tons to be the lead vehicle and "knock the shit out of anything that gets in our way." There had been reports of insurgents paying kids to jump in front of convoys to slow them down enough to set up an ambush.

When the CO got to me, he said, "Jane, how are you doing? How are you holding up?"

"Fine, sir."

"You're going to have to be vigilant out there, Jane. We're probably going to get ambushed, so you're going to need to be ready for anything.

Be prepared to leave in two hours. We're waiting on the fuel truck to come back, so once you see it roll up, get the Marines in your area prepared to get rolling."

"Yes, sir. Just one thing—I've heard the BBC reports on the radio just now, and it doesn't seem wise that we're pushing through here. We have no hardened vehicles and barely any ammo. Do we even know if the route up and Qalat Sikar are secured? I don't have the warm and fuzzy about this sir."

"That's what we're being told, Jane. We've been given the Warning Order. I know it doesn't seem logical, but we have to trust the system." He paused, looked around, and then said, "Let me share something with you—just between us, so don't go passing this to the Marines, because you'll get them scared. You see those Cobras and Hueys about a thousand meters out?" For the last ten minutes the only movement near us had been a stream of helicopters on the far edge of the airfield. Many of us were wondering what was going on.

"Yes, sir."

"That's Jalibah airfield. Those are medevac teams with Cobra escorts. They're bringing mass casualties in right now from An Nasiriyah. There are a lot of Marines getting killed out there right now. But, you know, there are more Fedayeen bodies in that count than Marines. A Marine armored unit is in there right now pounding the shit out of the Iraqis. Yes, we're rolling in right behind them, but they are in front of us. It does sound insane. Believe one thing, Jane. We're going to pound the shit out of them, too."

★ ★ ★

By my vehicle I silently waited. The other Marines tried to get some shut-eye before we pulled out, but there was no way I could sleep after what my CO said. My mind raced over missed training opportunities. If we came under attack, our unit had no formal ground training, and I questioned whether the junior Marines would know what to do. Did my Marines know how to do a skirmish formation? A flanking position? I didn't know if they knew these things. I was embarrassed that I hadn't taken a day or two to teach them the basics of platoon and squad tactics. Time hit the two-hour mark when we were supposed to go forward. But the fuel truck still wasn't back. There was nothing in the black distance ahead. Hours seemed to roll by, and my eyes kept shifting back to the medevac helicopters. I felt awful for the Marines in the fight. Why the hell weren't we flying for them now? We could be scouting out the battlefield for them instead of sitting on the side of the road. Closing my eyes, I tried to calm down. Next to me, my two Corporals were wide-awake and seemed nervous.

"You two should get some sleep—I have a hunch that we're not moving."

"Ma'am, I thought we were just waiting for the fuel truck to return."

"True, but something tells me that because it's already dark we're going to hole up here for the night," I lied.

The Corporals seemed relieved, assuming I knew more than I did, and bedded down. Through the darkness, I saw a vehicle in the distance, surely the fuel truck. But it was not. It was another scout vehicle. I walked over to the CO's vehicle in hopes of hearing whatever news there was. Most of the officers had also gathered.

"Are you the UAV squadron?" asked the Lieutenant from the courier team.

"Yes, I'm Lieutenant Colonel Mykleby," said my CO.

"The group CO told me to tell you to stand fast," he said nervously.

"We have a FragO, and that gives me the authority from my higher headquarters to move forward—we're supposed to have left already!"

"Every unit that's tried to go through there has gotten lit up, sir. Tanks are rolling through there now. The Marine Aircraft Group (MAG) CO said he wants you to wait until morning until further word."

"What the fuck, Lieutenant! We were ordered to roll several hours ago. If the fuel truck had been back, we would've left. Why is he just finding out this intel now?"

"Sir, I don't know, but I can relay the message. . . ."

"Tell him we'll hold fast, but also tell him we want our birds up in the air now; we can fly from this spot."

"Aye, sir. I'll tell him."

That conversation was to me like telling the firing squad they were not going to execute us today. Did anyone have a clue that we were about to go through An Nasiriyah *before* the armored units? Jesus, I just lost any faith I had in higher command. It was as though higher had some checklist with times and dates, and they just decided we had to meet the deadline. Did they even look at the situations board? We would not have been adequately prepared to deal with that threat. It seemed like there was mass confusion going on around us. I was reminded of the fact that I had never heard the operational briefing past the first seventy-two to ninety-six hours. Since we had accomplished that mission in only forty-eight hours, apparently no one had mapped out the contingency if our forces in An Nasiriyah got bogged down. I walked back to inform my Marines about what was going on.

We found out the following day that a light armored reconnaissance unit (LAR) and lead elements of 2nd Marines had been attacked in An Nasiriyah and had to partially withdraw. They already had eighteen casualties and thirty injuries. In the morning I watched a continuous stream of helicopters bring casualties to the airfield. The fact that they were Marines' bodies nauseated me. My former confidence in the upper echelon had yielded to a sickening feeling of dread, and I suddenly felt as though I had to be the one to look out for our unit.

"Those are our brothers," I thought, "but we would have had more casualties."

It was now 24 March, and things did not look so good. We heard that 10th Marines artillery had fired on the 1st Battalion, 2nd Marines infantry unit, convoys were being ambushed continually, and all the areas we had passed through had now been classified "unsecured." We felt completely surrounded and cut off from the rest of the Marine Corps. The MWCS-28 communications squadron had joined us on the side of the road, but they hadn't had the good fortune we did; they had taken fire several times to get to where we were. The communications officers told us what they knew, which was basically more rumors of ambushes and attacks along the routes. One of the officers, Lieutenant Winter, told me they were supposed to push up with us to Qalat Sikar but had gotten ambushed right off the road we were on and were ordered by higher to wait it out. He laughed when I told him we were supposed to have left yesterday for Qalat Sikar.

"You're so lucky, dude. If you had gone, you would all have been dead."

"I know, believe me."

The fuel truck had arrived eight hours late. I still wonder if my CO deliberately delayed that fuel truck to buy us time or whether it was just a stroke of luck.

★   ★   ★

That afternoon, our unit and the communications squadron were given a warning order to relocate to Jalibah airfield, where we would temporarily fly missions in support of the battle at An Nasiriyah. Task Force Tarawa, or 2nd Marine Expeditionary Brigade (MEB), was given this area of operations, and we were now in direct support of them. We were back in the fight.

Just thirty kilometers north of us, on the route we were supposed to have taken, Marines were taking heavy casualties. Lieutenant Colonel Grabowski, the CO of 1st Battalion, 2nd Marines, received the order to attack through the city to seize the two key bridges and rescue the stranded Army convoy. Moments meant everything. Lieutenant Carlson, a close friend from The Basic School and a tank platoon commander, received the order that, in less than two hours, he would detach from Company Alpha and attach in support of the 2nd Light Armored Reconnaissance Battalion and begin advancing. Lieutenant Carlson got his tank team assembled and set out from his current position, thirty kilometers south of the city. As they approached the city, he began clearing the enemy obstacles blocking the road using his tank platoon assets. The four tanks moved through the area. About twenty kilometers behind them, 2nd Light Armored Reconnaissance (LAR) was just south of An Nasiriyah, preparing for the attack. Lieutenant Stone, a forward observer who was attached to LAR, had established a hasty defense with the unit just a couple hours prior. As they stopped in a circular defensive position known as a "coil," they started to receive incoming fire. The Iraqi forces had seized the initiative and were attempting to infiltrate into LAR's position. Once Lieutenant Carlson heard that a LAR unit was being attacked, he changed his position and directed the fire of his four tanks to the enemy's location. The battle continued for twelve hours. As the sun began to set, the enemy forces rolled up in buses with their high beams on. The fight lasted all night. Throughout the night, our forces used fixed- and rotary-wing close air support, artillery, and mortars. Lieutenant Carlson's tanks became the anchor for the battalion defense and pushed the enemy out of LAR's position, keeping them from supporting the developing fight in An Nasiriyah. While the Battle of the Coil remains a relatively unknown story, it is part of the Battle for An Nasiriyah, which was to become the most decisive battle during the major combat operations phase.

★   ★   ★

There were some nights I couldn't sleep at all, even though I was exhausted. Before racking out, my mind shifted to thoughts about death and how frightened I had been at moments, knowing that this could be it. It didn't help that nothing felt like home and that the only thing that was home to me was this empty spot in my truck. I pulled my boots off, got into my sleeping bag, and stared into the night sky. I wondered if I was the only one in the universe who had ever slept in this spot in the desert before. Or maybe I was the first one who had ever been here, passing this lonely, miserable spot. I mean, I was out in the middle of the desert, where it seemed as if nothing had ever been before, and I wondered who else might have walked here and what that spot's history had been.

I was in the middle of the desert in Iraq. This small space in the universe was really vacant and mine alone. I thought that if the world were broken up into a giant grid of meters, each meter would have its own history. For Muslims, the Kabah was its center, a holy meter where thousands focused their prayers. In Israel, along several meters, there was sadness on the Wailing Wall. In Jerusalem, the Holy Sepulcher; in America—how many meters did the Oval Office take? Each meter on earth held its own unique history, and this one was mine, this one meter of insignificant sand I slept on. One day, there would be a meter that I died on, and another in which I was buried. Right now, Iraqis and our forces were killing on meters marking their important spots on the earth. This war was nothing but meters. On my meter I fell into a short, dreamless sleep and woke when I heard a civilian truck moving in the distance. Since we could see several klicks in each direction, we could see if Iraqi vehicles were coming near our convoy. As the vehicle came approached, we saw an Iraqi bus, probably Bedouin, pull down the road, trying to get past our position. Some of the SNCOs jumped up with their weapons and stopped the vehicle.

"Jane, get the hell over here, *now!*" I heard my CO call. Since I was the only one in the squadron who knew any Arabic, I was the designated interrogator/translator. We didn't rate a real one. When we were still in Kuwait, I taught an Arabic customs and courtesies class, a class on Islam, and the official rules of engagement brief, but this was something altogether new for me. Jumping off the five-ton, I grabbed my M16 and ran over in front of the vehicle, which was now surrounded by Marines who had assumed prone defensive positions. My CO told me to do something.

It had been almost eleven years since I had to speak Egyptian Arabic, so I was a little rusty. The whole squadron was watching with their M16s pointed in my direction. In the panic, I tried to come up with a plan. Holding my arm out straight ahead, I waved it up and down, palm facing down. That was the hand signal to stop in Iraq. The vehicle had now come to a halt in front of me.

I seemed to have instantaneously forgotten every Arabic word I once knew. I had to dig up something. The word I screamed out was "Yellah!" which means "come here" or "let's go." In not so many words, I told them to kneel down in front of me and put their hands on their heads. I realized later that making them kneel indicated to them that they were about to be executed, as the Ba'ath party members used this position for executions. But they mirrored me anyway. Shit, I was fucking this up. There were eight disheveled Iraqi men in front of me now. The gypsy caravan vehicle they were riding in looked like they had taken the engine from a bus and soldered scrap medal and plywood sheets together to form its body. Bright, multicolored Islamic designs decorated the exterior. As I instructed the men, other Marines boarded the bus and checked the interior. The men appeared to be Bedouins, ranging from about twenty-five to sixty-five in age. One fat Bedouin could not kneel, and he motioned that his knees were injured.

"Where are you going?" I asked in Egyptian Arabic. As I surveyed the group, it appeared they were a family—a grandfather, father, cousins, and perhaps sons. The father was the one who responded.

"Baayt," he said, motioning that his home was to the south. As he was explaining, the Marines checking the gypsy wagon shouted that it was clear, but filled with goats, sheep, and piles of feces.

The CO, who was next to me, asked what they said.

"Sir, they are farmers trying to go home to the south."

As soon as I said that, other Marines in the distance motioned that another vehicle had been stopped, a white Toyota pickup with about ten suspicious-looking young Arab men. Some of the NCOs were pantomiming to them to put their hands on their heads and step away from the vehicle. My CO ran over to the new vehicle with Corporal Valois, his driver. The NCOs had surrounded this new group of military-aged men in civilian clothing. One was dressed conspicuously all in black. We had been warned that the Fedayeen dressed like this. The CO yelled for me to come over.

The new group in front of me looked frightened and demoralized. Crouched down, they looked around nervously as I got on one knee about fifteen feet in front of them and pointed my weapon away from them. The Marines in my unit had them flanked all around. The Sergeant Major and another SNCO checked their vehicle and found medical supplies and some articles of clothing, one that looked like a military jacket. I told them not to be afraid. As soon as I had calmed them down, I realized they were staring at me, and it dawned on me that they probably thought it was strange that I was a female. One of the younger ones, a man in his late twenties, looked at me in amazement. I said to them, "Everything's good."

This seemed to relax them, and the young man said back to me, "Saddam, mish quiuzz." The young man motioned with his hand slicing across his neck. I smiled.

"Military?" I pointed to them. They all shook their heads no.

"Doctors?" The one dressed in black said yes. They looked around nervously. They were clearly either deserters or aiding deserters, but that was not necessarily a reason to hold them. Once again I reassured the group. "Everything's all right—just wait here a while," I said again in Arabic. They seemed to think it was funny this time.

"What?" I asked. Although none of them had spoken English, the man in black, a handsome, thin Arab in his mid-thirties said, "Madam, Egypt Arabia?"

It occurred to me that hearing a Westerner speak Egyptian Arabic must have seemed strange to them. Later, during an Iraqi Arabic class, I found out that most Iraqis speak only their own dialect; however, many Iraqis recognize and understand Egyptian Arabic because it is the language used in most Arabic cinema and television.

"Where are you going?" I asked again in Arabic.

"An Nasiriyah."

"Why?"

"Baaytak," the man in black answered again, meaning he was going home.

"Nasiriyah, mish quiezz," I said, telling them that Nasiriyah was not safe.

"La'a, Nasiriyah, qwizz." The Iraqi seemed insulted.

I turned to the Sergeant Major Rew next to me and said, "Damn, I think I just told him his hometown sucks." The Iraqi didn't seem to have taken it to heart, though.

In the meantime, one of the medics walked over to the vehicle to inspect the medicine and was carrying some things away. I shouted over to him, "Hey, don't do that. Bring it back to the vehicle. The rules of engagement say not to remove anything from the vehicles because they'll think you're stealing it." The Iraqi men seemed pretty shocked, as they had never seen a female ordering men around before. They smiled and laughed to themselves.

"Ma'am," said the medic, "I just wanted to let Doc see the medical supplies."

"Then call him over to the vehicle, but don't take their shit."

About half an hour had passed, and the CO was determining whether to turn the Iraqis over to the rear detaining area for further interrogation. The last truck was clearly filled with a group of men who were deserters from the Iraqi Army—or worse. Although the nights had been freezing so far in Iraq, days were beginning to get uncomfortably hot, especially with our MOPP suits, uniforms, and flak jackets. One of the detainees, who looked like he was about eighteen, asked in Arabic for some water. I called for some Marines to round up water and MREs. We didn't have a lot of food ourselves, but we expected to be resupplied as needed. The Iraqis grabbed the MREs and water eagerly and struggled to open them. They tore them open with their bare hands, eagerly getting to the food.

"Jesus, these people are starving!" the Marines around me agreed as we watched them tear into the MREs. The Sergeant Major was next to me now.

"They like the chicken!" I made sure they didn't get any pork MREs.

"Yeah, and the peanut butter!" One of the Iraqis, obviously unfamiliar with the MRE, erroneously thought everything in the package was edible. He removed the MRE heater, which was poisonous, from the package and stuck it in his mouth. The Sergeant Major almost burst out in hysterics.

"Good lord! Did you see that? He just ate an MRE heater." The man spat it out after trying to bite into it and seemed a bit upset. I almost lost my cool myself. After the Sergeant Major and I had regained our composure, I got up to brief the CO.

"Sir, they don't seem to be a threat."

"Let them go—tell them as one group at a time that they can leave."

I went over to the first group of males in the Toyota pickup and said, "You're finished, thank you."

The man in black, speaking for the group, replied in Arabic, "Good Arabic, thank you, peace to you." They all held their hands over their hearts in gratitude. Corporal Valois, who had been near me, in the prone position, covering me the whole time, looked at me and asked, "What did they say, ma'am?"

"They like my Arabic, and they were surprised I was a female!"

"Ma'am, that was really awesome."

"Thanks for covering me," I told him.

Corporal Valois was one of those quiet, warrior Marines who spoke only out of necessity. He was a handsome, Aryan-looking kid with a strong jaw, and physically fit. He was handpicked to be the CO's driver because he was strong and smart as hell.

I walked over to the second group of Iraqis, who seemed overjoyed and grateful that we had given them food and water. They had eaten everything and had taken the MRE trash with them. As they pulled away, we got the call to roll to Jalibah airfield, where we would start our first flights from Iraqi soil.

Only a couple klicks away, we set up the unit at Jalibah Air Base. We operated off a taxiway where an explosive ordnance demolition (EOD) team had found eighty-four Iraqi land mines. So after setting up our hasty flying position on a tiny concrete platform, we had to be extremely careful about where we went. The EOD team told us to stay on the actual runway since that was all that had been swept for mines. One wrong step and we could be dead. Our first flight taking off in Iraqi soil began on 24 March with a confirmation that our push north to Qalat Sikar would have been suicidal. As we flew over An Nasiriyah, there were no civilians out in what should have been a bustling city. Instead we saw emptiness and the strange eeriness of a city about to be besieged. Not a light was on.

Since An Nasiriyah was a choke point, gaining hold of the main road meant controlling all the road traffic from south of Baghdad to southern Iraq. An Nasiriyah was a historic city and had the distinction of being thought of as the "Garden of Eden," the fertile crescent where the Tigris and Euphrates met. Hammurabi, Nebuchadnezzar, Ishtar, Babylon, Ur, Nippur, Nineveh, and the *Epic of Gilgamesh* all shared their legacy in this alluvial plain. Mud thatch roofs, if there were roofs at all, topped the majority of houses. Even in this large city, Iraq had been isolated too long—most of the country was a once-prosperous land that never advanced from its golden age in 5,000 B.C.

★ ★ ★

Task Force Tarawa and RCT-2 had changed their focus entirely to concentrate on both An Nasiriyah and Souq Al Shyukh (market of the sheikh), two towns dominated by Ba'ath party influence. This influence, as we saw it, could best be described as a mafia that bullied the populace into doing what it wanted through lifelong intimidation tactics. It was so much a part of the common Iraqis' daily life that they seemed accustomed to dealing with this gangster mentality. The saving grace of it all, though, was that many of the locals were tribal people who wanted nothing to do with Ba'ath party members. Often, good Iraqis fell prey to the Ba'ath party—sometimes joining the party was the only way for businessmen to be successful. Many of the vehicles and valuables in the southern areas were owned by Ba'ath members, who bullied the population with threats of death or dismemberment. To wonder why the Iraqi people did not rise up against the Ba'ath party is to think like an American. These people were so destitute that they had nothing to protest. They had been stripped of all power and were living like vassals to feudal Ba'ath overlords.

As our bird pushed farther north, we noticed that the intersection between An Nasiriyah and Highway 7, the road that would have taken us to Qalat Sikar, was saturated with not only a battalion-sized enemy infantry, but five tanks, five BM-21s, numerous radars, and the Roland short-range air defense missile system.

"My God." I thought, and then said out loud to my Marines, "We would have been slaughtered."

I stepped away from the humvee for a moment to take a break from what I had seen. The morning air was still cool, and I had all my MOPP gear on. The thirty pounds of gear looked comical on me since I was so small. I cracked open an MRE labeled "cheese tortellini." I dropped an entire miniature bottle of hot sauce into it. It was my favorite meal, although I hesitate to use the word "favorite" in conjunction with MREs. It was the only meal I could still eat without feeling queasy. After two weeks of eating nothing but MREs, the chemical taste of the preservatives had made them nauseating to eat and hard to stomach. When we had crossed the line of departure between Iraq and Kuwait, our doctor had given us malaria pills to take as well. That antibiotic made me so sick that even if I took it on a full stomach, I would throw up. It had the same effect on others. No one even looked my way when, in the middle of my meal, I started dry heaving and threw up on some unexploded ordnance.

I was starting to lose weight rapidly. Most of my unit was. Although we had supplies for two to three MREs a day, I couldn't stomach more than one. I literally forced myself to eat. Since I was throwing up my food when I took the pills, my choice was to starve or to stop taking the pills. I figured that if I were to get malaria, I wouldn't be dying of anorexia. I tilted the bottle and spilled the pills on the ground. It was my small victory.

I laughed, remembering my travels to other malaria-infested countries. In Upper Egypt, I had taken a local ferry to Elephantine Island, and the locals had offered me water from a common cup they all shared and dipped in the murky Nile waters. I gladly took a glassful of water from a woman shrouded in black. As her veil slipped from the side of her face, an aged, near-toothless woman smiled back at me. She was wrinkled and aged from the sun, but her smile made her almost pretty. The water was sweet but lukewarm. No sooner had I drunk than I looked down at the dark water of the Nile to see a dead, festering cow carcass floating next to our boat. Its body was bloated, and its flesh was pulled out of the skin, revealing a yellow, rotting interior that smelled like vomit. I was sure I was going to get ridiculously sick but surprisingly did not. I thought about this as I grinned at the discarded pile of electric blue pills that lay there, alien against the soft hues of the desert. My feet brushed over the sand and covered them. I smiled, delighted, and returned to the mission.

★   ★   ★

In Arabic, Qalat Sikar literally means "fort of sugar." It was a town known for its sugar production. We still had a warning order to travel there as soon as possible. Fortunately, the CO bitched enough to higher about the fact that we had barely enough ammo for even the smallest of ambushes, and the helicopters brought us the resupply of ammunition we desperately needed. Route 7, the road to Qalat Sikar, was a two-lane highway with a canal running parallel to it from An Nasiriyah to Al Kut. The road was littered with small towns in which thousands of Fedayeen forces and Ba'ath party members were embedded. Intelligence told us that Saddam might have placed them there to draw coalition forces into the towns and engage them in guerrilla warfare. In the meantime, Saddam Hussein was pushing his forces into these regions to slow the American push toward Baghdad.

Things were getting so bad in this area that it had been renamed the "highway to hell." The area before An Nasiriyah was now known as "ambush alley" because every convoy that passed through there got ambushed. An Nasiriyah was, in fact, being compared to Hue City, a place where Marines during Vietnam had once fought bloody, fierce street battles.

Every hour, I was besieged by intelligence reports that the Ba'ath party from Souq Al Shyukh was making plans to attack Jalibah airfield. I was very uneasy on the inside, but on the outside, I did my job, devouring the mission and living vicariously through the eight-by-ten video monitor. Although I got to see things no one else in the war was seeing, it felt very much like playing a video game. The best part was that Debucher all but disappeared for the last few days, so I had a certain freedom that I hadn't known before.

Approximately one hundred thousand more troops were being sent to the area to reinforce the thin veil of security we had along supply routes. Apparently we had overextended ourselves. All the previously secured areas were now unsecured. Basra, Umm Qasr, and all the way up to our location were now filled with Fedayeen forces, Republican Guard forces, surface-to-air missiles, Scuds, and God knows what else. We were surrounded.

I had given the daily brief by the side of our humvee. The CO had made a circle of folding chairs that he called the combat operations center. In part of my brief, I mentioned the threats that surrounded us from all sides as well as what we would be looking for on our day's worth of missions with the UAV.

"You know, our airfield isn't secured, either, Lieutenant," my operations officer deadpanned. He didn't seem to like me much. He treated me like a child—probably because I was just a Second Lieutenant.

"So we're the security element on Jalibah, sir?"

"Basically," he said, adding, "The 15th MEU is supposed to come secure it in a few days."

"We got it, sir," I said flippantly. "We got MEF's southern flank; no need for them to hurry."

"Hey, Lieutenant, the Generals know what they are doing. It may seem like there's confusion, but the people who need to know are doing what needs to be done."

I remembered the leadership trait, "keep your troops informed," and I thought to myself, "I would never hold back that information from my Marines—why would they?"

Things were going so overwhelmingly sour that there was no need to panic; in fact, I was amazingly calm. I slept soundly that night for the first time, trusting and hoping that we would be lucky, if nothing else. While the media portrayed the "coalition blitzkrieg" across Iraq as successful, the behind-the-scenes mayhem I saw cast some serious doubt in my mind about what the long-term success would be. I had learned that General Mattis, the CG of the 1st Marine Division and our one beacon of hope, would use maneuver warfare techniques of tempo and speed in order to move so quickly through Iraq that the opposition would have no time to plan or react. The downside of this strategy was that because the frontline forces were moving so quickly, rear-echelon folks like us would end up meeting the resistance when they finally got organized. General Mattis, known fondly to the Marines as "Chaos," inspired confidence in us all and seemed to be willing to employ some rather daring, third-generation-style tactics. He was an interesting man, and everyone had a story about him. Unmarried, he was one of those warrior-monk types who was devoted, heart and soul, to the Corps. Most Marines seemed to have a love/hate relationship with him—he was unquestionably competent but thoroughly a hard-ass. Above all, he was a Marine's Marine and always would be part of every mission that involved his Marines. In one of his later speeches, he said: "Marines. The enemy will try to manipulate you into hating all Iraqis. Do not allow the enemy that victory. With strong discipline, solid faith, unwavering alertness, and undiminished chivalry to the innocent, we will carry out this mission. Remember, I have added, 'first do no harm' to our passwords of 'no better friend, no worse enemy.' Keep your honor clean as we gain information about the enemy from the Iraqi people. Then, armed with that information . . . we will move precisely against the enemy elements and crush them without harming the innocent."

The Marines in my unit seemed to be in good spirits despite the chaos around us, and I was jealous of their indifference. Many of the junior Marines walked around doing their jobs and had no clue about the larger picture. Some fixed the UAVs, chatting among themselves; others moved

MRE boxes off the truck for the squadron to eat, and others stood at parade rest while being chewed out by one of the gunnies. In the near distance, I could hear Staff Sergeant Smith yelling at his Marines. I found it a miracle that we could get communications systems up so quickly, so I considered Staff Sergeant Smith something of a miracle worker. He had erected a small sleeping area on the front of the communications vehicle—half a tent, folded and embellished with camouflaged netting. That way, he could monitor his Marines if the system went down, which it did often.

"Chicks dig me!" he would announce for all the Marines to hear.

"What chicks, Staff Sergeant?"

"Chicks . . . you know, my mom and wife for a start."

"But that's about it," Sergeant Wynn said mockingly.

"Hey Sergeant Wynn, did you hear about what the XO is doing?"

"No? What's up?"

"One of the Lance Corporals in the vehicle behind him said they saw him throwing rocks or even grenades at the kids."

"No fuckin' way!"

"That's what they said. The Lance Corporal said there was a kid with a weapon, and the XO took him out with one rock. Apparently he throws rocks to keep the kids away from the convoy."

"That's pretty freakin' hardcore shit."

Since the Marines couldn't dig fighting positions around the perimeter because of the mine garden that surrounded us, they had time to fix up their gear. Sergeant Wynn, our resident cook, not by military specialty but by choice, had set up a little cooking canteen under the ground control station. With camouflage netting and seven cube boxes, he made a little kitchen in a day. Having brought a camping stove and some pots and pans, Sergeant Wynn did what he could with the supplies he had and cooked up meals for himself and some of the Marines. Marines started calling him "the troll" because his tent area looked like a cave.

Within our small position, in the space of twenty-four hours, the Marines had created a city for themselves on our small landing strip. The minefields surrounding us protected us from an enemy attack, and our safe haven temporarily shielded us from the rest of Iraq.

★   ★   ★

The next morning, we got a call over the radio. "Pioneers 1, Pioneers 1, company-sized enemy force is moving five kilometers southwest of your pos in your direction," a Communications Sergeant screamed through our radios. Staff Sergeant Smith yelled the message back: "We've got a company-sized enemy force inbound!"

Everyone suddenly became frantic. We had just put a bird up, and many of the Marines began scrambling to get their weapons and set up a perimeter defense in the southwest sector of the airfield.

We notified the CO of the message. There were Cobras already in the air to scout out the threat. I grabbed my gear and assumed my spot, ready to defend and lead my Marines against a much larger force than our own. No problem. As we waited patiently for signs of an enemy force rolling through, my CO spotted me and called me over.

"Jane, I need you to take your Marines and continue this mission; we need to still be operational even though we have a threat out there."

"Roger that, sir," I said obediently.

Dubucher stood in the distance talking to another officer. Not only was his rifle slung over his shoulder, but he appeared oblivious to the potential attack. Sergeant Young, Sergeant Davila, and Corporal Warseck jumped back into our workspace and continued our mission. I watched the screen but listened with my ear half-cocked, awaiting the first round and then a volley of fire. None came. The Marines watched the perimeter of the landing strip in the prone position, their rifles pointing downrange. As we waited, an ominous wave of reddish debris was picked up in the wind. Very, very strange. With fewer than two hundred Marines, we made up only about a company's worth of men, so we were prepared for an intense firefight. Since we were the only forces at Jalibah, not including the Cobra pilots and the medevac team of medical staff, this was our fight.

As we waited with weapons drawn, communications got a call, and Staff Sergeant Smith came over. Shaking his head back and forth, he looked perturbed.

"Ma'am, you're not going to fucking believe this shit. The *threat* is just the Army bringing a company size of EPWs to the EPW holding area!"

"What the fuck??" I shook my head in disbelief, and ran over to tell my CO.

"False alarm, sir. It's just a gaggle of Iraqi POWs."

My CO threw his hands in the air. "What can you do? When are these folks in Kuwait ever going to get things straight? Jane, here's another one for your leadership book: don't report something as being true if you don't know it is."

As we waited for the attack that never came, the sky had turned dark. All of a sudden, gusts of wind rocked the equipment and threw the Marines off balance. The weather report issued for I MEF called for a huge sandstorm to blow through. This one called for 70-knot winds. My CO ordered everyone to pack up, as we were likely to move again. But we still had a bird in the air—and our bird had trouble landing in anything greater than 20 knots, let alone 70 knots.

The sandstorm seemed to come out of nowhere. We had seen miracles before, but now the sand was kicking up fiercely and feeding into every possible opening. My eyes, even with goggles on, were caked with sand as it whipped across my face. My shemagh, an Arab scarf we had been issued, shielded me from suffocating on the sheets of sand that blew across the horizon. It literally looked like it was raining sand. I fought my way toward my humvee parked twenty meters away. All my surroundings seemed to disappear, and all I saw was sheets of sand across my face. I kept my bearings only by looking down at the cement landing strip. Trying to get some relief from the pelting sand, I hid behind the front of the vehicle to watch the landing. Sergeant Young walked by, smiling and singing.

"Fly, fly away! You are the wind beneath my . . . ma'am? Why, hello, what are you doing there, ma'am?" The Southern cadence of his voice was almost singsong. His goggles were covered with sand, and his face was caked with mud.

"What does it look like I'm doing, Sergeant?" I shouted back.

"Oh damn, ma'am, hang in there! I'll see you later in the box!"

All of Staff Sergeant Wilson's talent as a UAV pilot could not prevent the bird from falling straight down from the sky like a paper airplane, 180 feet straight to the ground, as she came within hearing distance. Parts of it flew everywhere. Flights were called off temporarily, and we were ordered to bed down for the night, except for the unfortunate security patrol that walked the perimeter. As I lay down in my sleeping bag, covered in a bivy sack now filled with sand, the lightning began above us. It was like some kind of apocalypse. The sand and mud whipping through the air sounded like a freight train. The world seemed to be ending as the sky was embellished with quarter-sized hail, adding to the total effect of misery. I tried as best as I could to cocoon myself in the warm but sandy sleeping bag. As if the weather could get any worse, the red sky opened up with a downpour, and I could feel sheets of rain pelting down on my "waterproof" bivy sack. Hours passed as I drifted in and out of consciousness. It was the longest and worst sleep I'd had since the war began.

When I awoke to the sand-filled dawn, I realized my uniform, boots, and all my things had been completely soaked despite my attempt to cover them with a waterproof poncho. Although the wind had died down, there was still little visibility, and the air was heavy with moist debris. I shook the mud off my uniform and put on the soaking wet rags that were my clothes. It was freezing. My boots had completely filled with water, which I dumped off the side of the truck. It was too cold to put them on, so I grabbed my rubber MOPP boots. My ridiculous getup drew some smiles on an otherwise miserable morning. Major Cepeda, looking as cool and collected as ever, gave me the eye as he lit a cigarette.

"Lieutenant, you know you look ridiculous, right?"

"Yes, sir."

"I'm just making sure you knew."

"Thanks, sir." The CO thought it was even funnier and called over some of the other officers. Afterward, Colonel Mykleby decided to use "Boots" as my call sign, which I hated. Even after I told them that the one-time badass Emperor Caligula's name meant "little boot," they said it didn't matter because "Boots" was funny, and I hated the name, the two necessary criteria for a call sign to stick. I always responded with evil eyes and dirty looks when they called me that.

The freak twenty-four-hour storm had stalled our operations. Units ahead of us had pushed too far ahead, and the supply lines couldn't catch up. The loss of tempo triggered an operation pause or what was euphemistically referred to as "going firm." My unit was fairly fat on food, having a seven-day supply of three meals per Marine per day. North of us, elements of RCT-1 had already exhausted their food supply—we were told that many of them were down to fewer than one MRE a day, and some had no food at all. We donated four days of our supply to them, which the helicopters next to us lifted to their positions. We decided we'd rather go without food than have the critical frontline forces without it.

The war wasn't halted, though, and the rumor of a large Ba'ath party attack weighed heavily on our minds. We'd been told that the enemy forces were meeting in Souq Al Shyukh, with plans to attack Jalibah. Poor visibility or not, we had to fly.

Our mission was to determine if there was usual activity in the vicinity of Souq Al Shyukh. Our bird launched under conditions in which we normally never launch a bird. We lifted the bird up into the dark, invisible, swampy night.

From the last helicopter drop, we had received new cameras for the birds, and even with their remarkable clarity, the visibility at five thousand feet was nonexistent. Sand still saturated the air like thick fog. Our XO, Major Cepeda, took the mission. He had a combination of inner calm mixed with the suaveness of a professional hit man. If he hadn't been a Marine, he'd surely be a casino owner in Vegas. He had been a recruiter for many years, and could sweet-talk a pacifist into signing away his life to the Corps.

"Hell, let's drop her down to two thousand feet."

"Two thousand feet, sir?"

"Sure, why the hell not?" That was about as low as we had ever flown. Still, we couldn't see anything. The sky was caked with a thick, sandy haze we had never experienced before. I checked the weather report and found out the ceiling was still at one thousand feet.

"Sir, the ceiling is at one thousand feet."

"Let's take her lower, then!" We called the Direct Air Support Center (DASC), which is the command and control center responsible for all air operations that support ground forces, and made sure we were cleared to go that low. They told us we were the only ones flying that night.

"We have the skies to ourselves, sir. We're good."

As the bird flew lower, buildings and hot objects became faintly visible. Because we were so low, everything seemed much larger than what we were used to.

"Fuck it. Let's take her down," the XO said, and took the UAV down to six hundred feet. At that height, people in the city would feel as if an invisible chain saw was orbiting above them. Sergeant Veneleck shot me a dirty look, "Ma'am, I'm not sure how smart it is to fly this low."

I just shrugged. "Too late," I said.

"Jesus! We better hope there's nothing tall in the area!" Sergeant Young echoed his concern. But suddenly things became clearer, and we could see objects directly below the camera. At this level, we were practically on top of anything moving below us. On some rooftops in Souq Al Shyukh, scouts heard the UAV and jumped on their cell phones to report what was going on. We were clearly frightening people. Civilians darted into their homes, people ran off the rooftops, women stopped feeding livestock and scurried back into their houses, and the animals themselves ran frantically around their corrals. We saw people run outside their homes to see what the noise was, then shut their doors in terror. Clearly, word had gotten out: if you hear us nearby, artillery usually followed.

Again we swooped down to a low altitude and tried to find the location of the enemy fire. I studied the terrain carefully, looking for anything. One of the Sergeants on the mission started cracking jokes, so in a fit of anger I said, "Shut the hell up and take this seriously. Marines are getting shot at right now."

By the faint red light of our enclosed area, it was hard to make out details, but he immediately got flushed and said, "Yes, ma'am."

I was getting seriously pissed off. To make matters worse, we couldn't see anything. We passed over An Nasiriyah to the southern sector, near where 507th Maintenance Company was ambushed, and skirted the whole phalanx, but there was nothing. The city was still, the Marines in place by the bridge. We lowered again to six hundred feet to the grid where we'd heard Marines were receiving fire, but the damn weather obscured everything. We began seeing volleys of fire exchanged and then flashes of fire, but we couldn't pinpoint its origin. After an hour of searching, we were forced to return to base.

12

A FIERY CRASH

All war is deception. —Sun Tzu

Our series of bad luck continued. It was the end of March and the coalition forces still had not lifted the operational pause. RCT-1's CO had been fired due to what we were told was a lack of initiative to push up Highway 7. I had heard from a Lieutenant friend that the real reason he had been fired was that when General Mattis called him on the fourth day of fighting, RCT-1's CO was so exhausted after not sleeping for four nights that when he got on the tactical phone with Mattis, he was speaking gibberish. Mattis fired him on the spot. Mattis replaced him with a new Colonel who led the charge of his regiment to push north. Ambushes continued all along the highway, including Communications Squadron 28, the unit that had been traveling near us, which was ambushed four times with mortar fire, a RPG attack, and machine-gun fire. They sustained one casualty and one wounded.

Even less fortunate was Marine Wing Support Squadron 371. They had traveled that route early in the morning and were ambushed at Ash Shatrah after one of their vehicles drove into a ditch. The passenger, or A-driver, tried to get out, but in their confusion while taking fire (other Marines saw the vehicle take a direct RPG), they left the Marine and the vehicle. The missing Marine's name was Sergeant Rodriquez. I woke up to this news. To make matters worse, two helicopters, one CH-46 and one Cobra, crashed moments later. We were to conduct a TRAP mission to locate the downed aircrafts and the missing Marine.

Our first stop was the helicopter crashes. We located the CH-46, which by that time had already been found by other pilots. The Cobra pilots had escaped without injury, so we moved on to look for Sergeant Rodriquez, the A-driver. Ash Shatrah was a town of about forty thousand citizens and a strong Ba'ath party presence. We found the abandoned truck on the side of the road and circled it. As we made our second pass, about fifteen Iraqis jumped out from a palm tree oasis across the street. They evidently had heard the UAV and wanted to make a show. They started jumping up and down on top of the truck like a group of savage animals as we watched. One of the Iraqis smashed the windows with a stick. They waved at us, cheering at their victory, while signaling to us a clear message of "fuck you."

But Sergeant Rodriquez was nowhere to be found. We heard that headquarters had declared him KIA the next day. They probably had proof that he had not escaped.

Many of us felt the disorder of this war was caused by what was described as "the humane war." That is, America had grown weary of causing or receiving casualities and tried to minimize the inevitable result of all wars, which was death. Although in theory it was good that we were conscious of the rules of engagement and trying to use the necessary force in the right proportion, we were also losing the shock, awe, and fear that had allowed us to roll through the previous Gulf War in ninety-six hours. Since our tempo had come to a standstill, Iraqis were regrouping, too. Some of my fellow squadron mates began speculating that it almost would have been better to make an example of a town, like Souq Al Shyukh, as Asad had done with Hama in Syria during his attempt to restore order among the militia groups. Asad and his military warned the citizens of the city to leave before it was leveled. No one left. Within twenty-four hours, Asad destroyed the city, leaving thousands of casualties. Cruel as the thought was, the terrorist factions had wedged themselves into the heart of the city, and it was our challenge to extract that malignant force before it poisoned the people.

It's easy to lay blame on a culture when the particularities of their circumstances are so foreign from our own. It's easy for a military commander to say, "Let's bomb a city" or "Why don't these people just leave?" when the circumstances aren't taken into consideration. The average Iraqi has nowhere to go. It is easy for us to say we would leave if we knew our city would be bombed. But we could rent a room in a hotel or even camp out in a vehicle along the road. These people lived in mud huts, some without roofs. If they owned a goat or some land, they were better off than the average Iraqi. Most did not own vehicles, and if they did, the Ba'ath party could take them away. The Ba'ath party, to make matters worse, hid Scuds, chemical weapons, artillery pieces, and other military equipment in people's backyards, homes, schools, and mosques to deliberately complicate targeting efforts and rules of engagement. The remaining Ba'athist elements were exploiting the gaps in U.S. military strategy and our attempt to engage in a "humane war." In the process, they were also destroying their own people.

Our series of bad events culminated during an evening mission on the night of 30 March. All the news we had been hearing on BBC was bad. We knew the speeches we heard from the Iraqi propaganda minister making outrageous claims that the Iraqi forces were repelling the Americans were false. Still, the casualties were disheartening, and the forty-eight hour PauseEx that prevented us from moving forward put doubts in my mind about our success. It had already been eleven days since my last shower. I couldn't smell myself past the layers of caked sand on my clothing—our water supply was too low to wash any clothes. Besides, I had no privacy, so changing clothes wasn't an option. I lived like an animal. I hadn't shaved my legs or groomed myself in months. My hair was an itchy, matted mess. I didn't care at this point if I had to cut it all off. It didn't matter anymore. These things were trivial. Survival and mission were the two essentials.

★　★　★

It was about 2000, a couple hours after sunset the following day, and I had just joined my Marines in a mission that would take the bird into An Nasiriyah again. Just as I sat down to get oriented and to understand our new mission, we heard in the distance the sound of a large object approaching our position. Suddenly, a fiery ball of flames was hurling toward us. It was as if a meteor had descended upon the earth, forming a crater, sparks of igneous light dancing on the air like hell's furies in flight. I ran over to where I had seen the object in the sky. Moments seemed suspended in time, and on the periphery of my vision, a fiery object, arms outstretched like a phoenix, came flying out of the flames and then extinguished its light as it fell to the ground and got up again. Soon I realized it was a man enveloped in flames. Bam! A horrendous explosion and screams of panic followed. The impact was less than one hundred meters away. Our whole squadron was mobilized, grabbing flaks and weapons and making sure everyone was accounted for. Without hesitation, one of our Marines ran into the uncleared, mined sand area and covered the man with a cloth to douse the fire. Then, in the near distance, we saw a helicopter in flames. We weren't quite sure what had happened, and personnel were running around everywhere, adding to the confusion. Had we been attacked? My CO came around the corner and ordered the Marines on mission back to work. I walked back to my work area and told the remaining Marines what had happened. My team continued the mission and did not move from our spot.

We heard the CO return shortly and get on our tactical phone and say to the Direct Air Support Center (DASC), "A Huey just crashed into our position. They are getting a body count now." We didn't know if anyone on our team had gotten hurt until Sergeant Wynn came in, and in a panic, told the CO that all members of our unit were accounted for but that Marines had died in the crash. The CO continued on the tactical phone, "DASC, this is the Squadron Actual. Three KIA and one WIA. No one at our squadron was hurt. The Huey swerved to avoid us last minute during an onboard fire. There could have been a lot more casualties if the pilot had not done that. The pilot and two other crew members are dead. Only the fourth crew member survived. He jumped out of the aircraft before impact, and his leg may be broken. He was on fire and has first-degree burns. There's blood coming out of his nose. That's all to report, more details to follow. Out."

As we continued the mission, the image of the Marine on fire kept entering my mind. Medevac crews were taking the bodies away in body bags. I thought about their families, who had no idea their loved ones had just died. I was surprised that the surviving Marine miraculously had only a broken ankle and burns. He jumped from the burning aircraft just in time. Messages appeared on chat, questioning me for information on the crash.

"Jane, don't report any information," my CO said. "Let the system work itself. If those Marines from his squadron find out without the CO passing it, they may get all worked up. Worse, they could call back to the States and tell their families who it was."

The Marine Corps had a set process in which the next of kin were informed of a Marine's death. They would be the first informed, and no information would be released about the death until this happened. Marines in dress blues were required to personally appear at the doorstep of the family member and inform them of the death of their son or daughter or spouse. They would also be there to provide emotional support and guide them through the funeral and benefits process. My good friend, Lieutenant Jonathan George, was the collections officer for the deceased Marines, and I had chatted with him over our secure chat network since the war began. He came on the tactical network and pressed for details.

"I know who they are, so you don't have to tell me," he wrote.

"My CO asked me not to report details—he doesn't want to spread this before the family is notified."

"I know. Just tell me one thing. . . . Was it a fiery crash?"

"Yes." He did not respond for a while.

"Jesus, those were my friends in there. This is unbelievable."

Just then, Sergeant Young belted out, "That's the way the story goes. Pop! Goes the weasel!"

"Shut the fuck up! Have you no fucking sense of awareness?" Sergeant Leppan shouted back at him. And there was, after that, silence. Sergeant Young realized his mistake and quickly changed his demeanor.

Silence was broken an hour later when a helicopter flew in with Colonel Oliver North and a media crew at the scene of the crash to report it. The carnage of the downed helicopter was the background for their story. We were all so shaken by the crash that Colonel North's appearance went unnoticed by most of us.

Commanding Officer
Lieutenant Colonel Scott Mykleby

Executive Officer
Major Sal Cepeda

Doc Casey

*Leadership
(left to right):
Major Cepeda,
Sergeant Major Rew,
and Lieutenant
Colonel Mykleby.*

*The UAV Squadron in
Ad Diwaniyah.*

The Commanding Officer addressing the squadron before the push to Iraq.

The Sergeant Major (left) and Commanding Officer (right) getting ready to step off for deployment to Kuwait and Iraq.

A mural of Sadaam Hussien in the camp at Ad Diwaniyah.

Some of the first signs upon entering Iraq.

The first group of detainees that the author spoke with. She is in the distance running toward the new group.

Iraqi children by the water treatment plant.

Left to right: Lieutenant Euring, Captain Hamill, the author, and Sergeant Major Rew on the Tigris River.

Left to right: Captain Chontosh, the author, Lance Corporal McCormick, and Lance Corporal Kerman at their awards ceremony. Source: USMC photographer.

Burned-out vehicles on the way to the Tigris River.

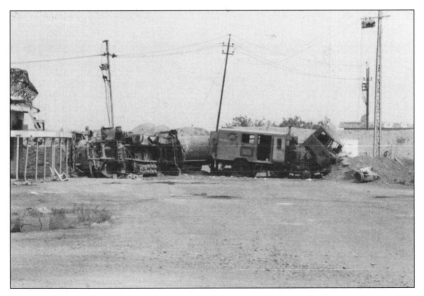

The roadblock of vehicles to the north of An Nasiriyah originally seen with the UAV.

The first stop in Iraq. Marines get some sleep before our planned trip through An Nasiriyah.

The passage through the ominous An Nasiriyah area to get to Qalat Sikar.

The author and her husband in Ad Diwaniyah after being reunited for the first time after major combat operations were declared over.

Sergeant Major Rew and the author near a destroyed Iraqi tank outside An Nasiriyah.

The author in Al Kut.

UAV air maintenance crew getting the UAV prepared for flight.

Captain Devallion Piper "getting some."

The Pioneer UAV in the desert in Iraq.

The author in front of the U.S. regional outpost in Babylon.

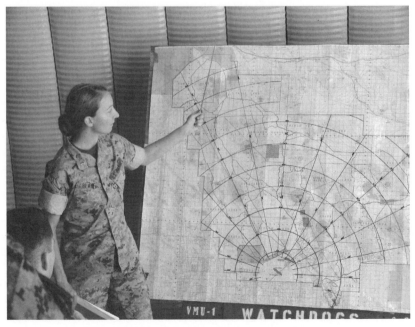

The author briefing the potential threats in the area.

13

GARDEN OF EDEN

A fire devoureth before them; and behind them a flame burneth: the
land is as the garden of Eden before them, and behind them a desolate
wilderness; yea, and nothing shall escape them.

—The Old Testament

I distinctly remember one of our first classes at The Basic School. Two
hundred and fifty new officers all sat in a classroom, expectantly waiting
for our instructor. A silence fell over the room when he entered. A self-
assured Captain stepped in front of us and said without emotion, "Before
your first tour is up, 25 percent of you will get out of the Marine Corps.
At least three of you will get DUIs . . . and two of you in this classroom
will be dead." I looked around the room. Could that be true? Here we
were, young, healthy Lieutenants with our lives ahead of us, practically
indestructible warriors.

When we graduated from The Basic School, many of us would part
ways, as we were assigned to different duty stations in the Marine Corps.
Thirty of us lucky warriors, including many of my closest friends, got stationed in the infamous Twentynine Palms. But before we could settle in,
suddenly we all got deployed to Iraq. There were already those who got
Purple Hearts, and indeed, some who did not make it back at all. Our class
of 250 already met the statistics.

As the weather cleared, so did our streak of bad luck. The tactical
pause had lifted, and soon we were on our way again. The next morning, I
was not surprised when we got the FragO to move up to Qalat Sikar. Ner-
vousness flooded me like never before. A clammy sweat covered my skin,
and images of us getting ambushed entered my brain. I was sure higher was

about to push us through another area they didn't realize was unsecured. RCT-1 was only at Ash Shatrah, sixty kilometers below the city we had to get to, clearing the way.

We spent the day packing the gear, followed by a late-night mission that I stayed up for. We had only minimal gear out for the mission; the rest of the airfield was in darkness. My small red light illuminated the inside of our enclosed humvee, where I was alone on the laptop doing some research and looking at the current events situation. Lieutenant George, my friend from MAG-39, came on chat again.

"Dash-2, are you there?"

"What's up, George?"

"Not much. I tracked your husband down on the friendly forces tracker—he's pushing up Highway 8 right now near Shak Hantush. They're all right and only meeting light resistance. How's Iraq?"

"Not bad. Thanks for looking out for me. How's Kuwait?"

"Hanging in there; I'll be coming up to Jalibah tomorrow."

"We're going up to Qalat Sikar tomorrow without an escort."

"Already? Be careful. You know that hasn't been secured yet?"

"Yes, I know, but there's nothing I can do. I told my CO; we're trying to work our connections and get us an escort."

"There's supposed to be a lot of Fedayeen en route—around Ash Shatrah."

"I heard . . . thanks for looking out for us. Hey, can you promise me something?"

"What do you need?"

"Promise me that if I get killed, you'll tell Peter that he was the best thing that ever happened in my life."

"Damn, Jane, don't say those things. You're going to be fine. I understand, though, and I promise I will, but it won't come to that. You'll be fine. Hey, if something happens to me, too, tell my wife that I was thinking of her and our dogs."

"I will. But George . . ."

"Yeah?"

"You're in freaking Kuwait. I'm about to go up ambush alley—I don't know, but I think you're not in the shit right now."

"We already lost nine Marines in my squadron; we've lost more than any other wing unit. There's no such thing as safety anywhere out here. There's only the illusion of the front line in this war; the front line is everywhere."

"You're right, George. Kuwait just seems safer than here, but you're right. Be careful, and find me on chat when you get communications set up."

"I will, man. You stay safe. Out."

★   ★   ★

Our last flight before we packed the rest of our gear was very telling. There was still a hell of a lot of stuff facing us on the way. It looked like we were about to undertake a suicide mission. Task Force Tarawa offered us escorts to travel through Nasiriyah, and RCT-1 said they would pick us up around Ash Shatrah, with Amtrac escorts supported by Hueys. With that much firepower, my fears decreased.

Our flight started with a tour of An Nasiriyah. The 15th MEU was supposed to secure the western side of the city tomorrow and take the second hospital. The city had blackouts periodically, and we were told these were indications of Fedayeen attacks on convoys. Something was different tonight. While random fires and explosions riddled with gunfire still lit up the city, there was civilian activity, too. Electricity was finally partially restored, the first time in a week, and the streets were filled with activity. Something was going on.

Task Force Tarawa came on chat and told us we would be part of the attempted rescue of POWs at the Saddam Hospital in the center of An Nasiriyah. An informant, an Iraqi medical professional, had escaped to warn the coalition forces that PFC Jessica Lynch and other POWs were being held at the hospital. The man had allegedly been trying to tell the Marines at the checkpoint for days but could not get to them because of the security perimeter and the blockage that did not allow vehicles to pass through. According to a grunt who had been part of the recovery of the 507th vehicles, Lynch and her team of Army supply folks had been ambushed by some Fedayeen forces after the lead vehicle in her convoy got lost. The story he had heard, which he vouched was the only authentic story, told of Lynch running from her vehicle after it crashed into another vehicle while the convoy was taking fire. He said she then ran into a nearby neighborhood where some Iraqis tried to help her. Not understanding the language, she thought they were trying to hurt her and fired at them. They retaliated by firing shots at her and brought her injured body to the hospital. The grunt officer was sent by Task Force Tarawa to look on while we flew over the hospital and located any possible enemy positions or personnel and a helicopter landing zone (HLZ) for the rescue mission. The Iraqi man who helped detail Lynch's location would later be given political asylum with his family in a safe country.

Since we were only a short distance from the hospital, it took just a couple minutes for us to get eyes on the area. We saw a Red Cross symbol marking an HLZ on the roof of the hospital. First part accomplished. There appeared to be no activity around the hospital. As we reported the information to Task Force Tarawa, they told us to remain in place. "We're going to do the extract now and we want you all there."

Half an hour later, helicopters showed up at the hospital, and we could see the special forces pouring out on the rooftops, going in to extract Lynch and other POWs. In another half hour, we watched them pour out, carrying a stretcher and what was presumably Lynch's body. We learned later that bodies of POWs were found buried next to the hospital and, of course, Lynch was very much alive.

Because of our success, Task Force Tarawa asked us to put up another bird to monitor a possible ambush being set up on the northern perimeter of town. As our bird flew north, we saw vehicles laid across the highway. Burned-out bus shells and trashed vehicles had been dragged into the center of the road to form a barricade reminiscent of scenes from the movie *Mad Max*. It clearly looked like an ambush for the RCT-1 forces that were about to move up Highway 7. As we flew farther along the road, we saw armored vehicles and then a defense in depth: armed infantry dug in along the side of the road, and pickup trucks ferrying militia to support their position. Then, from the south, two armored vehicles approached the barricaded area side by side.

"Those could be friendlies!" one of the Marines said.

"The armor?"

"Yes. Let's get a closer look," one of the imagery analysts said to the payload operator. He moved the camera so it focused on the armored vehicles, but it was still hard to see details. Then something interesting happened. We saw the two vehicles moving parallel to each other in perfect syncopation. We zoomed out to get a better look. They maintained the interval as they sped along, and when they approached the junction to the blockade, they broke off simultaneously. Each looped around with symmetrical ease, mirroring the other, one facing west and one east, blocking both flanks. We sat breathless. From the back hatch of each armored vehicle poured twenty personnel. Then they regrouped, providing consolidated 360-degree coverage. An individual stood in the middle, and then the circle formed two columns and patrolled with a leader in the center. They came to a tactical security halt. The men instantly got into a linear skirmishers posture and closed the gap immediately, forming a line of individuals advancing side by side.

I don't know if words can describe what it was like to watch a perfectly orchestrated platoon about to go into assault, but it's probably akin to a climactic moment in a symphony or a ballet. Those were friendlies on the ground. Not just any friendlies, but Marines. The armored vehicles now seemed to have obviously recognizable silhouettes. All the fears that had plagued me about the high echelon's ineptitude were cast aside when I saw the grunts go off into a firefight. They sure as hell knew what they were doing. Marines made war an art form. I watched as the grunts moved in, and I knew that no matter how much the plan was screwed up, the infantryman's decisive actions would win this war.

I typed to the chat network, "Friendlies, Marines, and Amtracs are about to go into an assault. Do you want us to provide coverage as they approach the enemy position?"

"Not necessary—the enemy position you reported earlier has already been destroyed; the grunts will have what's left of the area secured. Press north."

★   ★   ★

1 April 2003—that was our day to drive to Qalat Sikar on the highway to hell. Someone was obviously playing a cruel joke on us. But I tried not to worry as our convoy pulled out of Jalibah at 0300. We rolled up to the highway. The sky was still an eerie red, and it filled the surroundings with an aura of death. As we drove away from the false sense of safety we felt at Jalibah, I fed rounds into my magazines and checked my weapons to make sure they were functional. I rocked my finger back and forth over the safety of my pistol. I held it in my left hand as we drove forward, practicing scenarios in my head of what I would do if ambushed. My finger fell dangerously near the trigger as I moved the safety to the firing position at every perceived threat. At my feet, several grenades lay scattered between Corporal Reynolds and me. Corporal Cano stood fearlessly above us; the belt of rounds from his .50 caliber dangled across our sand-encrusted windshield. This was it.

As we drove on, my mind wandered to thoughts of my husband. Where was he now? Probably close, but still unreachable. We were still not in the danger zone. Without the others seeing, I pulled out a small photo of Peter. We were in our dress blues from last year's Marine Corps Ball. I barely recognized the face I saw in the picture. The handsome dress blues he wore had golden and silver flair, metals and ribbons, all bound together with the sharp smartness of the patent leather Sam Browne belt that made him look like an aristocrat. Behind him, the red, white, and blue of the flag stood out in contrast to his dark uniform. When I thought of him without the photo, I could no longer picture his face. That little photo held a whole world that I could enter in my imagination. But as soon as my eyes were off the photograph, I'd shake myself from the illusion and find myself in a much worse reality—entering Nasiriyah. This day was all the reality I had; this moment was all the hope my life contained. To wake up surrounded by enemies who want to kill you is, at best, a living hell.

Dawn broke, and the horizon was littered with adobe mud shacks like some primal token of a decayed civilization. Rows of roofless or flat-roof mud huts stood side by side without adornment. Iraq's peasant class, the Shi'ites, occupied them all. The barren land sustained them, and the dirty, fetid water that flowed through the tributaries of the Euphrates was their water source. Women in black carried large metal buckets on their heads. Children clad in colorful hues of purple and crimson tended flocks of sheep and goats in the distance. They turned their heads curiously at the far-off rumble of the convoy of Americans. A man, clad in a white dishdasha and a red gingham headdress, stood on a berm watching his family and the Americans, perhaps wondering what changes we would bring. Atop the Shi'ite mud shacks, the only colors were the green, black, and red flags that waved above. They all had symbolic meaning for the Shi'ites: black mourned the death of family members associated with Ashura, the ten days of remembrance; green represented the house of the Prophet Mohammed, indicating that they were loyal Muslims; and red stood for the bloodshed by Imam Hussein in remembrance of the blood that was spilled during the Battle of Karbala. Different combinations of these flags adorned many of the mud homes—sometimes there was only a black one, sometimes all three. I looked through my rearview mirror and behind me in Major Cepeda's vehicle, I could see him throwing candy out the window for the children, even though he told everyone he was lobbing grenades.

We had to make a stop at Task Force Tarawa's headquarters to get an armored escort through An Nasiriyah. The place was not yet secured, they informed us, and the northern bridge was receiving small arms fire. After about an hour of waiting, Lieutenant Colonel Mykleby made the decision to leave without the escort. No one seemed to be paying much attention to us. As we were pulling out, four humvees pulled out in front of us and told us they were our security convoy. Our CO got out of his vehicle, took one look at the unarmored vehicles, shook his head, and told them to get lost. We were going it alone.

He came on the radio: "Well, Marines, now that we've wasted several hours for nothing, we're going through An Nasiriyah unescorted. The 15th MEU is moving through later today to secure the city, so keep your eyes and ears open. The city is still taking fire, and an ambush is likely. The convoy ahead of us already received small arms fire. Maintain a strong posture, and we will get through this. Out."

★   ★   ★

We sat a few klicks south of the city, waiting for the go-ahead. As we waited, truckloads of EPWs were brought into the camp. Their hands were bound together by duct tape and zip ties. Their heads were covered with burlap sacks. The former Ba'ath party or military EPWs who had already been brought into the compound had the sacks removed from their heads. Lifeless eyes spoke of resignation and despair. Their distant stares into the horizon were filled with thoughts I couldn't fathom.

Our vehicles started up again, and we began edging forward. Wafts of diesel fumes saturated the air. I had become accustomed to the smell, but I still wanted to vomit. My heart started pounding again. I tried to prepare for the possibility of getting shot at, but that's pretty stupid because you can't really prepare for that. It was commonly believed in grunt circles that dumb luck is the reason why some people get shot and others don't. Marines would talk about this all the time. One moment, you're safe; the next moment, a round whizzes by and destroys your life. One round hits a Marine, and in a matter of inches and moments, one round spares another. It was all a matter of dumb luck. I was hoping there wasn't a round out there for me.

We rolled toward the bridge area. A sign in English said: "An Nasiriyah—Welcome." What the fuck? Welcome? Really? These fuckers had a real sense of humor. There was gunfire echoing in the distance. We rolled past the armored ambush area, with burning hulks on the road, bombed-out houses with just metal skeletal frames remaining. The roadblock of buses and armor had been destroyed. We rolled past overturned tanks and burned-up armor, then through the infamous palm grove known as "ambush alley." Strangely, the place was a little oasis of palm trees and flowering bushes that had managed to survive the firefights. It was actually eerily beautiful. But the mud homes still smoldered from yesterday's fires. My blood was flowing fast as we advanced down the road toward the first bridge. Because the area was so dense with vegetation, it was clear why it was a good ambush site. We thought we were alone, but throughout the route, friendly tanks and armored vehicles guarded the way. To each side, metal carcasses of abandoned or destroyed vehicles lay on their sides. This is where we had viewed countless firefights from the UAV. The Marines on the bridge didn't smile but stared as we advanced past them. As we crossed the Euphrates, one of the great rivers of the world, I saw a building in the distance, its side covered with a giant mural of Saddam Hussein.

A viridian river calmly ran through the war-torn city. Our convoy kept its dispersion, evenly spaced in case of attack, as we crossed into the interior of the city. This was near where the Army convoy of soldiers got ambushed. I scanned the mud alleys for threats. Then, to our front, I saw a large mob of Iraqis forming along the sides of the roads. We reduced the distance between the vehicles as we got closer. I fully expected something to go down at any moment, but the unexpected happened. All the Iraqi people on the side of the road smiled and waved at us. Some cheered us on. This wasn't at all the reaction I had expected. Children ran out in pairs to greet us and waved ebulliently as we road rode by. Mothers cheered. Women in black hijabs waved. The whole neighborhood watched as though we were on parade. The joy of the people we saw and the spirit of their seemingly wholehearted welcome surprised us. As we passed over the second bridge, I breathed a deep sigh of relief. I had expected shots to be exchanged. What had changed between today and yesterday?

★   ★   ★

On the side of the road I saw elements of Marine infantry and Amtrac units manning hasty trenches along the roads. They stared at us intensely as we passed by. By the expressions on their faces, it looked like they had seen some shit go down.

We crept on to the northern edge of the city where we had seen the vehicle roadblocks yesterday, and as we had expected, they had been pushed far enough off the road for us to get through. We weaved our vehicles left and right past the maze of overturned truck and bus hulks. Our convoy continued up the highway of hell, alone and unafraid. Every village we passed gave us the same friendly waves as they looked on in amazement. I always waved back—hell, this was their first impression of Americans. It was all smiles and cheers from the Iraqis until we reached Ash Shatrah.

This was the town I feared would not offer us the same greeting. It was where, a day before, we had seen the mob and the Amtracs. We learned later that the 1st Reconnaissance Unit had secured the town only a couple hours earlier, and that the Ba'ath members we had seen fleeing were a result of their attack. Our convoy immediately came to a halt when we saw 1st Marines, Kilo Company about to take fire in the middle of the road. They warned us on the radio that the battle was still going on. We were told to immediately file our vehicles in behind the line of Amtracs and Marines ready to assault. In the distance, masses of Iraqi civilians gathered at the gateway to the city. The civilians in the front of the crowd looked friendly and cheered and waved to us. Many of the civilians in the distance looked like they had just taken off their Republican Guard uniforms. We could always tell because they kept their black combat boots on. Some of them looked like they wanted to fight us. Cobras fired Hellfire missiles about three hundred meters into the town, and gunfire could be heard in the near distance. The attack was still in progress.

This would be it, I was sure. The entire Amtrac Company lay down in the prone position with M16A2 service rifles and assorted crew-served weaponry pointed toward the town. We immediately dismounted and jumped into prone positions on the ground, our weapons pointed ahead. Many of the Marines in my unit covered the flank, the gap area through which we had driven. They joined the other Marines in the prone position. Explosions were coming from inside the city. To find out what was going on, I walked over to the CO, who was talking to the Amtrac CO behind the cover of the armored vehicles.

"Hey, sir, we've been expecting you," the Major said to my CO. "We're all pushing north, and they said you guys need an escort."

"Thanks, we do. Looks like this area is hot."

"We're out here with the PsyOps team; they're trying to interrogate the Iraqis to figure out what the situation is. . . . They're still looking for enemy pockets within the city." I looked over and saw that their humvees were mounted with speaker systems. Speeches in Arabic echoed.

"We discovered some AAA sites within the city that the Cobras are taking out right now," he continued. "Apart from that, we chased out some Ba'ath party members. From what these people have been telling me"—he pointed over to one of the sheiks—"it looks like the Ba'ath party has fled this entire region. In case you were wondering why all these people have suddenly reemerged from their homes today, it's because the Saddam loyalists have left. This is the first time since the war started that we've heard the call to prayer."

"The people seemed friendly to us today. We had heard all kinds of stories about convoys getting ambushed," my CO added.

"They were ambushing until today. Our HUMINT sources say the Ba'ath party decided to stop fighting for now in order to regroup. They estimate that they intend to counterattack when coalition forces pull out. We have heard reports about foreign fighters and insurgent groups joining together."

"Yeah, that's just their way of surrendering while saving face!"

"Also, sir, we believe we found Sergeant Rodriguez."

"Wasn't he the one from MWSS-371 who got left behind?"

"Yes, he was."

"They declared him KIA, I thought?"

"Yes, well, the Iraqis over there say that they have his body and that he's in the building over there. The Hueys that just pulled in are here to medevac him out."

"Did he make it all right?"

"No, sir." He paused and winced. "Sir, they found his body crucified and tied up to a wall in one of the buildings. He's KIA, sir. These folks claimed they found him and buried his body behind this building on my map here."

"Jesus."

"I know . . . it fuckin' tears me up."

After about half an hour, the Amtracs provided security while the Cobras landed. We were told we would be rolling between the Amtracs because much of the area to the north was not secured. Most of our Marines lay interspersed with the infantry. Some of the infantry guys looked strangely at the females beside them, ready to fight. From behind me, I heard some yelling and fell back to see what was going on. One of our Sergeants was yelling at a female in the unit, Lance Corporal Gonzalez, who apparently was in shock and so oblivious to the whole situation that she remained inside her humvee with her headphones on. The XO arrived at the same time I did.

"Sir and ma'am," the Sergeant said, out of breath, "look what I found!"

The XO, who couldn't believe she was just sitting there, said, "Marine, what the hell do you think you are doing?"

"Listening to music, sir."

"Listening to fucking music? I can see that! Do you have any idea what's happening around you right now?"

"Not really, sir."

"Not fucking really? Have you taken a look around and noticed the whole squadron is in the prone position?"

"Oh, yeah, I guess so, sir," she said as she looked out of the vehicle.

"Have you lost your mind, Marine? What do you think you should be doing right now?"

"I don't know, sir." Her eyes shifted back and forth in confusion. The XO was infuriated. The Sergeant stepped in between.

"Sir, if you don't mind, I can take care of this."

"Have at it, Sergeant, but if I come back and she's still in the vehicle, she's going straight for court-martial."

"Roger that, sir." The XO and I walked away from the vehicle. We could hear the Sergeant yelling at her at the top of his lungs. We watched her in the distance join the Marines in the prone position. I felt especially embarrassed that it was a female Marine. A cowardly female Marine was just what we needed in front of the grunts. Freaking awesome.

Some Marines were just not equipped for combat, and that was becoming apparent as things heated up. Sure, I wanted to go home, but I didn't lose my shit, so to speak. Some of the Marines, and even a couple of the SNCOs and officers, seemed stressed. But it was predictable—they were the folks who got high-strung over administrative tasks in garrison. In a combat environment, they were downright skittish. All you had to do was approach them and ask a question, and they would start yelling. I tried to stay away from those folks at all cost.

The CO ordered us to mount the vehicles and told us we would be pushing north. In every town we passed through to get to Qalat Sikar, Iraqis seemed overjoyed to see us. They must have stood outside their homes all day waiting for a convoy, just so they could wave and chase the vehicles for food or souvenirs. The children lined up along the sides of the road, all with dirty, unwashed faces and half starved, but with hope in their faces. They were different than the other children we had seen. Many of these children were blond and had light-colored eyes. One of the Staff Sergeants said legend had it that the Gulf War veterans got a little extra on the side with the native women. It was true that many of the fair-skinned children were about twelve years old, but just as many were very young. They smiled and waved like the other children and did not notice differences among themselves. They came in the hundreds—it seemed as if every child in the city had come out to see us. Above all, I felt for the first time that we were doing the right thing, that we were going to make a difference.

14

KILLBOX

Whoever battles monsters should take care not to become a monster, too, for if you stare long enough into the Abyss, the Abyss stares also into you.

—Friedrich Nietzsche

When our bird was in the air, we were like gods, hovering over the battle space, watching friendlies and enemies move around, and calling in information that would change the dynamics below. But when our eyes shifted off the video screen, we returned to the reality that we were on the ground, that our imaginary world inside the screen was just that, and that we were entirely vulnerable. The war I knew seemed like a video game, playing out in a surreal world as I watched. Crossing to Qalat Sikar, we were no longer part of that video game world.

Surprisingly, we had made it to Qalat Sikar in one piece. There were only a few Marines in advance of us, such as a reconnaissance element. We set up in four hours and were ready to fly again, this time in support of I MEF's anticipated battle in Al Kut. In this area we were warned to be on alert for chemical attacks, since there had been warnings that Saddam would deploy chemical weapons in this region. Being next to swamplands, the bugs and humidity were kicking. It didn't help that we still had to wear our heavy MOPP suits.

Al Kut was what we thought would be the decisive battle—in other words, the tipping point at which the Iraqi opposition would decide to continue to fight or surrender. But that battle proved to be An Nasiriyah. As RCT-1, RCT-5, and RCT-7 enveloped the city from all sides, we would fly in advance to determine the threat ahead. The 7th Marines became the main effort, which put me on edge, knowing my husband was among them. The next day of flying was in support of RCT-1, which had escorted us to Qalat Sikar. After General Mattis, the CG of 1st Marine Division, fired the CO of 1st Marines, their new CO was to take decisive measures to move up Highway 7 as fast as possible to seize Al Kut.

Since we had barely gotten any sleep in the last few days, most of the non-mission-essential Marines racked out. Hungry today to find targets for RCT-1, I watched attentively for any indication of a threat. As we traced the road, we suddenly came to a bunch of white vehicles with a few personnel around.

"Stop—right there!" I said to the payload operator on the headset.

"It's just a bunch of civilians, ma'am." The people on the ground were all wearing black and had a motorcycle.

"No, they're not. That's how the Ba'ath party operates. They are scouts, possibly forward observers, and there could be artillery around."

"OK, ma'am, whatever you say." They weren't entirely convinced, but what I had heard from the reconnaissance team that briefed me was to watch for groups of male "civilians" in white vehicles or motorcycles driving around in obvious no-go areas. They told me these small groups of Fedayeen were trained forward observers and were actually spotting for the artillery and mortar rounds. I was certain that this was the case now.

"How far out would they emplace mortars and artillery from this position, Sergeant Leppan?"

"Mortars—three to four kilometers out (check), D-30s—twenty kilometers, and 59-1—forty kilometers."

"Payload, let's trace an arch in the northwest direction at those distances."

"Aye, ma'am."

At three to four kilometers, we saw infantry on the side of the road along the canal area. We radioed it in. Then at twenty kilometers, two batteries' worth of D-30s. Hundreds of Iraqi military hovered around the artillery tubes, preparing to load them. Knowing that Marines were just about thirty kilometers south, I wasn't going to let these bastards fire on my boys.

"Shit, they're ready to fire."

"Are we doing a fire mission, ma'am?"

"Yes! Go wake up the CO!"

Before the CO even got there, they had contacted the Fire Direction Center (FDC), an area at headquarters where they decided how best to execute a target: by aircraft, artillery, or other method. We were ready to put rounds downrange. We had only minutes. Our boys were pushing up the road fast, and it was either going to be our boys or their boys that died here. When the CO walked in the tent area, still groggy, and gave the

OK, we were ready to do a fire mission. Below on the screen, was an enemy D-30 artillery battery plus personnel in the open. Five, seven, twelve, maybe twenty personnel walked around the artillery site. This would be a live target. Vehicles moved around throughout, and it seemed as if they hadn't heard us in the sky. They were setting up the guns to fire down below. In the meantime, we waited patiently for the go-ahead from the artillery unit that would be supporting our mission. The FDC acted as the go-between for us and the artillery unit. The artillery unit told us to orbit directly above the target. We had minutes, but the artillery unit acted fast. Before we knew it, our artillery unit said they had shots out.

As we orbited above, we got notice that rounds were about to impact. Then it happened: splash! Rings of artillery rounds danced on the ground, hitting the enemy battery squarely. Large plumes of smoke obfuscated the ground area. With only one adjustment, we fired for effect. Like a fireworks display, impact after impact flashed in the target area in a devastatingly beautiful way. I looked on in both fascination and horror.

"End of mission, record as target, stand by for BDA," I typed dispassionately.

As the artillery smoke cleared, dozens of dead bodies lay lifeless by the trails of the guns. As unreal as first it seemed, I had just initiated fire on these Iraqis. The bodies lay motionless by the destroyed gun tubes. I looked around at the Marines who were cheering, but I didn't feel anything. I just looked at the screen and the tiny black-and-white features of the enemy. Nothing was left of the battery. These bodies were crumpled around the site because I had called in the target. It had been effortless. In one instant, I had become their executioner.

★   ★   ★

There was blood on my hands now. It's something that I couldn't erase from my mind, my eyes, or my gut. Once you kill, you can't take it back. There's an implied destiny there, and that destiny is something dark. It's not as if I felt the veins of another pulsate under my knife and grow faint with its withdrawal. I didn't shoot them, either. They were not targets in the scope of my rifle. I killed them when I looked into the computer screen, and I saw them in the images from the UAV flying overhead. That was it. I called artillery on them when they tried to run. Their limbs were scattered on the trails of the guns. I didn't feel anything and it was done. But I couldn't take it back. I kept seeing flashes of those bodies in my mind. I know it meant something, but I didn't know what.

Our mission continued, and we traced back to the road where, toward Al Kut, we saw a whole Iraqi defensive structure, a company's worth of infantry dug in about ten kilometers across the canal from the Marines' current forward line of troops. Past that, they had mortars. They were planning to ambush RCT-1. Not anymore. I had to kill those Iraqis because they were about to kill my boys. I wasn't going to let them hurt my boys down there.

The UAV moved on to Al Kut. As we moved forward, we weren't finding anything in the city. We scanned over and over, but there was nothing; any remnants of a military were gone. We got an ad hoc tip that the Baghdad Infantry Division was relocating to the Al Kut area to support in that battle, so we scanned the main service routes on Highway 6. If I didn't see it myself, I wouldn't have believed it, but sure enough, a battalion's worth of buses, trucks, and military vehicles—about eight hundred Iraqi soldiers—were taking a break on the side of the road.

"Can we call arty on this?" I typed to Division.

"They're out of range."

"How about air?"

"Standby."

We waited for about ten minutes, and I asked again impatiently.

"We have a battalion of infantry in the open, with associated vehicles, getting ready to load up and go—what are you going to do, Division?"

I took off my headset and paced edgily back and forth. The communications systems were so antiquated that I couldn't believe the military didn't invest more money in this. When we find targets, we should be able to get fire down on them immediately; otherwise, we were wasting everyone's time.

Finally, the answer came. "We're getting Cobras to pursue and fire on them." But by that time, the Iraqi infantry had heard the noise of the UAV and were jumping into their vehicles.

"Where's the convoy?" Division asked.

"About to pull away to the east, down Highway 6."

I was pissed off about how this system ran—pissed off about everything. When we got a FragO, to physically move the squadron position ahead to An Numenyah, a forward operating base closer to Al Kut, I was too pissed off to care.

★   ★   ★

War is always surreal. Nothing is as it appears, and your senses are in a state of hyperalertness. Whether it's the smell of gunpowder, the firefights, the screams, the foreigners, or just the strangeness of the air—war is a trip. The night that we arrived in An Numenyah was no exception. We had arrived too late to set up the position, so we stayed semipacked in our vehicles. It was 3 April 2003. I jumped out of my sleeping bag in my roofless five-ton truck to the sound of the night sky falling on top of me. I grabbed my gear and walked over to the command post. Once again, my unit was in the middle of nowhere, all by itself. My CO was standing alone staring up at the sky.

"What's going on, sir?"

"It sounds like a pair of fighter jets in a dogfight."

Just then, we got a radio message from the DASC telling us we couldn't launch another UAV because of a surface-to-air missile (SAM) threat. That night in the sky, we heard the noise of coalition aircraft dodging SAMs above us. Strange, haunting tones shifted from the Doppler effect and colors streaked across the open horizon as we all stood there, silently marveling at the light show above as the pilots freed themselves from the guided ordnance that pursued them. My CO explained all of this to me as we watched the sky.

"Hey, Boots. Come here. You see those streaks of red light?"

"Yes, sir."

"That's the chaff the pilot is dispensing to trick the SAM into falsely sensing it instead of the aircraft."

"That's pretty intense, sir."

"It is. Listen to that, Jane." It sounded like a motor rapidly decelerating and then accelerating again.

"What is that sound?"

"That's the pilot pulling Gs to evade the threat." The gyrations of a fighter pilot pulling g-forces made the sky sound like whale song.

"Didn't Captain Scott O'Grady have to do that before you and your team went to rescue him?"

"Something like it, Jane. But he didn't have much time before he was shot down."

My CO was very modest about the rescue and didn't like talking about it. But I could tell by how intently he was watching the sky that it had been a significant event in his life. One thing was sure, I was lucky to have him as a CO, and he was becoming something of a father figure to me. It didn't occur to me until this moment, but I had yet to see him lose control. He was always cool and collected. The Marines, including me, respected him for that.

★ ★ ★

Al Kut and An Numenyah were the potential areas for Saddam to employ weapons of mass destruction. We fully expected to get gassed. Before we left, we learned that our sister UAV squadron not only engaged in fire at a location near Ad Diwaniyah but also received a barrage of indirect fire from a nearby enemy artillery position and then engaged in small arms fire. We somehow had been lucky thus far, but I heard the murmurs of some dimwitted Staff Sergeant saying, "Damn! They're going to rate combat action ribbons! Why can't we get in a firefight?"

I was glad we had not yet been shot at. From my perspective, the best option would be if we could accomplish the mission without ever firing a round. After all, we were supposed to be liberating the Iraqi people, not killing them. Yes, the Ba'ath party members were all worthy of a fate worse than death, but the fewer Marines that fell into harm's way, the better. It was about what essential risks were necessary for Marines to accomplish the mission, not how many Iraqis we could kill in the process. Don't get me wrong—I was no pacifist; I just didn't want to see this thing escalate into Islamic jihad because some Private got trigger-happy and killed innocent children. Nor did I want to see my brothers in arms lured into an ambush. These were not just Marines; the Marines who were leading this fight for Imperial MEF were some of my best friends in the world. The 250 Lieutenants with whom I went through officer training were spread out all over the units on the front line. This was our war, so we should at least try to do things right.

15

NATIONAL GEOGRAPHIC

*Whoever kills another one without justifiable cause, surely he is kill-
ing all of humanity. And whoever saves the life of another one, surely
he saves the lives of all of humanity.*

—From the Qur'an, Sura Al Ma'aidah: Ayah 32

By 4 April, we had crawled across many more miles in Iraq and received the same happy greeting in the villages. I was actually beginning to think we'd make it through. With sixty-four Marines dead and one hundred wounded, there had been fewer casualties so far than the media predicted. No one liked to talk about the Iraqi civilian and military casualties. They were unknown numbers to us. While the Marines continued pushing through Iraq, sometimes in the wake of the Army units, they were often met by ambushes. We were sweeping up the unfinished messes in cities the Army units failed to secure. They had left areas exposed, and the Marines could no longer trust that those areas were safe. As the Marines were seizing hold of the southern route to Baghdad, the Army's 3rd Infantry Division had just reached the city's suburbs.

Once we got to An Numenyah, we would be able to fly into Baghdad, a first in Marine Corps history. One thing was for sure: the media had been right about the population's hatred of Saddam Hussein. The murals bearing Saddam's likeness that filled the cities were defaced, and villagers greeted us with cheers and pleas for food and water. Little girls in long, colorful dresses danced dangerously close to the street, waving their hands in the air. Grabbing some snacks, I threw them to the children on the side of the road. We had done right with Iraq; I was sure of it now and whole-heartedly believed in its liberation.

Mail had stopped coming—we hadn't received any for a month. I had only received two letters from Peter in the two months that had passed in this place, and they were all dated during the time when he was still in Kuwait. What the fuck? Others had gotten care packages and letters, and I had received nothing. I tried not to be bitter, though; I lived with the prospect that I could run into him any day.

At An Numenyah, future home of MEF main headquarters, hundreds of convoys were arranged in a giant cluster of military logistical wonders. I had never seen a military spectacle like this. Thousands upon thousands of Marines were assembled in this small area, most lined up by unit. Marines from infantry all the way to wing support were stretched out as far as the eye could see. We found our place, weaving through convoys, and spent hour upon excruciating hour waiting. We advanced several hundred feet in a couple hours, baked by 104° temperatures. With my ear to the radio, I drifted to sleep until suddenly awakened by the announcement that we were "on the move" again. Damn it, I needed caffeine.

★   ★   ★

By nightfall, we had finally arrived at our position. They gave us a spot where the large C-130s, transport aircraft, landed at the end of the runway. Landing between C-130s and helicopters can be a bit disconcerting, especially when you have a small plane that could be crushed by the wind wake alone. But we found our space on the runway, even though the Harriers and C-130s rumbling on top of us urged us out of the way. The first time a C-130 was landing, it touched down about fifty feet in front of us. Sergeant Young jumped off the runway and landed in the scrub in the sand. He got up, brushed the sand off, and started whistling. We didn't give a damn anymore. We just wanted to get our bird up in the air again.

Before we set up, we passed a convoy of Amtracs that seemed amazed to see females again because they couldn't stop staring at me. They waved and pointed and smiled, strangely reminiscent of the Iraqis who had acted similarly. Hundreds of young men stood in some state of undress, hanging up their dirty clothes on hasty laundry lines of 550 cord strung between their vehicles. After staring them down, Corporal Reynolds said to me, "Ma'am, they're probably thinking, 'Oh, damn, she's a Lieutenant!'"

"I don't think they care about my rank at this moment, Corporal."

Despite the ogling, the camaraderie between our units was apparent when one of the Amtrac SNCOs who was standing on top of one of the vehicles shouted out, "Hey UAVs, go get some for us!" Other grunts echoed, "Go get some!" or "Take the fucking enemy out for us!" Evidently, we had gotten quite a reputation. For a moment I no longer felt like a nasty wing POG. Sweet.

When we had finally gotten our gear set up, our first flight in An Numenyah would be to Baghdad and over the Al Hillah area in Babylon. As a child I had often rummaged through my grandmother's *National Geographic* magazines, ripping out articles and pictures of amazing places I wanted to explore. I had dreams of being an adventurer and travel writer, going to the corners of the earth and knowing every facet of the world. I wanted to understand the ways people lived and why they believed in the things they did. I had particularly loved pictures of the Middle East. Since the time I was a small child, pictures of Jordan and Egypt adorned my walls. To fulfill the promises I had made to myself as a child, I saved every penny I earned and traveled to all those places after I graduated from high school. Petra, Thermopylae, Troy, and Ephesus: however, the one place I dreamed of but never saw was the Ishtar Gate in Babylon. To me, that was a place of legend. Ishtar was one of the original matron goddesses of fertility and war. Surprisingly, for such an oppressed area, the legend of Babylon includes another female: the founding queen of Babylon, Semiramis. The legend tells of an orphaned girl, abandoned in the desert and raised by birds, hence her name, meaning "beloved by doves." After the governor of Syria, Onnes, found her abandoned, he was instantly smitten, and they wed in Nineveh. Onnes traveled to Bactria, now Afghanistan, during a military campaign, and asked Semiramis to follow him. But Onnes's inability to act put his army in a stalemate. Seizing the initiative in a surprise attack, Semiramis took charge of part of the military and seized the city. After Onnes committed suicide, Semiramis wed King Ninus, and they ruled the empire together. After the king's death, Semiramis became the sole ruler of an empire that comprised most of Mesopotamia. Semiramis made her empire prosper and became the founder of Babylon. In many ways, she was considered the female Alexander the Great. Since then, Babylon represented one of the earliest civilizations in human history. At the entrance to the city, the Ishtar Gate was constructed, honoring its goddess of fertility. That beautiful azure gate was something I had always dreamed about seeing, but my parents told me as a child that Iraq was, and would always be, off limits.

"They are fanatics there—you'll never be able to see it."

"Do you think the gate is still there?"

"The original is in Berlin. The Iraqis probably destroyed all the archaeological sites. With the Iran-Iraq war going on, all that historical stuff is probably gone."

Still, I vowed one day I would see Babylon. It meant a lot to me as a child, and even as an adult, Babylon was that unknown world where civilization was born and had flourished. I had to believe that some of those things I dreamed of seeing as a kid were still out there and not destroyed.

So here I was, in the middle of a war, concerned about some historical site. But it was more than that. As one of the earliest civilizations, Babylon was a testament to both the progress and history of mankind. Most people can trace their history back to this place where law, calendars, languages, science, literature, and civilization were born. What was the purpose of any war, if the history of the struggles of man were forgotten? Babylon was our history; it was the story of us and them. As we flew our bird over Al Hillah, I scanned for that historic center. But I didn't see it.

★   ★   ★

Although I did not see Babylon—I feared it had been destroyed—we flew over Baghdad and were awestruck. We had never flown over a city of this magnitude. There were thousands of buildings and homes and a tangled web of streets and highways feeding out of the central arteries. A river meandered its way through the center of the city. Saddam's palaces, government buildings, and parks were all visible from our vantage point. Below was Rashid airfield, Division Objective Raven. Division had finally gotten to the periphery of Baghdad and was now consolidating in order to seize the airfield. It was on the outskirts to the east of Baghdad near the Diyala River. The Marines would set up a forward position from there to prepare for the assault into Baghdad. The Army units would swing into Baghdad from the south while the Marines flanked the city from the northeast.

We scanned the airfield and saw metal hulks of burned-out enemy equipment. Farther down, eight intact aircraft stood at the ready. We identified them as MIG-23s. But upon further investigation, we realized that they were abandoned and nonoperational. However, some bigwig at the CFLCC decided these were hot targets, even though we explained that they were derelict.

"This is a big find," one of the field grade officers said. We weren't too interested, as we knew they couldn't fly. Some had huge holes in the wings, and others had parts missing. We didn't bother asking for artillery or air support. But before we knew it, they were calling for an air interdiction mission using B-52s to destroy them.

"Maybe we shouldn't ask for air or arty anymore, because we seem to get it faster when we don't ask," I said sarcastically. My shift was about to end, so I decided to call it a night and left it for the other collections officer to handle.

When I awoke a couple hours later, a Marine Corps historian and some press were interviewing one of my Marines, Sergeant Beaty, regarding his excellent job in finding those MIG-23s. I was amused, considering it was actually Sergeant Young who had found them. Sergeant Beaty sat speechless—he knew he merely happened to be present when the B-52s dropped the bombs on the site, looking for battle damage. Of all the things our squadron had accomplished in the last few weeks, we found it funny that they thought this was the important one. They voted Sergeant Beaty "imagery analyst of the year" and handed him a trophy. He was so flabbergasted by the situation that he didn't set them straight.

"Just humor them, Sergeant Beaty," I said. "Let them think it's important; we won't bother reminding them again that the MIG-23s weren't operational!"

The only time we thought of the MIG-23 air strike after that was when we had to go back and report battle damage assessment (BDA) on the damn things, and it turned out that for all the fuss about the "strategic threat" we diverted, the B-52s only managed to hit one! Chances are, the real purpose of these MIGs was to deny us the use of the airfield or to make it look occupied. Well, the members of CFLCC had gotten their names in the history books for their contributions to the war, all for taking down one nonflying MIG.

★　★　★

By that time, things got freaking crazy again. The Army 3rd Infantry Division captured the Republican Guard headquarters and the Baghdad International Airport. The interim government was expected to show up even before Baghdad had fallen. 1st Marine Division had gotten into their attack positions and would be taking Baghdad soon. The Grand Ayatollah Sistani, a key Shi'ite Iraqi leader, issued a pro-coalition fatwa calling a cease-fire on all hostilities against U.S. forces. Cities were revolting against pro-Saddam forces, and things were at last turning in our favor. We had finally almost broken the back of the Ba'ath regime.

Our camera kept taking electromagnetic interference hits from all the electrical activity around. We were never quite sure what started this, be it radio towers nearby, other aircraft, or the weather. But at last we had a clear view, then we moved down to Al Hillah again, where they wanted us to look at one of the palaces they destroyed.

"Which palace?"

"The one near the archaeological ruins, near the old gate."

"The ruins of Babylon and the Ishtar Gate?"

"Yes, that one." A palace had indeed been there, one of Saddam's many. Thousands of feet below our UAV was that ancient artifact, left intact through war and centuries of change. There was Babylon and the Gate of Ishtar, the proud blue gates that were a shadow of what was once there. I looked on in awe.

But Babylon was the only positive thing in a country that was being transformed before our eyes. The war surrounded us, and we were starting to feel the effects of fatigue. Everyone looked emaciated, and our muscles grew thin with lack of exercise. Our faces became tan and leathery, and we all knew that our bodies would be permanently weathered by the conditions in Iraq. I looked at my reflection in the small mirror on the five-ton truck. It was the first time I really had a chance to rest and take care of myself. I hadn't showered in eighteen days, and my hair was a matted, sand-filled mess that itched like crazy. I was so filthy I could rub the dirt off my arms. I couldn't even remember when I last changed my socks. Everyone was dirty, but some smelled worse than others. It was getting to the point where you didn't even want to stand next to certain folks. Although the end of the war seemed near, home was not. Planners had estimated that after the end of hostilities, we would remain in Iraq at least three more months. The only thing I really cared about anymore was that somewhere nearby my husband was OK.

16

A TURNING POINT

Never forget that no military leader has ever become great without audacity.

—Karl von Clausewitz

We were supposed to push north again to a place called Salman Pak, which was a peninsula of land about eight kilometers, a place long famous for its Fedayeen terrorist training camp. Instead of my unit packing up again, we were able to fly over the site from where we were. We were supporting RCT-7, our boys from Twentynine Palms. This was the first time during the war that we rejoined our brothers from 7th Marines and had artillery support from none other than 3/11, my husband's unit. I knew that any targets I now found, my husband would kill with artillery rounds.

According to sources, Salman Pak was supposed to be home to one to two thousand of those elite Fedayeen fighters. We would fly in advance of 7th Marines on their movement to Salman Pak, looking for any threats or unusual activity along the way. But the initial reports sounded exaggerated, so I didn't expect to see what we found.

The peninsula of Salman Pak was a small, lush oasis in the otherwise arid country of Iraq. Mansions lined the main route, which looped around the entire perimeter of the peninsula, following the water's edge. The whole area was slightly smaller than Manhattan and filled with pools and fountains, verandas, and docks with boats. Flying over, it looked like the Iraqi Beverly Hills. Fecund earth gave way to well-kept farms with pruned citrus groves and date palms. It was like nothing we had seen in Iraq before. However, an eerie fact remained—there was no one outside. No civilians or military personnel were visible. It was as if the peninsula had been abandoned.

Flying farther, deep into the area, we began seeing nicely arranged barracks-type structures and headquarters buildings, much like The Basic School in Quantico. Then we saw a physical training track, an outdoor weights area, and an obstacle course. Farther down the road was the rifle and pistol range. We saw the silhouettes of targets much like our own in the distance. Farther ahead, a 727 aircraft stood in the middle of a football-sized field. Its tail had been cut open to provide access into the aircraft. Evidently this was their terrorist training aircraft. We had never seen anything like it before. Only two hundred meters ahead, a row of display vehicles stood. Much like we had in Quantico, as well: an an-tiaircraft artillery piece, an SA-8 surface-to-air missile, a T-72 tank, an armored personnel carrier, and a T-54/55 tank were arranged in a row, mirroring the best equipment Iraq had to offer. They were obviously decoys. We then came to the administrative building. After our infantry brothers came through here, we would later learn that they found a tor-ture chamber, an interrogation room, and an armory full of hundreds of brand-new AK-47s.

"Do you see anyone at all?" Captain Nettles from 7th Marines asked. Recall that he was the one who helped me before the war kicked off.

"Not a soul."

"Hey, just to tell you, it's great working with our Twentynine Palms team again!"

"I'm with you. If it was up to us, we would always be supporting our brothers from home."

"We're going to start rolling through from the northeast corner of the peninsula and make a loop, sweeping the area," 7th Marines added. "Can you cover us about five to seven kilometers ahead?"

"No problem, we will lead ahead of your assault."

We positioned the bird to fly the route ahead of them and traced the road. We still saw no enemy personnel. Evidently the Fedayeen training school was empty.

"Pioneers?"

"Yes?"

"3/11 is going to start taking out targets along our route."

"Do you need us to adjust their fire?'

"No need—they're taking out preplanned targets."

"Roger. . . . We'll spot for BDA."

"Good to go."

No sooner had he said that than the sky was ablaze with thousands of dual-purpose improved conventional munitions (DPICM) rounds firing for effect. DPICM was the ideal killing round for troops that were dug in. The opulence of Salman Pak was being destroyed. Headquarters buildings blazed as gas lines burst open in showers of flame. The surrounding area was enveloped in continuous destruction. The whole peninsula was in flames.

The 7th Marines' push into Salman Pak was indicative of the rest of the problem-free progress the Marines were making through Iraq. Our tenacity and tempo did not allow the enemy the time to reposition, let alone hold meetings to reconsolidate. Our incredible green machine was set in motion, and we were destroying the threat without even being engaged. All the enemy had time to do was run. With 7th Marines advancing unhampered by hostile contact, the regiments, aided by Army's 3rd Infantry Division to the south, began surrounding the city of Baghdad for an all-out assault. All our units were gaining tempo and moving in for the final push.

Our next flight was to confirm or deny the existence of enemy massed along the Diyala River—a small but strategic choke point into Baghdad—and to determine the condition of the bridges in the vicinity. We moved into the target area and flew to the two strategic bridges; these were the only two bridges that allowed vehicles to pass from the east side of the river into the city. The southernmost bridge was the one that 1st Marine Division envisioned using. On our first pass over the other bridge, we saw something.

"It looks like personnel and trucks hidden in a palm grove," I said. "Do you want us to adjust fire on it?"

"No, we don't want to ruin our element of surprise yet," Division responded.

"Well, I hope we didn't just ruin it for you!"

"No, we're not planning on using that bridge anyway."

"Then why did you want to see it?"

"We know how much noise you guys make flying over things. Now they think we're interested."

On the last circuit around, we got a close-up picture.

"Looks like they've got dynamite rigged all over the western side."

"Are you sure?"

"Yes. We think they're planning to blow the bridge. It makes sense—the best place for the enemy to blow it would be on their side."

We took a couple pictures and moved to the southern bridge, a strategic line of communication for 1st Marine Division.

Although I MEF seemed very concerned that the bridges were rigged, they assured us that even if they were blown, they would have engineering assets to fix them. The southernmost bridge consisted of three spanned-deck girders; the center section was rigged with explosives. Since this was the main bridge into the city, we were sure it would be blown. As we moved forward, we saw that the Iraqis had set up trucks and possible indirect fire positions, all oriented toward the bridge to delay our passage into the city.

The next day, the bridge was blown as we had expected. This was the Marines' main crossing point into Baghdad, and without it, the assault could be delayed for days. This ultimately would be disastrous, giving the Iraqi forces a couple days to consolidate and build up their strength; they could easy create chaos for the Marines trying to cross this choke point. We needed a bridge up *now*.

Because 1st Marine Division asked us to watch the bridge for twenty-four hours, thus getting advanced eyes on it, Marine engineers set themselves up to fix it before our troops were set to cross, and they had enough time to plan and build a pontoon bridge to cross.

★   ★   ★

Built like a brick shithouse, Marine Lieutenant Paul Bock, who stood about six foot, four inches, had gone to officer training with me, and everyone thought he would go straight to infantry. But Bock was a prior Staff Sergeant in the infantry, and his knees were giving him trouble again. Not only that, his family was dead set against it, having already been through countless combat deployments since the Gulf War.

Infantry was one of his last choices when it came time for military occupation selection (MOS) because he knew that our instructors would try to put him there. When MOS selection day came, he was relieved when he was assigned as an engineer officer.

Attached to 1st Combat Engineer Battalion and also in support of 1st Tank Battalion, Lieutenant Bock, despite his MOS choice, found himself moving alongside the grunts during combat. He was on the ground when it came time to build the pontoon bridge across the Diyala River. As 1st Tanks set up a defensive position along the northern bridge we had flown over, Bock's team moved forward but were blocked by an antitank mine-field. The Iraqi forces, knowing that this choke point would be key, had set up a defense in depth. As soon as Bock and his team crossed the Iraqi "trigger line," the Iraqis sent small arms fire downrange to harass them as they tried to clear the minefield. But when they set the line charge that would blow the mines, it failed to detonate.

One of Bock's Marines came to his side. "Sir, the line charge didn't go off! What do you want us to do now, sir?" As he said this, more incoming rounds landed in their position, and the large explosion of a RPG went off nearby.

"Set more line charges."

The mine-clearing vehicle set three more line charges, and they moved back to a secured position. *Boom!* The percussive blast shook their bodies and made their ears ring. They failed to clear a straight line through the minefield, but Bock decided to move through anyway, and his team detonated the remaining mines by hand. At the bridge area, Bock radioed for the Engineer Support Battalion, which included vehicles with bridge kits attached. Within hours, they had set up a pontoon bridge, and the assault on Baghdad began on time.

As our forces moved across the makeshift bridge, we were given a FragO to move back to Qalat Sikar in support of Task Force Tarawa again. Higher had determined that there would be a big battle in Al Amarah, a city on the Iraq-Iran border to the northeast. So as my husband crossed into Baghdad, I moved back east and tried not to look back.

★ ★ ★

The few days we were in Al Amarah were, for the most part, uneventful. Units that were supposed to capitulate instead abandoned their equipment, the young men stripping themselves of their uniforms and going home to blend in with society. We saw endless streams of young men who had deserted their posts walking in groups along the sides of the roads. Some removed their boots and walked barefoot; most carried nothing, not even water. By 7 April, Al Amarah had erupted with activity. We saw a mob of hundreds, even thousands, of civilians carrying flags and running through the streets. At first we didn't know what to make of it. Then we got an intelligence report saying that civilians were rising up against Saddam's supporters. The situation was further confused because the Iraqis had hung banners and signs that said, "Remember Hussein."

"Why would they want to remember Saddam Hussein?"

"They're pro-Ba'athist or something. I don't know." And then some genius figured it out—or rather, he asked one of the Iraqis. "Hussein" didn't refer to Saddam, but to Imam Hussein, the revered martyr of the Shi'ites.

In Al Amarah, events were imploding as the Iraqi civilians rose up to take control of their city. Here it was happening in front of our eyes. They would rally support from those in the homes and businesses, calling everyone to the streets, but many could not keep up as they ran through the city. The main group attacked any retreating vehicles that came along Highway 6. They swarmed the vehicles until they were certain they did not harbor pro-Saddam or Ba'ath party members. We watched the insurgent group move across town. As they came into the main square, they were led and flanked by motorcycles that hunted the people who fled. In the square we saw them swarm an individual and club him to death. They knocked him to the ground and beat him until a pool of blood collected around him. A shot went off, and the crowd dispersed. We looked for bodies, but there were too many individuals around. The group's energy never seemed to wane; they continued to run through the streets, waving black and red flags. Watching from the safety of our screen, I knew that this marked the beginning of the end. Like a wildfire, soon to ignite across Iraq, the same stories were being told. Cities were rising up and pushing out the Ba'athists.

★ ★ ★

On that day in Baghdad, a thirty-foot crater was all that remained from two BLU-109s (bunker busters) and two joint direct attack munitions (JDAMS) that were dropped by a B-1B into the Mansur district of Baghdad. It was believed that a meeting between Saddam, his two sons, and high-ranking officials had been taking place at the time. They were reported dead. But we were not sure. All we heard on BBC radio was that the Marines, rather than being repelled by the Republican Guard, had seized Baghdad with such tenacity that the enemy only had time to run.

Units crossed the pontoon bridge with incredible speed, just hours after we had imaged it with the UAV. The 3rd Battalion, 4th Marines—more Twentynine Palms grunts—were one of the first to cross the river that day. One of our friends, Lieutenant Pat Spencer, was a forward observer with 3/4. Spencer was a crazy, unlucky, but incredibly proficient Marine from Oregon. Once, while running the obstacle course during a competition, he had become so focused running toward a wall as quickly as he could that he forgot to jump over it and knocked himself out.

That day, Spencer, sweat drenched and heart racing, sprinted his way across the damaged and swaying footbridge. Concrete and debris from the exploded bridge littered the way. As he crossed over the Diyala River, he jumped over wood planks and open holes that emptied thirty feet below into the river. Every fifth step, Spencer turned around to scream for his Marines to stay close behind, but they were always evenly spaced, staggered to the left and right, like an unbroken chain. Their faces were gaunt and they were panting, trying to keep pace, but surging from the adrenaline. Spencer turned back just in time to stop himself from falling into a three-foot gap in the bridge.

"Hole!" he shouted back, the sound fading into the dissonance of tank rounds and artillery barrages hitting the enemy armor straight ahead. The moment was chaotic, but just ahead, Spencer could make out the end of the bridge that spilled out onto the edges of Baghdad. As his feet hit the dirt, rounds impacted around him, but he brought his platoon safely to a berm by a nearby building. He wiped the sweat from his Roman nose, twice broken years before. His usually pale skin was hidden behind layers of caked dirt and the brassy sheen of his sunburnt face. His shaved head cooled him, but not enough, from the intense heat, the sprint, and his multilayered protective equipment. The platoon paused, regrouped, and formed patrols into Baghdad.

Spencer would spend the next couple days jumping from one rooftop to another with his team. With binoculars in hand, he would call for artillery fires to suppress Iraqi RPG and small arms fire attacks as his unit and others moved into the area. After almost falling off a couple roofs, Spencer took a team of his Marines and an interpreter into Baghdad to scout out the "old city," known as the Sheikh Omar district. The interpreter informed Spencer that this area contained a mixed group of people, and Spencer's team confronted looters, friendly newly liberated Iraqis, and the Fedayeen.

Part of what made Spencer a great leader was his unconventional solutions to problems, although they sometimes backfired. On one particular patrol in Baghdad, Spencer was clearing a building with his Marines when he came upon a safe in a Ba'ath party building. Spencer wanted to blow the safe open so he could see if there was anything important inside. None of his Marines had any experience with demolition work, but they'd had instruction from some combat engineers on how to use the C-4 they were carrying.

Hollywood nonsense aside, you don't just stick a digital timer in a block of plastic explosives and walk away. Detonating C-4 requires a detonation cord tied to a fuse cord, which is hollow plastic tubing filled with black powder. The fuse cord is ignited with a small device with a pull ring. Pull the ring, the fuse burns, and when it hits the detonation cord, the small explosion causes the C-4 to detonate in a much larger secondary explosion. Playing with C-4 like this is simple, but there is a hitch. The fuse cord, like so many other pieces of equipment Marines stake their lives on, is manufactured by the lowest bidder and is notoriously inconsistent in how quickly it burns. So Spencer cut a length of fuse, ignited it, and timed it to determine its burn rate. Then he timed himself running from the safe to the doorway and slamming the door. He cut the appropriate amount of fuse cord with some extra for safety. Now came the tricky part.

Spencer turned to his scout observer, Corporal Wormington, and said, "Hey, Worm, how much C-4 you think I should use?"

"Fuck, sir, I dunno."

Having thus thoroughly mulled over the various ins and outs of the delicate issue of how much plastic explosive is needed to blow up a floor safe without destroying its contents, Spencer fell back on his artillery training and decided to rely on the time-tested, Marine-approved principle: more is better. He slapped an entire block of C-4 on the safe and rigged it to blow. He had his Marines get into the other room, all down on the deck, except for the two standing in the doorway who would pull Spencer into the room. Spencer finished setting up the explosives, checking one last time to ensure that he'd set it up properly. He took a breath, popped into a crouch, and pulled the ring on the igniter. He sprinted to the door, and his Marines yanked him into the adjacent room and down to the floor, slamming the door. Half a second after the door shut—*Boom!*—a huge explosion struck them like a punch in the chest. The explosion was so massive that Spencer and his Marines were all dazed. The door blew off its hinges, hitting the opposite wall twenty feet away. Disoriented from the blast, Spencer and his Marines looked at each other stupidly.

"Oh, shit! Fire! Fucking fire, assholes! Put it out!"

The obscenity broke through their daze, and they all jumped up to stomp out the small fires all over the room. Worm looked at Spencer and shouted, "SIR!"

Ears ringing, Spencer looked at him. "WHAT?"

"SIR, WHERE IS THE SAFE?"

Spencer was still out of it, shaken by the force of the explosion. His hearing was starting to come back. "Of course we're safe, Worm; we're on the seventh floor!"

Worm was slightly more lucid. "No, sir, the safe! The motherfucking safe! It's gone! Where is it?"

Pat looked where Worm was pointing, and sure enough, the safe was gone. Only then did he realize that the entire exterior wall had been destroyed. He walked over to the gaping hole and looked down at the plaza below. There was the safe, which had miraculously failed to hit the dozen or so Marines who had been below. They looked over the edge of the building at the safe. It had failed to open.

Lieutenants weren't allowed to use plastic explosives after that.

★ ★ ★

A few days later, Spencer was leading his Marines as they secured an abandoned hospital. They received an intelligence report that the building was being used as the command post of the Iraqi Intelligence Communications Unit and was likely occupied. They had to check every room, just to make sure no Fedayeen or Iraqi units were hiding out there, but by the time they'd swept everything but the basement, they were feeling confident no one was there. Pat led his Marines to the basement level, splitting up to check rooms individually to get it over and done with. Thinking they'd find nothing, they uncovered a room with secured documents, military maps, and communications equipment. Pat checked a few more rooms without incident. It was dark down there in the basement because the power was out, and it was getting a little spooky. Pat came to a room with a closed door and took a breath as he grabbed the doorknob. He turned the knob and took two fast steps into the room, his rifle at the ready as he looked into the darkness.

Without warning, an invisible hand yanked his weapon from his hands. Terrified that an Iraqi soldier was about to kill him with his own rifle, Pat began flailing around the room, unable to see anything, striking out at random in a desperate attempt to find and kill his unseen enemy. As he fought his way across the room, he screamed, "You motherfucker! I'll kill you! Give me back my weapon!" He continued to scream as he fought his way across the room.

His Marines came running as soon they heard him shout. They ran into the room, some with flashlights, and looked for someone to shoot. One of the Marines shouted, "Sir, what the fuck is happening?"

"Some motherfucker just stole my rifle! Yanked it right out of my hands! Find him!"

"Sir, there's no one in here! The room's empty!"

"Then who the fuck stole my rifle?"

As the adrenaline began to ebb from their bloodstreams, the Marines shone their flashlights around the room, trying to find the weapon. One of them saw it.

"Holy shit, sir! Look!" The Marine shone his flashlight on a piece of equipment on the far wall. Spencer's rifle was hanging from it at chest height.

Mystified, he walked over and grabbed it. It did not budge. He pulled, hard, with his foot against the medical machine, and the rifle reluctantly broke free. One of his Marines laughed and said, "Sir, it's an MRI."

Even without power, the MRI retained an electromagnetic field strong enough to pull the rifle out of Spencer's grip and across the room. Mortified, he swore his Marines to secrecy, a solemn oath that lasted until they ran into some other Marines. Word quickly spread about the incident, and Spencer was forced to tell and retell the story several times. To add insult to injury, his rifle had become magnetically charged, and he was now unable to go on patrol without his rifle picking up nails and other small metal debris everywhere he went.

★ ★ ★

As 1st Tanks rolled into the streets of Baghdad, they were not greeted by a fury of rounds but by flowers thrown on top of the tanks. On the other side of Baghdad, the tanks rolled into Firdaus Square, and the symbolic twenty-foot statue of Saddam was dragged down by the Marines from 3rd Battalion, 4th Marines. The Iraqis quickly desecrated the toppled statue, some taking pieces as war trophies. Slogans denounced Saddam throughout the city—and across the country, as elements of Task Force Tarawa Marines secured Al Amarah without even firing a shot. Iraqis celebrated the arrival of Americans, hoping for a change after Saddam's regime.

The collapse of the twenty-five-year rule of Saddam Hussein was imminent. Signs were everywhere in Baghdad, and most insurgents were in hiding. There were no suicide bombers or unconventional forces that were willing to go up against the newly arrived coalition. Instead they stood in the shadows, glaring ominously. Men from other countries who had come to fight a jihad now found themselves alone and frightened in the streets of Baghdad. Some turned their vehicles around, and when confronted, said with terror-stricken faces that they were just trying to get home, back to Egypt, Syria, or Iran. But there were some who came resolved, their eyes transfixed and full of hate, waiting for their moment to rise up, regroup, and attack. We saw these men, lurking around corners, and we knew, when the time came, they would fight again.

Looting was rampant, government buildings were ransacked, war trophies were taken, and images of Saddam were defaced. Banks, hotels, museums, and libraries were left unguarded, and looters stole whatever they could. Despite these tragedies, it was a decisive moment in the end of a regime, and I MEF had seized the initiative by charging through. We were all relieved and took joy in the aftermath, which allowed us individually to relax and soak in some solitary moments. Knowing that Iraq was now secured was a relief, but the war was not over yet.

On the radio, we heard a BBC reporter question an Army officer, asking, "Is Saddam dead?" The Army officer replied, "Does it really matter? We're in his palace drinking his booze; he might as well be, 'cause for any self-respecting man, at this point, he'd be better off dead." The fact was, we were in Saddam's home now; it was just a matter of time before we found him.

Although Saddam had the classic defense in-depth plan leading to the gates of Baghdad, we had swept through too quickly for him to assemble his elite Republican Guards and regular armies. It was twenty-one days after the war had started, and, symbolically, this day had signaled the end.

A radio station was taken over in Baghdad, and Bush's message, translated into Arabic, was heard: "We will help you build a perfect and representative government that protects the rights of all citizens, and then our military forces will leave. You are good and gifted people, the heirs of a great civilization that contributes to all humanity. You deserve better than tyranny and corruption and torture chambers. You deserve to live as free people."

A new era had come. Other Arab nations were comparing Baghdad's fall with the Mongol invasion 745 years earlier. What was done could not be undone. The Middle East would never be the same again. Or so we thought.

★ ★ ★

We got an order to move back to An Numenyah. The war had entered Phase IVa, which signalized "reconstitution," but there was talk of us moving to Tikrit, Saddam's birthplace. The war was supposed to culminate there, as most of the Republican Guards were die-hard Saddam supporters, and resistance was expected to be heavy. Farther north, the Kurds, fighters who were called the Peshmerga, had overthrown the resistance and were now aiding the coalition special operations forces to oust the last remnants of the regime. We learned that the Kurds had captured northern Iraq, including Kirkuk. That left Tikrit.

The MOPP level was lowered to zero, which meant that for the first time in three weeks, we took off our MOPP suits and put our cammies back on. After wearing the same clothing for the better part of a month, you could smell a Marine coming from half a klick, but the simple joy of shedding the heavy, stifling chemical suit in favor of clean, light desert cammies more than made up for it. I was completely dehydrated again. It was the only way to survive the convoys without pissing on myself. My mind wandered to better days as we packed up to convoy back to An Numenyah. Now that much of the fear had subsided, I couldn't stop thinking about my husband. Where was he? Was he still alive? Had he been injured? Did he kill anyone? Having him in my life and in Iraq fighting this war changed everything for me. Here I was, married for two weeks and then rushed off to war. I had met the right man at last, and then unlucky timing had pulled us apart. My platinum wedding band, inscribed with "semper fidelis," was all I had to remind me—that and a wrinkled photograph of him in his blues and that damned unopened letter. I missed him but I didn't even know if he was alive.

Looking down at my mud-caked arms reminded me of my appearance. We were getting dirtier by the day. My trousers were covered with dried dirt and my face was caked with a layer of it. Thankfully, my period had miraculously stopped. I wasn't sure if it was due to stress or malnourishment, but many of the females were in the same situation. The only other time I remembered my period stopping was in boot camp when most of the females, strangely, lost theirs the moment they entered boot camp, when they stepped on the yellow footprints in Parris Island. The few remaining women who still had theirs had become syncopated, so the entire platoon was on the same cycle.

America seemed so far away, such an illusion. This was the only life I imagined having now. Living a life in the war zone, fighting a war that had multilayered front lines. Now, from our offensive standpoint, the front line was how far your platform could reach into the depths of the battle space. For the enemy, the front line was how far they could sneak past secured areas and attack the rear-echelon supply lines.

The enemy's center of gravity had been their chameleon-like ability to blend into the populace and then resurface after the larger, stronger forces had left. Their critical vulnerability had been not amassing enough troops to sustain morale. But this was good, because thus far, there were few deaths on both sides. I was relieved to have been spared the living nightmare of chemical warfare; I had been haunted by visions of drowning on dry land as my lungs choked with mucus from chlorine gas, of the agony as my muscles spasmed hard enough to break my spine after a VX attack, of feeling my blood clot inside my veins after inhaling a blood agent. After taking a moment to savor the respite from the looming fear of death and destruction, I steeled myself and resolved not to relax and call it a victory until every Marine and military member stepped off a plane back in the United States.

On our drive to An Numenyah, we encountered the same Iraqi faces who watched us roll through. But as we made a stop along Highway 1, we saw a trailer full of FROG-7 missiles right across from my vehicle. "What the hell?" I thought. Soon enough, while I was busy snapping pictures of it, an officer from the EOD unit, dressed in full MOPP with gas mask, rolled by in a humvee.

"Be advised, you can't stop here; those missiles have nerve agents in them!"

"Holy shit! Roger that, we'll move," said our Master Sergeant.

We had known there was a possibility of weapons of mass destruction here, but this was our first direct contact with them. That same day, we heard reports of unrefined uranium found in a nuclear research facility south of Baghdad.

Rumors abounded during this phase of the war about weapons of mass destruction, particularly chemical weapons. Scuttlebutt circulated about a coalition logistics depot near Basra that had been discovered to have significant amounts of nerve agent. Every day someone would tell of newly discovered documents detailing the secret locations of reserves of weapons of mass destruction or of underground bunkers filled with enriched uranium. I never saw a goddamn thing and can only conclude that these were all baseless rumors.

As we continued the convoy, we came to a tactical herringbone halt after running up to a grunt unit in front of us. As we were staggered, diagonally lined, I pulled out my binoculars to see what the delay was. I could see that a group of Iraqi vehicles had driven through the grunts, but at the end of the grunts' convoy, they had blocked them from moving past us, and Marines had circled the vehicles and were pointing weapons at the Iraqis. A large Iraqi woman in a black, flowing abaya exited the lead vehicle with a young boy. She was crying and waving her hands wildly in the air. As a Marine officer approached her with his interpreter, she seemed even more enraged.

"What do you think is going on, ma'am?" asked Corporal Reynolds, who also had his binoculars out.

"I don't know. . . . She's upset about something."

Corporal Reynolds scanned the vehicles.

"Check out all those colored boxes in the vehicles." The boxes were multicolored in red, green, black, and gold, intricately detailed with Arabic designs, as delicate as henna.

"What are they?"

"Storage containers?"

"No, I think they're coffins."

My binoculars moved back to the animated conversation between the Iraqis and the ranking officer. There were several Iraqis now pleading with Marines. As they appeared to come to an agreement, the Marines waved them through, giving them the go-ahead to move between our vehicles. We got the word on the radio to let them pass and not to point weapons at them.

"They're letting them through our convoy?" Corporal Cano asked. For security reasons, there was strict SOP about not allowing Iraqis to break rank into our convoy.

"Apparently so."

Ten Toyotas passed through, some station wagons, some GAZ, most painted in the distinctive white and orange that was so popular in Iraq. Inside the vehicles that passed, the families, in a funeral procession, their eyes glazed over and tired, looked through us. I would find out later that the coffins were civilian casualties of war, some children, and that all the bodies had been washed and wrapped in white cloth and then put in decorated wooden caskets. The Shi'ites were bringing the bodies to the holy cemetery of Najaf, the largest and most historic Shi'ite cemetery in the world.

★   ★   ★

As the bodies of the Iraqis moved past us, our reverence for their loss could neither be expressed nor truly understood. We watched them stone-faced but not unaffected. Back in America, our own sacred cemetery in Arlington was being filled with our own brothers and sisters. Flag-draped coffins were met at Dover Air Force Base, where Marines, like my friend Lieutenant Hembrick, met the bodies to determine who would receive them and to ensure that they were afforded the proper dignity. Lieutenant Nicole Hembrick, a beautiful, dark-skinned, athletic woman, was one of those people whose ethnicity was impossible to pinpoint, but whose sharp features spoke of classic beauty. In her blues, she was in every way the billboard picture of a Marine Corps Officer. She had not gone to combat this time. But her job was no less than that, as she read her manifest roster with fifteen Marines' names on it. On the list, she not only knew their names by heart, but read their vitals on the sheet before her: blood type, hair color, eye color, Social Security number, hometown, age, and next of kin.

"Oh God," she thought as she looked down the list to see how young these boys were. Twenty-one, twenty, twenty-three, eighteen—some not even old enough to drink. Hembrick was a prior like me, but she had been a Staff Sergeant. She had grown up in the Corps and watched so many young men and women grow up beside her. And now, here they were, coming back to her in a way she had hoped never to see.

The funeral detail was made up of enlisted Marines in blues from "Eighth and I," the oldest post in the corps. Assigned the primary duty of carrying Marines killed in action off the plane as well as laying them to rest if they were buried in Arlington National Cemetery, they proudly stood by their motto, "The last to let you down." While the other services used eight people to carry a coffin, the burly Marines used six-man teams. The detail ceremoniously lifted the caskets one by one out of the C-130. The caskets draped in red, white, and blue were religiously lifted, and the Marines and other service members who handled them wore white gloves and moved with a rigid delicacy. Hembrick's job meant coming here to meet casualities, which arrived frequently. No matter how many times she would meet the bodies, she had to hold back her emotions. But there were so many this time: to how many more families would she have to hand over the casket of their Marine?

★   ★   ★

Sun-soaked Iraqi children peddled cigarettes and Iraqi dinars as souvenirs on the sides of the streets, their faces gleaming with the newness of our arrival. Some Iraqis flaunted prized alcohol in front of us, which we hadn't had since leaving America. Kuwait and Iraq were dry zones for us, and alcohol was not authorized. Damn, how good just a glass or two would be. The Iraqi kids flashed peace signs and gang signs that they had learned from the Americans. Weird.

An Numenyah had already changed in the few days since we had left it. MEF forward had moved in, and with it thousands of Marines. They gave us a small side road to use as a landing strip for the UAVs, and we were parked next to the TRAP team of CH-46s and Harriers, vertical takeoff and short takeoff combat aircraft, whose engines hummed all night and sounded like a wind tunnel next to our ears. It was almost impossible to sleep.

Instead of our usual twenty-four-hour flight schedule, we had only two flights a day, as both Baghdad and Al Kut's conventional threats had disappeared. An occasional suicide bomber killed or injured coalition forces, but for the most part, 9 April 2003, had been the decisive day of victory. But to me, the only decisive day was seeing Peter again. My mind did not measure victory in terms of war but only in the success of reunion. I kept his unopened letter these last few months in my flak jacket. I held it in my hands, pondering for a moment whether to open it, and then put it away.

Morale rose when, on 12 April, we got our first showers after not bathing for over a month. Hot tray rations were served once a day now, our first relief from a steady diet of MREs in almost a month and a half. Tray rations are inedible, as well, but at least they're hot. A scandal erupted when it was discovered that our squadron logistics chief, a Staff NCO, had been lying about the availability of tray rations. The squadron leadership hassled him continually about getting some hot chow for the Marines, and he consistently said that the logistics bubbas responsible for keeping us flush with beans, bullets, and Band-Aids didn't have any to give us. When one of our officers asked logistics what the fuck was so hard about executing their primary mission, the baffled logisticians were taken aback. They replied that that they had had been offering us hot chow for weeks, but our logistics chief told them we didn't want it. He had been scamming to avoid all the coordination work, running from one unit to the next and bringing the chow to us. He was relieved of duty most ricky-tick, but the reason was kept quiet after the Sergeant Major pointed out that the Marines might slit his throat in the dark. Hot chow was that important.

Mail had also come for the first time—finally—and I was handed a letter from Peter. I ripped it open. It was dated 14 March, before the war kicked off. The letter read:

> Have I mentioned yet that I love you? I do, you know, with all my heart and soul. I cannot wait until the day when we can resume a normal life and put this nonsense into dim and distant memory. Let's find a little corner of the world, you and me, that we can carve our lives out of and be happy together. I have many ambitions and aspirations, but my greatest one is to live my life with you, my wife. What do you say? Sound good? It does to me. I miss you, baby, and live only to hold you in my arms again.
> All my love, your husband,
> Peter

17

THEIR BLOOD HAD WASHED OUT

No bastard ever won a war by dying for his country. He won it by
making the other poor dumb bastard die for his country.

—General George S. Patton

As soon as "major combat operations" were declared over, it seemed that
the tempo of our life changed. Instead of doing offensive operations, it
seemed as though we were just waiting around as though we had won. It
was as though once the leaders called an end to operations, we could just
pack up and pull over to the side of the road and call it a day. I wondered if
the Iraqis got the memo that the fight was over, or maybe we just called the
war over prematurely. I was getting bored out of my mind. Despite the end
of operations, we weren't going anywhere. I fought the agony of depres-
sion, as even the prospect of leaving was a distant truth. My Marines were
all feeling it. I tried to be positive when I was around them. Talk began
of Phase IVB—post hostilities. The Marine Expeditionary Force planners
came up with a time line they called "time phased force deployment data,"
or TPFDD, which was a fancy way of outlining what every unit needed to
do in order to go home.

Entering Phase IVB meant we were concentrating now on the humanitarian effort of nation building, retrograde, and reconstruction. We
were told it would be at least three months before we would return to
America. We assumed it was because they wanted us to help with the
humanitarian effort. Other units were already starting to pack up to move
back to Kuwait, but there was no talk yet of us moving anywhere. Everything was at a standstill. Although hostilities had all but ended, it was now
just an interminable wait to go home.

★   ★   ★

A call came from 3rd Battalion, 2nd Marines, a Marine infantry unit parked on the edge of the Tigris, saying they had found an enemy UAV. Excited by the prospect of doing anything to break up the monotony of the day, I pulled together a group of Marines to accompany me on a convoy to retrieve the UAV. We had our doubts about it, but we had no trouble rounding up a group to go get it. When all was said and done, we had thirty volunteers. Lieutenant Colonel Mykleby gave his blessing and instructions in case we got ambushed along the way. The Sergeant Major even decided to come along.

We loaded our vehicles with essential personnel, like the NBC chief, the Communications Gunny, and all the nonessential personnel. Some of the administration and S-3 Marines just wanted to get the hell out of base camp. Before we knew it, we were booking down the road, dodging Iraqi vendors peddling cigarettes and dinars. They shouted out to us, "Mister, mister, money, money!" Three kilometers before we reached the river, our convoy came to standstill; a whole company was trying to push through ahead of us.

While we were stopped, one of the Staff Sergeants called me over. "Hey, ma'am, you know some Arabic. Can you talk to this Iraqi kid?"

"I'll see what I can do."

I was an odd sight among the grunts. A company of male Marines stared at me, following my movements like the Iraqis followed ours—a kind of surreal and blatant stare. I walked over to the group of Arabs and started wheeling and dealing with them in Arabic, keeping the mob of Iraqi children at a disciplined distance.

"Wahid—Wahid," I said to the children, which meant "one at a time." They listened—after all, how many Western women had they encountered?

They traded dinars for dollars and flags for trinkets. When it was a smiling, big-eyed Iraqi kid's turn, he said to me, "Mister, mister—oh, no . . . madam! Madam, madam, I love you! Madam, I love you!"

Everyone laughed, especially Sergeant Major Rew. "You have a fan, ma'am!"

"He's a little young for me!" The Iraqis started swarming again, so I had to act fast. I bartered for a lot of the Marines. Even the grunts joined in. Suddenly, I was in the middle of a mob of two-way traders.

"Get me whatever you can for twenty bucks, ma'am."

I showed the bill to the Iraqi child, but he shook his head, indicating "no deal." Instead, he pointed to the dollar.

"One dollar?" I asked.

"Yes, yes!"

"They don't seem to understand that $20 is twenty $1 bills!" No matter how I tried to explain it to the Iraqi children, they only wanted the dollar bills. So we traded dollars for big stacks of dinars, which were now virtually worthless to them. We made sure they got the better deal; after all, what did we have to spend our dollars on anyway?

We got back on our vehicles and moved forward. Soon we came to the bridge area in the town of An Numenyah at the southern edge of the Tigris. The area was lush and exotic, full of date palms and sorghum plants, a green oasis juxtaposed with the burning hulks of Iraqi equipment that lay abandoned. We moved under the underpass into 3rd Battalion, 2nd Marines position in a beautiful, lush palm grove. We followed a barbed wire–lined road, which led to a foliage-laden cove where coalition vehicles blended into the surrounding vegetation. It was unusually peaceful, as if there were no war at all here. Exotic tropical flowers were everywhere. We pulled our vehicles to the side of the dirt path and walked in a patrol, our weapons at the ready. The stillness of the air was punctuated only by the sound of wild birds. Shade, stenciled by the tall palm fronds high above, sheltered us. Then, from out of the bushes, infantry suddenly surrounded us. A Captain effortlessly pushed his way out of the undergrowth, and behind him, a Lieutenant Colonel approached.

"Who are you looking for?"

"We were called because of a report by 3/2 of a downed UAV, sir."

"Downed UAV? What the hell does that have to do with us? Do we know anything about a UAV?" He looked angrily toward the entourage of officers who stood behind him.

The Major who materialized out of the bushes looked at him and closed his eyes quickly to indicate "no." The CO disappeared into the foliage, and the Major motioned for us to follow.

"Come with us." The officer led us to a narrow dirt path flanked by tangles of elaborately laid barbed wire. We followed the maze of foliage until it opened into a sanctuary of tents, a company command post. The Marines stared at us despondently; there was a strange somberness among these men. It was as though we were intruders on another gang's turf. I was met again by that glare I like to call the "what the hell is a woman doing here?" look. However, once Captain Hamill stated our business, they eased up.

"We're here because you called us on the radio. You called about a possible enemy UAV. . . ."

"An enemy UAV? Perhaps the deuce knows. Sergeant Aaronson, escort the officers to the Intelligence Officer. But only the officers and the Sergeant Major . . . the rest of you—you can wait by the vehicles."

"Aye, sir."

Our men disappeared back to the vehicle area. Out of the shadows of the combat operations center emerged a familiar face—one I suddenly recognized as one of my officer training platoon mates, Lieutenant Euring, who was the Battalion Adjutant. Instantly, things became less tense, and the senior officers stepped back, seeing that the company grade officers knew each other.

Lieutenant Euring and I shook hands and made small talk about the war. "Let's walk down the path, Lieutenant Blair," he said cautiously, eyeing the brass in the distance and carefully leading me away.

"What's up with your leadership?"

"We're a little on edge."

"I heard you lost a few men."

"We lost ten, with thirty more WIA—we've been the hardest hit unit."

"Jesus, I'm sorry. I didn't know."

"They're still counting bodies—and fuck, one of the wounded just died."

I learned that they had been the ones who had walked into the firefights of ambush alley and seized and secured the bridge. They had lived through the worst of the fighting. They had seen their brothers die before them.

The adjutant told me, "I had to write all these letters to the families: 'Dear so and so, your son died. . . .'"

"It seems like just yesterday we were at The Basic School together and they were telling us we would go to war."

"Yeah, but we never believed them."

"True, we didn't know . . . until September. . . ."

★ ★ ★

It was true that out of our Fox Company class of 250 Lieutenants, probably 175 were out here right now. We, the young leaders, were the tactical leaders of the frontline units. We had been at TBS in September 2001— September 11 to be precise. We were getting ready to start classes when one of the Lieutenants came hustling from one of the barracks rooms.

"Hey, are you guys all watching the news?"

"No, what's up?"

"Someone crashed a plane into the side of the World Trade Center."

"You're kidding me? Like a Cessna plane?"

"I'm not sure; it just happened, but one of the towers is on fire."

We walked over to his room, discussing how idiotic the pilot must have been to have the ill fortune of crashing into the World Trade Center accidentally. As we came in the room, though, our laughter died. We walked in just as another plane flew into the other tower.

"Was that a playback?"

"No, this is live."

"I don't understand."

"That was a second plane."

We didn't stop staring at the television for twenty-four hours. As more Lieutenants heard the news, more people filtered in. The room had become packed with our classmates as we sat there, stunned at what was unfolding before our eyes. About sixty Marines hovered around a single television, watching and waiting. A female Lieutenant friend of mine came in the room and sat next to me. We watched together in horror as the towers fell, one first and then the other. The only sounds in the room were from a couple of the Marines who were moved to tears. Together, a room full of classmates watched in horror, unable to do anything.

September 11 had been personal for me. I was from New York City. I used to work across the street from the World Trade Center and had friends who worked in the building. True stories that surface about 9/11 showed us how interconnected our world really is. Peter's uncle was with the New York Police Department, and he was involved in 9/11 and watched many of his buddies die. More than a dozen people Peter knew, directly or indirectly, were killed that day, from the father of his brother's friend to a girl Peter had gone to school with since kindergarten. As we watched television that day, my best friend, Unni, was in New York, fleeing the towers. During the attack, Unni, a smart, beautiful Danish mathematician and stock analyst, was at work at one of the largest investment banking firms in the world. The office had two locations: across the street from the World Trade Center and in one of the towers. She had been in the building across from the towers when the planes crashed into them. Many of her coworkers were still inside the towers. Before she left, she got a call from her ex-boyfriend in the north tower.

"I'm OK," he said to her on the phone.

He called her before he had a chance to call his mom. As the tower began to collapse, he was still inside. Peter's friend Brooke was showing up for her first day of work when her tower was struck. She was never seen again. Thousands of people, innocent people, were in those towers that day, all with friends and families who watched them die.

My friend Unni escaped. She fled her building and looked back up at the flaming towers, watching in horror as descending bodies slammed into cars and the pavement around her. Her feet couldn't move fast enough to get away from the crashes that surrounded her. The first tower seemed to melt and explode and began quickly sliding down around her. Unni, horrified, couldn't run. Her feet weren't moving fast enough as debris crashed around her, and soon she was overtaken by waves of suffocating ashes that turned the world black. For a moment, she thought she was dead, in some gray world, until she collected her senses. Moments seemed to last forever, and she saw pale, dark figures emerging from the gray. As the air cleared, Unni walked again, this time in no particular direction because she couldn't tell where she was. She stopped in front of her reflection in a storefront and saw that her pale, silvery blondness had turned grayish like the undead. Everyone around her walked in a daze, some crying, some screaming, some running, some staggering, and others calling for help. Sirens and alarms blared up and down the streets, and Unni just walked.

When she returned to work the week after 9/11, the streets were littered with signs, walls were filled with flags, candles, mementos, and posters emblazoned with missing relatives, loved ones feared dead. Thousands of missing faces lined the walls. Unni walked quickly to work, trying not to look, trying to forget. All those faces, all those she did not know, but she frantically searched for one face she did know. Where was he? So many faces that were obviously now dead passed before her eyes. She stopped and stared, and tears of rage filled her. She turned around and walked back to her apartment. She didn't return to work again.

While Unni was in New York, my classmates and I watched, and we slowly realized that this was the day our training wheels came off. Our training would be practice for a war that we would fight. The global war on terrorism was our war, and with every ambush and live-fire exercise we did, our real enemy was out there waiting for us.

★   ★   ★

Captain Hamill and I followed Lieutenant Euring to a primitive site within the barbed-wire area, where a DRASH tent stood alone. Several Marines stood guarding what looked like wire cages. In the back of the cage an Iraqi man sat, wearing only underwear, a burlap bag over his head, his head pressed toward his breast as though in prayer, his hands tied behind his back with zip ties. What the fuck? I stared in disbelief.

"That's Mohammad."

"Mohammad?"

"Look closer." I stared at the seated man; his fit body showed that he had not been starving.

"What am I looking for?"

"You see the tattoo on his arm?"

"Oh yes, I see it now." There was a heart design with strange-looking wings. It looked almost like a love tattoo.

"He's Fedayeen Saddam, one of Saddam's "men of sacrifice." That's the tattoo that they all have." I stared a bit and then walked into the S-2 tent. A Captain met us inside. His name looked familiar, but I had never seen him before.

"Hey, you're the Predator UAV folks!"

"The Pioneer UAV—yes, that's us."

"Oh right, Pioneer. Predator's the Air Force UAV, right? Shit, I'm always messing that up. I'm the one who called you on the radio. So you're going to take it, right?"

"Can we see it first?"

"Yeah, yeah. No problem. Follow me." We followed him farther along the dirt path until it opened up past the brush borders where Marines had dug foxholes. They had their weapons pointed north toward the Tigris, which now was visible about two hundred meters in the distance. The five of us—Captain Hamill, the intelligence officer, Lieutenant Euring, the Sergeant Major, and I—walked into a dense palm grove down a small trail. The place was so saturated with humidity and vegetation that it was almost tropical, much like I envisioned the Garden of Eden. Light rays bounced in gentle arcs upon flowers and plants, but the trees formed a dense cover over us. Sweat dripped uncontrollably over our bodies. There was only the sound of our feet and the small chartreuse-colored birds that chirped and flew curiously by our side.

Finally, we reached the bank of the Tigris River, and echoes of the war surrounded us. Enemy equipment littered the banks of the river. We moved forward along a concrete walkway to where the UAV was seen. Marines patrolling along the bank passed us. Once again, they gave me "the look."

We reached the UAV, and Captain Hamill, a Cobra pilot, took a look at it. It was a large, cylindrical gray-colored metal aircraft with swept movable wings with about a five-foot wingspan. Captain Hamill shook his head.

"This is not enemy equipment. This is not even a UAV. This is a joint standoff munition."

"I'm sorry, what does that mean?"

"It's a coalition missile!"

"Oh, shit. I didn't know. We saw the damn thing on the deck, and it looks like a UAV. . . . Well, do you guys want it?"

"Not really . . . what the fuck we going to do with this thing?"

"We can't leave it here."

"Well, thanks, but we don't want your shit. It's definitely not a UAV."

We laughed and started walking around the underpass toward the bridge. There was a wider path that circled around, leading back to the vehicles. Marines in this area manned firing positions. Beside the bridge, a deserted T-54 stood vacant. As we stood near it, we heard our UAV pass us in the air.

"They're spying on us, Sergeant Major Rew," I said.

"Yes, I think they are, ma'am." We smiled.

"Am I the only one who's pissed off that they tried to pawn their trash off on us?" Captain Hamill asked.

"I think you are pretty much the only one," Sergeant Major Rew smirked.

"It could have been cool to take back to the Marines. . . ."

After the grunts invited some of my unit's intelligence analysts to come back and identify the enemy tanks for them, we pulled away. I wished Lieutenant Euring good luck, and as we were pulling out, the Intelligence Captain came and halted our vehicles.

"My Marines brought over the enemy UAV in case you changed your minds," he said.

"You mean *joint munition*," said Captain Hamill, still pissed off.

The Sergeant Major looked at him, giving him the eye.

"All right, who gives a fuck? Marines, help the Captain load the freakin' thing into the seven-ton."

18

STAR-SPANGLED BANNER

Any solution for the Iraqi problem cannot be reached without Arabs and Arab participation.

—Amr Moussa

Surprisingly, with all the work our UAV squadron had done during the war, we had gotten little recognition from the media or higher command. True, people who worked directly with us appreciated our work. But we had just finished a string of missions that yielded little intelligence. Some inexperienced people had taken over our missions, and they had tasked us with impossible missions, such as locating an individual in a crowd or weapons on individuals. Our camera didn't have the capability of seeing these things. I walked away from the mission frustrated, heading toward the air maintenance Marines who were hard at work, fixing a UAV. It was the first time I noticed that they had strategically placed the joint munition among the UAVs with writing on it that said, "If you think this is a UAV, then this work area is off-limits to you."

Near the landing strip, I saw my CO talking to a group of high-ranking individuals, including one general. The general pointed at the CO and then up toward the flag hanging on one of the vehicles. I walked back toward the collections vehicle, but I could still hear part of their conversation.

"Who told you to go and hang U.S. flags all over your unit, Mick?"

"We have only one hanging up, General."

"Didn't anyone tell you that it's not authorized in Iraq? It's offensive. You shouldn't be parading American flags in front of Iraqis. We're not here to conquer, just to liberate. Listen, you're Buck's brother, right?"

"Yes, sir."

"Well, I certainly expect more out of Buck's brother than you and your gypsy caravan unit you're running over here. Look at this mess—you have cots out everywhere, no tents up for your troops, and what the hell is that hippie bracelet you are wearing on your wrist, Lieutenant Colonel?"

"My son gave this to me, sir, for good luck. Look, sir, we just got here, and we've been packing up and tearing down at a moment's notice to move to new locations. We don't even have tents, and we operate a lot differently than the other wing units here."

"Yes, I can see that." The General eyeballed the area and then looked down at his watch.

"Clean up this mess so the next General isn't embarrassed by your lack of order, because apparently you like disobeying orders. I have a plane to catch."

"Sir, I'll clean up. Thanks for visiting."

There was no thank-you, no comment that our unit had done a great job. He didn't even tour the unit to thank the Marines. The General, on his first day in Iraq, took a quick tour of the units, got straight back on a plane, and returned to his hotel in Bahrain. My CO was livid, but he saw that I had heard part of the conversation and walked over to me.

"Boots, put this one down in your leadership book of things never to do when you pick up rank. What did you think about that?"

"I can't believe he said that to you, sir. Especially about the flag. We're in a secured coalition position with no Iraqis around. It's the first flag we've had up. Who will be offended?"

"If we had lost any Marines, or even had someone wounded, I would have punched him in the face!"

"Can you imagine when he hits the grunt units, sir, and tells them the same thing?"

"He doesn't have the balls to go near the grunts. I can't believe he walked over here and said those things—no compliments, no recognition of our months of work, just 'police yourself.'"

I shook my head.

"Seriously, remember this one, Jane. It's a perfect example of the type of leadership that's not in touch with the pulse of what the Marines are doing. It's total misguided leadership. If you don't respect your subordinates, they won't return respect."

Lieutenant Bishop, the other female officer, was talking to the General in the distance.

"Come over with me, Jane." We walked near the General, and I was scared my CO was going to actually punch him in the face. The General,

looking at Bishop, recognized her as the daughter of a Colonel who used to work for him. He asked her, "Aren't you Colonel Bishop's daughter?"
"Yes I am, General. I didn't catch your name, sir?"
"I'm General Chaney."
"Nice to meet you, sir. How did you know who I am?"
"Your father works for me."

?" He was flabbergasted that she
The General was obviously in-
"I guess your CO doesn't teach

That sincerely pissed the General

eral!" the CO told all the officers
was pulled down and mysteriously

with 3rd Battalion, 5th Marines
or?" said a Lieutenant.
eutenants from another unit who
tell us what I was sure had to be
he war we had heard unbelievable
eer nonsense about Jessica Lynch
ing captured, to a Marine unit be-
ine Cobra helicopters—and none
ded and listened incredulously as
ir mouths shut. The story was so
amazing and unbelievable and detailed that we thought it might actually be true. I stepped out of the enclosed area and asked some of the other officers if they had ever heard of Brian Chontosh. Apparently everyone had. He was something of a legend now. The stories about him varied from him single-handedly gunning down a unit full of Iraqis, to leading his Marines to attack a group of Iraqis using the Iraqis' own weapons against them. One of the SNCOs smiled and said, "Chontosh? Great guy! I worked in my last unit with him; he's a real hard charger. Why are you asking?"
I later heard the story directly from Chontosh when I met him and his Marines. Now a Captain and Company Commander, Captain Brian

Chontosh is a prior enlisted Marine with such an air of competence and confidence that makes him stand out even among his fellow Marines, a group flush with those qualities. Chontosh is unassuming, funny, and humble about his Marine Corps career. His good looks and charismatic nature enhance his natural likeability. As best as I can remember the story, it went something like this.

At 0300 on 25 March 2003, Lieutenant Chontosh was leading his CAAT team up Highway 1 during the assault on Ad Diwaniyah, following in trace of a platoon of tanks. A Combined Anti-Armor Team (CAAT) is a special infantry team used in combination with tanks that is composed of combat armored vehicles with heavy machine guns and TOW missiles. They are a highly mobile team that provides security for convoys.

The officers planning the attack were concerned about the high level of resistance from the Iraqis and had called a "slingshot," meaning all available aircraft was standing by to assist their mission. Lance Corporal Armand E. McCormick was driving with Lieutenant Chontosh riding in the front passenger seat. McCormick was a strong Marine, the type that everyone likes and everyone tries to emulate. Lance Corporal Robert Kerman—oddly nicknamed "Xena" by the other Marines after the warrior princess played by Lucy Lawless—and Lance Corporal Kenneth Korte were riding in the backseat. Kerman had the boyish good looks of someone in his late teens or early twenties. In the ring mount turret, Corporal Thomas Franklin, called "Tank" because he's built like one, manned the M2 .50 caliber heavy machine gun. The day had already been filled with strange occurrences. The sky had turned red with the oncoming sandstorm, and an ill-omened patrol lay ahead. Although they were traveling down Highway 1, they had yet to be fired on—but more eerily, they hadn't seen any civilians, either. Something was going to happen. As they approached Ad Diwaniyah, Chontosh's CAAT team, being a highly mobile scout/reconnaissance team, was the lead element of their unit, with only a couple of lead tanks in front of them.

The battle started for Chontosh and his Marines when the tank platoon commander, another Lieutenant with the call sign "Blue-1," radioed that white pickup trucks were beginning to drop off Iraqis armed with AK-47s and RPGs on the road ahead of them. The tanks quickly stopped to engage the targets ahead, buttoning up and blocking the road to form a defensive position. The road was walled in on either side by dirt berms too high to drive over. Chontosh's vehicles were caught between tanks in front of and behind them. And then, suddenly, the CAAT platoon began receiving enemy fire. They were sitting smack in the middle of the kill zone of an ambush. At first, 120mm and 82mm mortars impacted on the road around them. Splashes of debris and asphalt flew everywhere. Then a swarm of RPGs rocketed around them, accompanied by heavy automatic weapons fire from both sides of the road. The second vehicle in the CAAT team was hit with a RPG, injuring Corporal Francisco Quintero and killing Navy Corpsman HM2 "Doc" Johnson, who was ominously in the seat where Lance Corporal Kerman usually sat.

Lieutenant Chontosh quickly realized that his team had to fight its way out of the kill zone. He looked around and saw a small break in the berm, just large enough for a humvee. He quickly passed verbal orders, which prompted Lance Corporal McCormick to drive through the berm and straight into enemy machine-gun fire. Corporal Franklin fired his .50 caliber, suppressing the enemy gunners as the humvee crested the berm and dropped into a trench line. Without hesitating, Lieutenant Chontosh ordered McCormick and Kerman to dismount and follow him and told Korte, the team's radio operator, to stay back and provide security for Corporal Franklin in the ring mount. Surrounded by Republican Guardsmen, Chontosh, McCormick, and Kerman took well-aimed, deliberate shots with their M-16A4 assault rifles and Beretta M9 pistols. They shot their way down three hundred meters of trench line, more than three football fields' worth of hostile terrain. While McCormick and Chontosh fought their way in the trench line, Kerman ran parallel with them on the top of the berm to provide flank security and to pick off the Iraqis running across the road toward the trench. The Iraqis could not believe that three Marines would be willing to attack so boldly and aggressively. As the Iraqis ran toward them into what they thought was a safe area, the three Marines ambushed them from inside the Iraqi berm. They quickly picked off Iraqi after Iraqi just as they raised their AK-47s to fire back. Despite not rating a pistol because of his rank, McCormick had one. Only officers usually rated pistols. McCormick was armed only with Chontosh's pistol, which he had traded earlier with his Lieutenant because he was the driver, and both McCormick and Chontosh thought a pistol would be in better hands with the driver who could only fire out the left side with his left hand while he was driving. For this reason, it was a popular decision during the war for officers to hand their drivers their pistols. Because McCormick didn't have his rifle, he saved his fire for the Iraqis attempting to counterattack into the trench as they crested a second berm beyond the one the Marines had crossed.

Too many Iraqis were running into their position. As Kerman continued to run down the trench line, pausing to pick off Iraqis with his M16-A4, Lieutenant Chontosh ran out of ammunition for both his M9 and M16.

McCormick also was out. Without thought, they picked up the discarded AK-47s from the dead Iraqis and began to fire, bringing death to the Iraqis with their own guns. They left a trail of death in their wake, though they didn't have time to look back. A new group of Iraqis, fleeing from the fire of other Marines, had crested the berm and were beginning to pour into the trench line. The Iraqis ran across the berm, and their faces lit up with surprise as they attempted to get their weapons. But Chontosh's team fired before they could take action. Again, McCormick and Chontosh both ran out of ammunition. Kerman, foraging for more weapons, found a RPG launcher with a grenade ready to fire and brought it to his Lieutenant.

"Sir, I don't know how to use it."

"Neither do I." But, seeing a new group of Iraqis about to attack them, Chontosh, without regard for his own life, fired the weapon he had never used before at an enemy machine gun, silencing the automatic weapon and the Iraqis.

While Lieutenant Chontosh and his two Marines fought their way down the trench line, Corporal Franklin continued to fire his .50 caliber machine gun as Korte guarded his flanks, shooting at the enemy as they revealed themselves at a fortified machine-gun position. Three Iraqis a short distance in front of the vehicle popped up out of a fighting position, wanting to surrender. Displaying unthinkable composure and restraint in such a chaotic environment, Lance Corporal Korte ordered them to drop their weapons. He used plastic restraints to secure their hands behind their backs and returned to provide security for Corporal Franklin, who had continued firing the entire time.

At this point, Chontosh, McCormick, and Kerman had reached another breach in the berm. Lieutenant Chontosh realized that India Company, one of 3rd Battalion, 5th Marines' three standard rifle companies, was about to assault through the berm. To avoid the possibility of fratricide, he ordered his Marines away from India Company's battle space and back to the humvee. As they moved back down the trench line, they stopped to kill wounded Iraqi troops that were feigning death, lying in wait for the opportunity to kill a Marine with his guard down. One was in the process of pulling the pin out of a grenade as he was shot.

By this time, Corporal Franklin had silenced the enemy machine-gun fire and shot Iraqis setting up mortar launchers in the distance, so the enemy position around them had been effectively destroyed. The Marines regrouped. Armed only with a single machine gun, semiautomatic rifles, two pistols, and whatever weapons they could pluck from the hands of the enemy dead, these five Marines, an Officer, an NCO, and three junior

Marines, one barely out of boot camp, had assaulted and destroyed a forti-fied, company-sized defensive position. They had killed more than twenty Republican Guardsmen, wounded many more, and driven the rest into the jaws of the battalion. Once the five of them had regrouped, they took the time to examine Korte's prisoners and discovered that one of them was a high-ranking General. His capture proved to be a major intelligence coup for the Marine Corps and the coalition as a whole—due entirely to a Lance Corporal who was not even old enough to buy a beer in the States.

For their actions that day, Corporal Franklin and Lance Corporal Korte were awarded the Navy Commendation Medal with a combat distinguishing device for valor. Lance Corporal McCormick and Lance Corporal Kerman were awarded the Silver Star Medal. First Lieutenant Brian Chontosh was one of a handful of servicemen from Operation Iraqi Freedom to receive the Navy Cross, our nation's second highest award for valor behind the Medal of Honor.

Like all good officers, he explains his success as a result of the hard work and outstanding qualities of the Marines he was leading that day. He never took credit for his team, even though his leadership led to its success. Because Chontosh and his Marines were unharmed during the assault, they undoubtedly would not be awarded the Medal of Honor. In a ceremony where the Commandant of the Marine Corps flew in a group of helicopters into the middle of a CAX to give them awards, they were surrounded by the entire battalion and a tent full of reporters, family, and high-ranking military. Months later, after we had all returned from deployment, he and his Marines humbly told me their story in a quiet corner in his unit's stor-age room.

19

ASHURA

What is raining? Blood.
From where? The Eyes.
How long? Day and Night.
Why? From Grief.
Grief for whom?
Grief for the king of Karbala.

—Qaan's elegy on the Death of Hussein

Black is the color in which Shi'as dress during the mourning period called Muharram. It is the season of sorrow, the remembrance of the slaying of Imam Hussein. The season makes Iraq's bleakness even darker, and we were lulled into its sadness. The solemn aftermath of war affected us all. We watched funeral processions and these ceremonies through the eyes of the UAV and the times when we left the wire on our convoys and traveled through the towns.

I counted the rocks on front of me, twenty in all, wishing they represented the days that remained until I went home. Damn, I'd been in the same spot too long. I was bored. I hadn't even seen Bishop or Debucher in days. Not knowing our future or having no control over it was killing our spirits, and we had visions of being here for years. One of the few things I enjoyed during the day—our flights—had become scarce. We just weren't seeing anything. The risk of putting a bird up outweighed the risk of crashing, and soon we were down to a mere two to three flights a day. As I was sitting around, my CO walked by. After some small talk, I asked him, "Sir, do we have any new missions?"

"Not exactly, Jane, but we're going to fly anyway. Everyone's happy that way. Just keep Task Force Tarawa happy, and we'll all be good."

This meant flying around Al Kut, looking at buildings and patterns of vehicles moving. But I was a pattern-analysis junkie and so were the Marines in my section. What was there one day was not the next. Groups of people, lines of cars, exchanges between individuals, and market flow were all symbols of the cultural intent, movement, and pattern of the city. Traffic patterns, I was sure, had deeper meaning. Watching the influx of vehicles into the city, Sergeant Leppan reported it to Task Force Tarawa. At first I thought it could be the return of citizens who had fled the city during the war. Then I began to lean on the hypothesis that meetings were taking place in the city, signaling a rebuilding and return to order.

Task Force Tarawa thought differently. "We are assessing that there is a buildup of terrorist factions, and there could be a pro-Saddam uprising of three thousand to five thousand individuals."

I didn't buy that theory. Logically speaking, the Ba'athists had moved away from a visible presence, especially of that magnitude. After watching what happened in Al Amarah, I was sure the citizens would repel such a group—rather, it would be a suicide mission for those Fedayeen. There's a hell of a lot you can see from the sky that you can't see from the ground. I suspected they were hiding now and would only resurface if the Ba'ath party reorganized itself. Given this state of disorder, I didn't believe they could formulate such a sophisticated network against both the citizens and the American military parked outside the city. They saw what we could do to them. They were waiting for the right moment.

Flying that night's mission, therefore, my hidden agenda was to disprove the almost-flippant hypothesis that higher was drawing from population displacement. Their theories always were worst-case scenarios or vague, overarching analysis based on themes. Our imagery from the UAV revealed things as they were in our omniscient view of the situation.

As we flew over Al Kut on 13 April 2003, there were large groups walking everywhere. The city was unusually animated. It looked like everyone was out. Families strolled casually on the waterfront. Iraqis were riding bikes, children were walking in groups, and everyone was going about their lives. It looked like a peaceful Friday night in America. We watched the seemingly tranquil city life, divorced from the war that had just been at their doorstep. It was if they had erased all signs of Saddam, torn him from their memory, and instantly tried to rebuild a life devoid of Saddam and us.

Then we saw unusually large groups of civilians. They were celebrating something, but we couldn't figure out what.

"Maybe they're celebrating their freedom?" one of the imagery analysts said.

"Shut the fuck up, goon. Celebrating their freedom? They don't give a shit about that," Sergeant Leppan said.

"Yeah, I can see it now. It's like *Gangs of New York*, after all the gangs are killed!"

"Fucking-A! I expect fireworks soon."

We flew over a group of several hundred personnel standing in front of a building. MEF and Task Force Tarawa were quick with questions: "Does it look like they're protesting?" "Do they have weapons?" "Is the crowd unruly?"

But the crowd, evidently composed of more women and children than men, looked like they were having a good time on a Friday night. So I answered, "It looks like they're in front of a movie theater or social hall. Everyone is very casual; families are strolling around in small groups. This does not appear to be a hostile crowd. We assess this is a family entertainment area."

We moved on. Startlingly, we came to another group. This time, several hundred individuals stood gathered in front of a large building. It looked like a performance of some sort, and the speaker appeared to be telling some kind of story. There were no protest banners, no signs, and no flag waving. Instead, the crowd appeared to be listening, clapping, and laughing at a speaker.

"What are they doing?"

"They're just listening, but they don't appear hostile. It looks like a lot of children and families."

"Roger."

Again, we moved on. We swept the city with our invisible eye. Unfocused and far away, the city appeared like a giant circuit, with small flashes of light and streams of movement everywhere. It was beautiful. When they asked us to look at the soccer stadium, we saw the strangest thing. A bunch of individuals was standing in a group, and in the center, several people looked like they were fighting. They were not just boxing, though; it looked like a death match. We could see the spray of blood coming off one man's face. As he was thrown to the ground, the other man continued to attack and kick him; as he retreated, the crowd parted, but the other man continued to kick him. Soon enough, the rampant street bashing finished, and the once-rowdy crowd gathered in a circle around a speaker. It looked like the opponents were lined up on each side of the speaker. Unfortunately, Task Force Tarawa beckoned us to move on, just as the badly beaten man was carried away by his Arab buddies. I reported in detail what I saw.

"This is a strange city," someone added.

"Yes, it is," said Task Force Tarawa.

We moved back to the large crowd by the movie theater, trying to figure it all out. One of the headquarters units on our secured chat system asked, "Do you think they're listening to Al Reef?" He was an insurgent leader who was rallying the people to rise up against the United States, but he had few supporters among the population.

"I don't think so." Just as I said this, the crowd disbanded and formed into smaller circles. About twenty circles of thirty or so people formed, and everyone's hands went up and down in unison in a strange tribal dance.

"They're dancing . . . in unison."

"Maybe it's a wedding; they dance in circles in weddings," I suggested. No one had any answers, so we decided to scan the rest of the city to see what else we could find. At an intersection where five main roads merged together, decorative lights were strewn up along the roads, so I added, "This is much bigger than a wedding. Maybe there's a festival going on, or they're celebrating liberation."

"Mass partying across the city!" one of the Marines chimed in.

Soon enough, on the other side of town, we saw another street party. Once again, everyone was dancing in unison. As we scanned the city of Al Kut, the story was the same everywhere. Wherever a group congregated, they were either dancing or performing the bizarre group-fighting rituals. Had there not been others watching, I would have thought I was finally losing it.

Finally, someone from I MEF asked, "Does anyone have any clue what's going on? Is it Mardi Gras in Al Kut?"

Task Force Tarawa came back with an answer. "My information officer came back with information from the local Shi'ite sheikh."

"Well, out with it." I MEF said. I myself wanted to know why they didn't tell us upfront.

Finally, we got an answer to our mystery. Task Force Tarawa replied, "Apparently, this is the start of the Ashura religious festival. Beating and dancing are both ways in which this festival is practiced."

"Is this a Shi'ite festival?" asked I MEF.

"Yes, it is celebrated annually."

"I think I'll take Christmas and getting gifts over mass beatings any day!" said I MEF.

"I think this is all very interesting," I added.

What I had seen made such an impact on me that I read everything I could find on the subject on my computer. The Iraqi Shi'ites, although they comprise the largest group of Muslims in Iraq, had once been tribal groups and had only been converted to Islam during the nineteenth century, near the end of the Ottoman Empire. Because of this, their religion combined the sharia, or Islamic laws, with their tribal folk religion. These folk beliefs, different from those of Shi'ites from other countries, reflected their once-nomadic past, and some still worshipped in shrines sacred to their ancestral past.

The Shi'as believe there is a succession of infallible imams, or rulers, that must have direct lineage to Mohammed. According to the Shi'as, the first imam was Mohammed's cousin Imam Ali. His son, Hussein, is seen as the first true Shi'ite. He was martyred during the Battle of Karbala in 680 A.D., and this marked the beginning of the Shi'as. The sheikhs, or tribal leaders, as we were beginning to find out, controlled Iraq and had the power to stabilize the region. The majority of Shi'as believe that they have been without a caliph since World War I, and they await the twelfth imam, who they believe awaits the right time to reemerge. But a religious faction of extremist Shi'ites had formed, a group of Islamic Iraqis called the Sadr Militia, claiming to be part of the Twelver Shi'ites. So in the midst of the chaos in Iraq, the leader of this group decided to rekindle a messianic tradition. This tradition is based on an eschatological system of beliefs regarding the return of the Mahdi, the great redeemer, who will bring justice to the world by destroying those who don't convert to the true religion of Islam. This belief has been perpetuated through violence by groups such as the one led by Muqtada Al-Sadr, a radical and powerful imam who violently opposed coalition forces with his Mahdi Army. This was the threat that we saw in our crosshairs.

★   ★   ★

But, at this moment, the Shi'as dancing on the ground were exuberant. They hoped this celebration also marked their freedom from Saddam's rule. Their bodies moved in unison and with joy. Colorful lights danced on their faces, and they formed a circle, holding hands. On this day, I didn't see anything violent, just a culture finally able to practice their Shi'a rituals. High above, I watched them and wished I was down there celebrating with them.

20

OCCUPATION

Trust in God and know that man is born to die, that heavens shall not remain, everything shall pass away, except the presence of God.

—Imam Hussein

We had officially entered into Phase IVB, which meant we were waiting for the Army to relieve us so we could make our push south and eventually go home. This was about the same time that General Franks declared "all major combat hostilities are over." As Tikrit was secured by a task force of Marines, my Operations Officer, CO, and XO met to determine the value of launching birds at all anymore. In the end, higher command determined that we might as well launch our UAVs until we had crashed or lost every last one of them.

Operation Iraqi Freedom had been declared a twenty-six-day air/ ground campaign to take out Saddam Hussein's government and liberate the Iraqi people from his tyranny. We had learned to manipulate the enemy by learning their critical vulnerabilities, and we were now focused on appealing to the needs of the Shi'ite majority in order to convince them that their lives would soon be free from tyranny. With our overwhelming tempo, we had disorganized the Iraqi military to the point that they not only didn't know where we were, but they didn't know where their own forces were. As long as we focused on rebuilding the nation and strengthening our ties with community leaders and sheikhs, we would continue to help the Iraqis.

But would we be able to sustain the local population's needs? Baghdad citizens were already demanding that we restore security and stop widespread looting, prevent theft, make citizens feel safe, allow the population some freedom of movement so they could resume their lives again. Above all, they wanted us to provide news on events, make improvements to their infrastructure, and fix the electricity, water, and food situation. Their demands were real but massive.

One of the most disheartening things that emerged from postwar Iraq was news that looters had ransacked the National Museum of Antiquities, taking with them countless artifacts. The library next to it was also plagued by looters who took manuscripts and cuneiforms, inscribed clay tablets dating back seven thousand years. The human history of our common ancestors was now little more than a nearly vacant museum. The missing piece of the *Epic of Gilgamesh* contained in the clay tablets supposedly had been there as well; now the classic tale would never be finished.

As museums and businesses were looted, bank vaults were also blown. Small children were dangled into the vaults from the arms of eager parents, hoping to get their share of the American dollars stored within. This time, U.S. forces interceded and saved $4,000,000 in U.S. currency. Stories like this spread across the country; some businesses were saved and others lost.

But the saddest story was the children. It is an unfortunate consequence of war that innocent children invariably become blameless victims. Some Arab news sources claimed thousands of children and civilians had died. Moreover, we heard about children who had been maimed and saw pictures of children with limbs and body parts missing.

As hostilities quelled, General Jay Garner was scheduled to take over as the newly appointed governor for the interim authority. His past was clouded by prior support for Ariel Sharon, whose supporters proclaimed he did the right thing when Palestinians in refugee camps were killed en masse by Christian Lebanese militias in 1983 in Beirut, Lebanon. Syria and other Arab nations were concerned that his presence would turn Iraq into some kind of pro-Israeli state. So far, the United States had taken significant measures to avoid bringing anything related to Israel into the war. I hoped the United States knew what they were doing by appointing him, but I doubted it. Such a past meant a lot to the Arabs, and it would be hard for them to reconcile. However, a Grand Baghdad Conference was scheduled in a few months, which would likely make Garner's rule more permanent.

As for the future of Iraq, leaders such as Ahmed Chalabi were all too eager to step up. Chalabi led a group called the Free Iraqi Fighters. He was also head of the exile opposition group, the Iraqi National Congress. He seemed a reasonable candidate to many, but because he had left Iraq in 1958, other Iraqis were skeptical of a man who had "abandoned" Iraq for so many years. Iraq's stability was uncertain. And then we were told we would no longer be "liberating" the people but "occupying" the country. We had no idea what this meant. No one explained it to us. But the Iraqis knew. Occupying was what the Mongols did in 1258 when they ransacked Baghdad and beat the caliph to death while he was wrapped in a carpet.

★ ★ ★

The initial occupation would be ninety days, and it was the first step in establishing an Iraqi interim authority. It would require two hundred staff members in a "green zone," a secured area in Baghdad, which would house the Coalition Provisional Authority, including the new American Embassy.

Relief forces started pouring in, much to our happiness. The U.S. Army's 4th Infantry Division moved through, and the 3rd Calvary Regiment was scheduled to arrive shortly. But where had the Iraqi military gone? We didn't know—perhaps they had assimilated back into the civilian world, only too happy to shed the dreaded Republican Guard uniforms. As for the upper echelon, it was possible that Syria let them in. In retaliation, we heard engineers closed the Iraqi pipeline into Syria. Rumors circulated that we would attack Syria next.

Already, reports of mysterious Saddam sightings had begun to occur. At the Adhamiya Mosque in North Baghdad, Iraqi witnesses said Saddam had pulled up in a convoy of three white sedans with tinted windows and proclaimed, "I am fighting alongside you in the same trenches." This made no sense to me; even if he was serious, the fighting was over. Wasn't it? But true or not, an air strike took care of the problem twelve hours later that killed eighteen Iraqis including Fedayeen, ironically, in the cemetery behind the mosque. Graves were adorned with bottles containing messages in which fellow Iraqis proclaimed them martyrs. Stories circulated of Saddam helping people and rallying support from communities.

It was now 17 April 2003. Our first stack of mail arrived, and we named the day "Iraqi Christmas." The CO celebrated with us by gathering all the Marines and helping to distribute the mail to them. He spoke to each Marine individually. He was like that. The Marines looked up to him because he genuinely cared for them. He loved them, in fact, and they loved him. You could see it on their faces. I watched Sergeant Veneleck, his eyes starry, smiling that natural smile that develops unconsciously when one looks at someone he admires. The CO had that effect on everyone. He ran his hand through his white-blond tuft of hair, and it stood straight up, like a shock of wheat blowing in the wind.

Eagerly I received a stack of letters, including six from my husband, dating as far back as 26 January. All of the letters were from before the war had started; evidently, the post office had indeed routed them to the United States before delivering them a mere eight kilometers away. Still the same story. I didn't know where Peter was or if he had survived. The majority of the troops received packages, and even those who didn't receive anything got their share from Marines who willingly shared their boxes. The Operations Officer's wife had been generous—she sent him a package a day, so he received a pallet of packages. It was impressive. After he offered the packages to all the junior Marines, he passed them to the officers. Inside, I foraged and found containers of delicacies such as biscotti, marinated olives, and sardines. He smiled at my delight.

"Lieutenant Blair, come here," he said. He had a stash of some of the more coveted delicacies like hummus, nuts, and cheeses. Prior to this, I thought he disliked me, but we found that we had a lot in common after all.

"Sir, this is a gold mine!" Apparently he and I were the only officers who shared a love of gourmet food, foreign films, and esoteric books. We watched some films that his wife had sent him on his work laptop. But everyone had gotten something they wanted; the packages were loaded with beef jerky, toiletries, trail mix, and all kinds of gedunk, Marine slang for candy and junk food. Within a few days we had gorged ourselves, and it was almost all gone.

Things for the Shi'ites were not quite the same. The Ashura festival was followed by the Arbaeen pilgrimage, marking the first time since 1979 that they had been able to make this holy pilgrimage. From An Najaf, their most holy city in Iraq, they traveled to Karbala, a city of great historic importance. Saddam had threatened torture and death to any Shi'a who made this pilgrimage while he was in power. Now, twenty thousand Shi'ites were expected to make the pilgrimage, and more than a million would participate in the event. The pilgrims would walk along the Euphrates and beat their chests as they approached the shrines. This symbolic gesture of hitting the right fist to the chest and then opening the hand and flicking it up in the air was part of their practice of self-mortification. We had seen these self-inflicted practices from the air. Thousands of men beat themselves in rhythmic circles, dancing while performing this ritual. Sometimes during Ashura, devotees would go so far as to cut themselves with knives, hit themselves with rods, and even crack their heads open with sticks, believing they were sharing the suffering of the prophet.

On the streets of Al Kut, we watched devout Shi'ites gather in the city hall square to practice mass prayer. Some, with Qur'ans in hand, read scripture. They prayed in unison, bowing east together, neatly lined up in rows of prayer. Their prayer rugs, lined up squarely, were like a giant network of faith, linked by Muslims head to toe. At night, citizens would rise up in groups and dance in circles, swinging their arms up and down and then beating their chests, all done in amazing cadenced unison.

Pilgrims who made it to the shrines would follow the Euphrates, visiting Ali's tomb and the shrine in Najaf. From the air, we saw the colossal mosque, its dome sparkling golden in the sun, the Ottoman tile in prophet green and sky blue, lined with intricate religious designs from its minaret towers to its base. Some would visit the holy shrine Abbas and Hussein in Karbala. All this happened, symbolically, in perfect timing with the end of the war and with our own Christian practice of Easter.

The Iranian, Tehran Keyhan, said of these practices many years ago, "During the recent Ashura . . . every street and alleyway you went into, there were crowds of mourners. You would see a group of Imam Hussein's devotees lost in their tears of sorrow, beating their chests in sadness, keeping the memory of the innocence of Hussein alive . . . to keep the memory of Karbala alive."

In the northern areas of Iraq, muezzins once again summoned the people to prayer. Despite the dangers from the war, they called "Allah Akbar" ("God is great") from the minarets that echoed the prayers of Islam five times a day. Farther north still, in the foothills of the Zagros Mountains, the Kurdish Pershmerga fighters had liberated the north. Their struggle for freedom had just begun, trying to carve a homeland for themselves. In Baghdad, some remained skeptical, unsure of their futures. One moment they were waving banners in support of Saddam, and now they were defacing every image.

★ ★ ★

In camps across Iraq, American troops cleaned weapons, listlessly passing the boredom of the day. Some flipped through letters from relatives and loved ones who felt farther than a world away. Others drowned themselves in the endless chain of cigarettes and dip to dull the pain. For me, one monotonous day blended into the next, my wish to go home fulfilled only in dreams of what seemed like my first full eight hours of sleep since I'd been here. Aircraft and vehicles came and went, both always plentiful, but new ones always passing through. Rumors of how long we would remain flickered in from both the Lance Corporal network, and the conversations I casually heard passed between senior Division Officers. Sadly, this was, in a way, our home.

A female CH-46 pilot who had been one of my tent mates in Ali Al Salem Air Base in Kuwait flew into our position one morning. She spotted us on the way to her unit's forward operating base.

"My God! I barely recognized you!" she said to me.

"Really?"

"You've all lost so much weight; your whole camp looks emaciated!"

"That's because we've been living on MREs for the last two months."

"That's rough; I can't imagine. But you know, everyone's been saying great things about you guys."

"What are they saying?"

"That you guys are saving a lot of lives out there. I'm envious of you all. You've been out here doing missions. You'll remember this, and people will remember what you've done. You've made history."

"MEF has made history," I replied. "We were just doing the best job we could so we could go home faster!"

She was right about the history-making aspect: 1st Marine Division and the forces on the ground had done this. She was also right about the weight loss. I looked around at everyone and realized that some folks had already lost more than forty pounds. I had been too busy to notice my own body, but my flesh was tight against my ribs, and my bones poked out everywhere. My hands looked skeletal. The few who had gained weight all happened to be logistics and supply folks in the S-4. I found out later that one of the Lance Corporals in supply was opening all the MRE boxes at night to steal the highly coveted hamburger MRE. Henceforth, he was known as "Hamburglar."

★ ★ ★

We had finally gotten showers, or at least the wing finally told us we could use theirs. Since it was now almost a month since my last shower, I was already past the point of caring. I had gotten used to my smell. I took the group of female Marines to the shower area within the secured perimeter about one or two kilometers away. As we pulled up in our high-back humvee, a group of infantrymen from the 2nd Light Armored Reconnaissance Unit began gawking at us. I gave them the evil eye, but some of the other females were not giving them the same look. They were flirting back. For some of them, this was the most attention they got from males in a long time.

It wasn't just that the balance between males and females was so uneven in the Marines, but also that most places Marines were stationed didn't

ines usually have the pick of the
its and divorce or single parent-
m home for the first time in his
his rational sensibilities. That's
itly get, the excessive interest
iys around college co-eds, and
of the female Marines they had

own share of failed dating ex-
: Basic School things had been
illy fit, college-educated males
ales for training. But the stakes
from dating other Lieutenants,
eet about it. I think that's how
iember, now my husband, was
ur friendship developing into
ieen me at my worst—wearing
face, hair matted with dirt, and
ie still fell in love with me.
ie strength of our relationship.
gether, we had been separated.
to be able to hold out against
those odds, but more important, you really have to be in love. The Marine
Corps has a disastrous failure rate for marriages, but Peter and I were trying to beat the odds. They say absence makes the heart grow fonder, but
I could shoot the idiot who told that lie. Separation just makes you realize
how little the rest of the bullshit in the world matters. I had been heartbro-
ken these last few months. I felt I could stay in Iraq forever, just as long as
he was here now.

My mind wandered back to the present, to the hormonally charged
infantrymen who were ogling my girls. One, an average-looking Joe Corporal, had the balls to approach them when I turned away.

"Hey, how's it goin' ladies?" he said. "You've gotta excuse me for
staring, ladies, but it's been almost three months since we've seen chicks,
and I just wanted to talk to say hi and to welcome you all to Iraq. We've
been out there for at least a month without anything. By the way, you
don't have a clean pair of socks I can have, do you?"

We had been out here just as long as they had, under the same conditions. True, we weren't infantrymen, but we had done everything and
gone everywhere they had. Apparently this guy thought we were fresh off

the boat. I walked around the vehicle just in time to intercept the sock transaction and said, "What are you doing, Corporal?"

"I'm trying to get a pair of socks," he responded with a complete lack of military courtesy. "We haven't been able to go to the PX in over a month."

"Really, where do you think we're coming from?"

"Uh, I'm not really sure. Kuwait?"

"We've been out there just as long as you have, no PX, no showers. So you're done. Move. *Now.*"

He looked at me strangely and turned around.

"Oh, and by the way, Corporal . . ."

"Yeah?'

"I'm an officer, so you better go to your officer and get some training on the proper customs and courtesies for addressing officers."

"Yes—"

"Unless you want me to do it for you?"

"No, ma'am."

He walked back toward the LAR vehicles, saying quite audibly to his fellow squad members, "The Lieutenant said no and to fuck off!" I heard them all laughing.

One of the females, Lance Corporal Gonzalez, was shocked, holding her only pair of clean socks in her hands. She had been the one flirting with them. "So can I still give him the socks, ma'am?" she asked me.

"No, Lance Corporal," I said. "They don't really want clean socks, but I want them to respect you."

We walked over to the shower tent. I was one of the shyest females about this stuff. There were holes all over the tent, and it would be easy to look inside if you really wanted to. The shower tents were fed water by giant bladders that looked like huge tan water balloons. Inside the tents, a water pipe with showerheads was rigged in a primitive fashion. God, I hated undressing in front of other females, but I desperately needed a shower. I entered last, towel wrapped securely, and finally rinsed the month-old dirt off my skin.

When we got back to the main camp, my CO asked how things went and I gave him a debriefing. I briefly mentioned that the females were getting harassed by the showers.

"*Harassed*? Come on . . . tell me what really happened," he said.

"Well, the young Marines come over and flirt. It's pretty harmless, but they can get pretty disrespectful."

"Well, Jane, what did you expect? Do what you have to do if they get out of hand, but remember this—"

"Yes, sir?"

"Remember, war has changed them, Jane. They're not quite the polite little gentlemen they used to be. They've been out here for two or three months like we have. But they've probably taken casualties. They may have even killed up close. They may not have been as lucky as us. Not that it's an excuse for their behavior now, but they're more aggressive now than they've been in their whole life. They're going to do things they've never had the sack to do before, and a lot of it will be wrong. Let them flirt, Jane. It's harmless enough. They're wound up to the extreme, and probably the best thing their leader could do is sit them in a fighting hole until they get bored enough to dull that aggression."

"I guess you're right, sir. I just don't think they realize we've been out here, too. It's frustrating, sir. They see females and automatically think we're straight from Kuwait."

"Probably they don't realize. But you know you've changed, too."

"I have, sir?"

"Oh, yes. Maybe you can't see it, but I do. You've changed a lot since you were in garrison. You don't see how aggressive you are now. We've all changed since we've been out here. Wait until we go back to America. People are going to think we've lost our minds!"

"They won't be right, though."

"They will be right! A civilian doesn't turn every corner expecting to shoot at someone wearing an Iraqi uniform or expect to be gassed at every moment. You can't live with that type of intensity, or people will think you're psychotic."

"I guess so, sir."

"They're going to look at us like we're some intense crazed lunatics. Trust me, I've seen it before. Coming home won't be the flowery parade you think it will. It will be full of frustration and for a while, you won't feel like you belong. You'll see. You'll wake up one night because you hear a dog barking down the block, and you'll low crawl to the door, thinking someone's coming to kill you. Then, one day, you'll finally unwind enough that things feel normal once more. Then you'll be able to go out in public again without thinking everyone wants to kill you."

"Kind of like a severe case of culture shock?"

"Exactly. You'll see. Just wait."

21

WHEN FREE MEN SHALL STAND

I have never met a group of men with cleaner bodies and dirtier minds, higher morale and lower morals than the Marines.

—Eleanor Roosevelt

There were things innately different about Marines. We had a reputation. In Belleau Wood, the Germans had given us the name *"Teufel Hunden,"* or devil dogs, because of our fierce fighting. Then there was our unyielding look in dress blues, with our impeccable white covers and gloves, shiny golden buttons, and eagle, globe, and anchor emblems, all bound together by the sharp lines of a cinched belt and tailored cut. While the uniform exemplified our ideals, we were so much more than a stereotypical image. The Marines were a motley crew of individuals bound together in a brotherhood based on the belief that being a Marine was among the toughest things in the world to do. But that belief is what held us together. It was the certainty that Marines had to be the toughest, meanest, and bravest sons-of-bitches in the world.

Captain Devallion Piper, an officer who had stayed in Kuwait during the major combat operations as a liaison officer at the wing-level headquarters finally joined us on 20 April 2003. He was one of the only Marines who felt like a friend in the unit, so I was glad to have him back. He was the whitest dark-green Marine you'd ever met, but he was also vibrant and full of stories and very much the glue that held the officers together. We were glad to have him back but teased him incessantly about "sitting out the war in Kuwait." Al Jaber, 3rd Marine Aircraft Wing (MAW) headquarters, was co-located on an Air Force base, which had all the luxuries not associated with war. There was a myth that the chow hall had a third-country national—basically a foreigner hired by the American government—whose sole job was to fill bowls with Häagen-Dazs ice cream. While we dreamed of cold water, 3rd MAW was getting ice cream with every meal. We made fun of Captain Piper but were genuinely glad to see him. He and I passed the empty time by looking at magazines that kind-hearted American citizens sent us from home.

"You know, I think a lot of people will be getting out of the Marine Corps after this war."

"Why do you say that?"

"Because most Marines join to go to war."

"You think so?"

"I know so. Face it, if you wanted to join the military to get college money and benefits, you'd join the damn Air Force."

"Some people joined the Corps for the uniforms!" I said jokingly.

"Yeah, we've got nice uniforms, but let's face it. When young men and women are choosing the service they join, they think: Air Force, interesting job, good money, living large; Navy and Army, benefits and good travel; Marines, I get to freakin' kill people!"

"We are crazy—that's true."

"Hell, just look around this squadron—no Marine here is normal. We're all a bunch of freaks. That's why it's so hard for us to socialize with civilians. Hell, this is the cult of ultimate machismo. That's why there's so many Hispanics in the Marine Corps over all the other services. It's because we all know the Marine Corps is the ultimate test of manhood. The men in the Corps say, 'Hell, I'm going to get me some of that! I'm going to kick asses for a living.' But when you think about it, they're all one sandwich short of a picnic basket."

"You've got a strange way of putting it," I laughed as he continued.

"But then you ask, 'What about the women in the Marine Corps?'"

"I didn't ask."

"Well, I'll tell you anyway: they're doubly crazed! They say, 'Men, pish! I can get just as much as they can get!' They, my friend, are the ultimate machismo freaks. They're two sandwiches short of a picnic basket!"

"Nice, very nice."

"It's true. Every Marine wants to prove their intestinal fortitude, and every Marine wants to go out and be a superstar, because that is what being a Marine is really about."

While my buddy was probably right, it was boredom and a lack of activity that comprised much of the day now, and that was a true killer of morale. I wouldn't wish this life on anyone. It had its amazing moments, don't get me wrong, but it was also a test of one's sanity. Especially when the days never ended out here.

★ ★ ★

There was talk of us pushing west to Ad Diwaniyah and marrying up with 1st Marine Division's consolidated position. Relief in place was happening all over the country. The Army's 4th Infantry Division finally made it to Baghdad, taking over Marines' positions. The British now had control of Basra and most of southern Iraq. But where there once had been active patrolling and meeting with locals, the Army now remained in its vehicles. Having just arrived about two weeks earlier, the Army units must have been overwhelmed with the task of distinguishing an Iraqi friend or foe. Going on our third month out here, we understood the dynamics of the culture on some level now. We had stopped the looting; made a presence, and we interacted with the people. But as we pulled away, the Iraqis were left with the cold indifference of the exterior of a tank as their defender.

Back in Al Kut, things became less prosperous. As locals waited patiently for a dramatic change from coalition occupation, they saw no immediate results. Electricity, fresh water, and the basic comforts of life were not available. The city, one of the largest, northernmost cities close to the Iranian border, was perfect for infiltration and border crossing. The Iranian Hezbollah and Syrian jihadists were becoming a problem in Karbala and An Najaf. In Al Kut, a self-appointed leader called Sayyad Abbas Al Reef spoke in local mosques, conveying a strong pro-Iranian message.

"You are not free until the U.S. leaves," he proclaimed. He commanded a small group of two to five hundred pro-Iranians called Hizb Al Dawa. He was the quintessential thug. Despite his false appeals to the people of Al Kut, they didn't appear to be buying it. Yes, they were afraid of him, but they also hated him.

Task Force Tarawa was losing the precious leverage they had in the city; one day, they allowed Al Reef's group to blockade them from an area they were patrolling. Al Reef took this opportunity to show the people that the Americans were afraid of him. Of course this wasn't the case, but the people lost hope in the coalition forces as protectors. Because of this, many of our missions were centered on city hall and the city center.

Meanwhile, in Al Kut, a meeting took place between local leaders and Brigadier General Notonski, the 2nd Marine Expeditionary Brigade's leader. We flew to the meeting place to find out if protests were taking place. The meeting was held in a building we described as "the B2 building," because it resembled a B2 bomber aircraft from our view above. It actually was the former mayor's house, which the Marine Corps had taken over and were using as a forward command post. But the B2 building name stuck and soon had spread. I wondered if I had started a mini-trend, as all of MEF was calling it that. We could tell that the meeting had gone well, because they took a group photo in front of the building afterward.

In the meeting, all the local leaders had been given a chance to speak. Al Reef was there and claimed, "The U.S. forces are not a welcome presence in Al Kut and have done nothing for Iraq." At which point the remaining local leaders responded, "We are grateful the Americans are here; it is you who have done nothing!"

Despite some of the leaders saying that they were grateful, the rest of the country seemed undecided. The Iraqis were glad for their freedom, but they definitely didn't seem to want American influence. In a way, it seemed their pride in many instances prevented them from saying thank you. Or maybe they just didn't fully trust us yet.

This was especially true in Tikrit, where a shadow regime was forming and local leaders were seizing control. Rather than attacking coalition forces, they bided their time, waiting for the moment to strike. They were ever watchful. Marines would patrol the cities and find families of innocent civilians massacred; the same families who had waved at the coalition forces earlier. Marines would find mutilated bodies on the streets, bodies in pieces, bodies of those who had supported the coalition. It was a thug's way of gaining support through fear, just as it had been with the Ba'ath party. The day would culminate in the discovery of a mass grave, all children, massacred in ways too horrible to imagine. Strange things were found everywhere—first it was a wing of an MIG-25 at Al Asad in the middle of the desert, then it was a group of MIGs half-buried and abandoned like forgotten artifacts. One patrol found $650,000,000 in one of Saddam's palaces.

An Najaf represented the Shi'ite hope for a new regime. Ayatollahs began moving into the city. Ayatollah Al Asifi, head of the Hizb Al Dawa—one of the leading political parties in Iraq—and Ayatollah Al Ha'iri both believed Iraq would be better as a secular government. Then there was Grand Ayatollah Sayyid Ali al-Husayni al-Sistani, who like former Grand Ayatollah Muhammad ibn Mahdi al-Hussaini al-Shirazi, was a charismatic Islamic leader who preached religious pluralism, human rights, and nonviolence. Sistani had even issued the fatwa prohibiting Muslims from waging attacks on coalition forces. An Najaf was one of the holiest of the Iraqi cities, housing the prominent Hawza in Najaf, or theological school. An Najaf looked like an ideal Iraqi city—a well-tended metropolis with neighborhoods, stadiums, mosques, and ancient history. It was a holy city and their most beloved.

Our first new mission on the transfer from Task Force Tarawa back to 1st Marine Division was to fly the route of the pilgrimage from Karbala to An Najaf. As we flew over Route 9, we saw hundreds of thousands of pilgrims. It was an amazing sight to behold; for the first time in twenty-three years, Shi'ites flocked to their holy sites in Karbala. I had never seen anything like this; it was monumental. The people below looked like a giant chain of black walking from Najaf to Karbala. The gilded dome of the Shi'ite shrine glimmered in our eyes; the multicolored tiled mosque of Hussein and Abbas's shrines was marked by the black flags that adorned its peaks. A million people moved and prayed below the shadow of our UAV, which glided in the sky unnoticed by those below. The mourning of Ashura was similar to Easter, marking the death of a man—only without the resurrection, without the joy and the hope. Where, then, was that hope for them?

Our camp had been made more permanent, and huge olive-drab canvas tents were erected, each meant to hold about thirty personnel. I was ordered to move into a tent designated as the "female tent," which, sadly, forced me out of my solitude in the topless five-ton truck. I had actually enjoyed my hours of peace in the warmth of my sleeping bag and Gor-Tex bivy sack, which had kept me dry. Now I had nowhere to escape, to drown myself in the pages of my journal or to think quietly about this strange state of being. In the female tent, one of the Marines, a female Corporal named Kassie Council, had set up a cot for me in the corner.

"Ma'am, we set up a spot for you. We put it in the corner so we wouldn't bother you so much with our noise."

I was grateful, but I was not looking forward to sharing a tent with a bunch of enlisted females. But it could have been worse. The officers' tent was full of rivalries, and men were such dirty slobs. Word was that Debucher was doing some kind of puppet show with finger bunnies and clothespins attached to genitalia, but I never asked for details. At least the women cleaned up after themselves. While I felt distanced and segregated from the officers, I didn't really want to hear them talk about women, see them in their skivvies, or see the "puppet shows." The mere thought weirded me out.

In the female tent, wafts of Victoria's Secret fruit-scented concoctions drifted through the air, and the women spoke softly about the men in their lives. Although it did make me long for womanly things like my Prada suit at home and my never-worn Louboutin shoes, I couldn't imagine wearing anything like that in the condition of dirtiness my body was in. I still didn't feel at ease. I preferred my solitude and seeing the night sky. The sky, at least, was constant. Above I could see the wash of stars that made up the band of the Milky Way. It was the same universe I stared at from back home. No matter where I traveled, it was the one thing I could count on, proving that I was just a small dot on a tiny planet barely moving in an infinitesimally small part of the cosmos.

Instead, here I was in some government-issued tent, listening to Marines talk about the same shit that they always talked about. I spent little time in the tent, drifting back to my area of seclusion by my truck at the edge of camp where I could see the expanses of the airfield and the Harriers and C-130s that flew in now, consistently delivering supplies to all the camps. The only sounds I could here was gunfire in the distance, and Sergeant Young singing "John the Revelator" softly a cappella. I enjoyed what little privacy I could find. It was almost dawn. Beyond were groves of palms and the occasional Bedouin I could see through my binoculars. As I pulled out my platoon commander's notebook, Peter's sealed envelope slipped out. I drummed it with my fingers, still wondering what was inside. Its edges were worn, and it had gotten dirty, more brown than manila now. I held it up to see if the gathering first light would reveal its secrets. But the paper was too thick, so my only choice was to open it. It was the only thing from Peter that I had with me. I wanted to keep my promise. But I couldn't. I barely knew him any longer. I wasn't going to debate it anymore. Fuck it. I could be dead tomorrow. I ripped open the envelope and read it. Inside, my husband had scribbled: "I know you are going to open the letter whether I die or not, so I love you. In the event that I am dead, shit, I guess I fucked up somehow. Sorry."

★   ★   ★

About the same time our tents were erected and we started getting T-rations once a day, Lieutenant Debucher reported to the medical tent, throwing up in all directions. He had grown a big hairy mustache, which made him look like a dirty perv from a '70s movie. They gave him some antibiotics, which made him vomit instantly. He was too weak to do anything, so he collapsed on his rack. He slept for two days, and we thought he was going to die. The docs reassured us it was just a bad virus—"Saddam's revenge," they called it. I would have been glad he got sick, except I knew I'd get whatever he had next.

Sure enough, the next day I woke up sick as a dog and went over to medical. That's how I came to know Doc Casey, a badass who was a Navy

SEAL for fifteen years before becoming a Navy doctor. Doc Casey was bald—not the fat, ugly, bald-guy type, but the badass Ajax type.

"What, you too?"

"I think so."

"Take this."

"Am I going to be down like the other Lieutenant?"

"Well . . . it affects everyone differently."

I looked into his tent area, where there were a couple of Marines with the same illness.

"Is it spreading?"

"Ten already; you're number eleven. Look on the bright side—everyone in camp is probably going to get it, and you'll get it done with early."

"*Great.*"

I felt like throwing up, but I didn't. I spent the day asleep on my cot and woke at night to find the camp infected. I felt much better. I had gotten off lightly. As I walked around, I saw some Marines lying on the ground, unable to walk; one Staff Sergeant lay half-dressed, moaning in pain on the sandy dirt. It looked like a zombie B movie. I went over to the Staff Sergeant to see if he was OK.

"Lieutenant," Doc Casey motioned me over. "Come here and let him be—we tried to move him, but he said he's going to throw up if he goes anywhere."

"So you're back from the dead?" Doc Casey asked me.

"More like the walking dead right now."

"You look a little pale, but you got off light—look at some of these guys."

"Jesus! They look bad!" Others lay about, in various stages of the sickness.

"Fortunately, it looks and feels much worse than it actually is."

"What is it?"

"Just a twenty-four-hour virus. Thirty infected and growing."

A Marine came over to the tent, almost crawling and near tears.

"Doc, I'm shitting constantly and fucking throwing up everywhere. I feel like complete shit."

"Take this, and you'll be knocked out like that Staff Sergeant over there."

He looked over with dismay at the Marine on the ground but took the medicine and walked away with a slow, zombie-like gait. We laughed.

"I know it's not right to laugh, but we look like *Night of the Living Dead!*"

★   ★   ★

By 22 April, we had stopped our missions altogether, as Iraq seemed to be in a settling period. Dust devils, or small tornadoes, swirled mysteriously around our camp. I was walking back from talking to my Marines when Sergeant Major Rew walked up to me with his usual John Wayne gait and said, "Hey, ma'am, I've been meaning to tell you something for a while."

"What's going on, Sergeant Major?" He got a twinkle in his eye and smirked before speaking.

"You know, I come from the grunts and was a drill instructor for some years. When my buddies heard I was going to the wing, they all made fun of me. They said, 'Oh God, Rew, I hope you have females in your unit, because it's messed up that they're in the Corps to begin with—and since you're now all messed up, it's only right that you get them.' They gave me a real freakin' hard time. So when I came to this unit, I had this impression that female Marines were going to be all jacked up. For the first year, all I wanted to do was transfer out. But the staff changed and we got a great CO, but when we got deployed I was really worried about the ten females. I thought, 'What kind of drama are they gonna put us through out there?' I had my worries, trust me. You know, when we had our anthrax shots, things changed—my perspective changed." He paused again and took off his cover for a moment to scratch his hair.

"In the grunt unit I was in before, a lot of the men refused to get their shot. Many of them made a lot of fuss. It's strange, but when we got our shots—with the females there right beside the males in line—not a single one of the men complained. It was amazing. It was as if they knew their manhood was at stake, as though the females made them braver. And then out here, I've noticed no difference with the females. There hasn't been a problem. In fact, the females seem to give the men no excuse for backing out or being afraid. They make everything work better; they just balance things out."

★   ★   ★

When the true apathy of the day kicked in and we reached an all-time low, the thought of the unknown wait before we could leave loomed heavy in our minds. Boot camp, even with the deliciously evil tortures we endured, was better because at least we knew when it would end. But now, time was our warden, and boredom was our prison with no exit in sight. There was already talk of most of the Marine Corps going home. The 24th Marine Expeditionary Unit was already on its way, and although ticker-tape parades almost certainly awaited the bulk of the returning forces, we felt our homecoming would be the anticlimactic, forgotten return. 1st Marine Division would leave a contingency force of a regiment behind. 1/4, 2/5, 3/5, 1/7, and 3/7 infantry units were chosen to become the Joint Task Force 7 that would remain until September at least. Artillery and other units would be back home within thirty days. But some General, far removed from our level, thought we were useful and doing something. In reality, we hadn't flown in days.

There were two fears that beset me daily: The first was the natural, untrustworthy feeling that some enemy unit would counterattack. Every day, Iranian influence flowed into all factions of the country, and the situation looked grim at best. I wondered if we had made much difference at all or just replaced one thug group with another. The people of Iraq were skeptical of everyone—Saddam, the United States, local leaders. They wanted to see results, not just hear words.

My second fear was a much deeper, more pervasive fear, one that haunted me in dreams and sometimes in the long hours of the day. It was the fear that my new husband and I would never be the same, that somehow our relationship would go sour due to our separation. Logically, I knew nothing could be further from the truth—Peter was my lifeblood, my hope, and my reason for staying alive. But the longing, the heartsickness was unbearable. I could no longer remember him clearly in my mind; I just had an image of a once-perfect time. The war would change us, but I had no way of knowing how.

I couldn't call the States and couldn't expect letters. He was somewhere in Iraq, maybe thirty miles away, but there was no way to talk. Once our squadron had gotten phone privileges, everyone had stories of calls and mail from home, but I had no calls to make and no letters to receive. My husband was nowhere to be found. He was somewhere on the banks of the Diyala River or in Baghdad, that was all I knew. How could I be sure of his thoughts, his intentions? The war had clouded my reasoning and distorted reality. Perhaps it was the same for him. Maybe he no longer needed me, maybe his band of brothers and fervor for the Corps had vanquished his passion for me. In my heart I didn't believe this, but I wanted to be prepared for the worst. We hadn't reached the point in our relationship where there's a symbiotic understanding. We had so little time together—and then this.

Part of my fear lay in the fact that Peter would invariably be home before me. He would be waiting at home, perhaps for months. Rumors had circulated that the Marines who didn't have spouses or girlfriends waiting for them would be greeted by "huggers" who would offer other services to them as well. I shook my head as the thought entered my mind. It was dusk, and I walked over to my empty tent—most of the females were out doing one job or another. I perched on some boxes stacked against one of the trucks. I was high enough to see around the camp. Grabbing an MRE, I cracked it open and ate only the main meal. I almost gagged as it went down my throat. Several of the officers sat below me, disturbing my few moments of silence. They were laughing and talking about how many clothespins they could clip to their genitals, and a few were betting as to who would be the "winner" among them. They evidently hadn't noticed me above them. I watched them check out a female pilot who walked by and heard them talk about how hot she was and the things they wanted to do to her. What losers. I felt sorry for them. I thought things like this would change when I became an officer, but maybe not. Here we were in the middle of a combat zone, and they were ogling females just like they had in junior high.

My mind wandered again to Peter. I cursed myself for being so jealous. I had no reason to be, yet I had little faith, given the men in my past and the men I was constantly around. The majority of their morals were suspect; why should I think my husband's would be otherwise? But I had to believe he was different—I had to trust him. The harder I tried, the more disconcerting thoughts entered my mind: Would I come home and find no one at the gates to greet me? Would I find the world changed? Would I enter our new home and find him gone? Or worse, would I find him drunk and in bed with another woman, like so many other Marines had in the past?

I was getting angry thinking all these things. This fragile world was so weak. I really doubted whether this war would change anything. Did the thousands of wars fought before this one really make a difference? Technology had changed things. But it was the same struggle against wills, resolved only by violence. War, sex, disease, struggle, survival, and death seem to be part of the inexplicable human condition. The absurdity of it all was hard to shake off. Only the brief flares of joy made all the effort worthwhile. When the blind philosopher Diogenes the Cynic wandered the streets of Corinth, he held out his lamp to the world and said, "I am looking for an honest man!" but no one answered.

★ ★ ★

All my negative thinking seemed trivial when compared to the average Iraqi's life. None of the Marines liked to think or talk about it. Instead, most Marines luxuriated in ignorance of what was going on immediately around them. Mission was all that mattered. Give Marines the pagan joys of *Playboy*, Game Boy, and tobacco, and they were in their happy place. Part of what makes America so great is that we have luxury. It was wonderful to think we came from a country with so many possibilities. Here it was different. There were Iraqi refugees wandering, single and homeless, often without cars—or tongues, or limbs—because of the horrific impact of Saddam's regime. Their problems were not when they would return to a good life, but when they would get water or food. My life was blessed compared to the small Iraqi child, caught in crossfire, lying on the ground, comatose but alive, wondering what happened. Or compared to the Corporal, whose wife was eight months pregnant and sick, knowing that with months to go, he would not witness the birth, enduring those precious hours alone. So I tried not to complain too much. It was true everyone had their problems; many of my Marines had been given their one morale phone call for the first time last week, and news wasn't always so good. Some would go home to find their spouses had left them, their money had been spent, and a new men or women had moved into their places. Faith was the only thing I had to hold on to, and I had to believe in my husband. For all I knew, he could be dead. The last letter I received from him was about the private world of men, speaking of the Marines with whom he served. He wrote about Marines who were packed in their tents "nut to butt," trading porn, cigarettes, and a fair amount of griping about the living situation in their unit. He wrote about the designated area for wrestling matches and the curtained area for private moments, pragmatically dubbed "the whack shack." These comprised my only correspondence from him. They were very distant and impersonal, but they were all I had.

Every Marine had an illusion that got them through the day, sometimes through the moment. Moment by moment was how we lived.

22

MORTARS IN THE GARDEN

War is a racket.

—General Smedley Butler, United States Marine Corps

B y 25 April, our convoy was once again packed up to leave. Our next stop was Ad Diwaniyah. 1st Marine Division had consolidated, and the relief in place had pushed them to the middle of the country in a predominately Shi'ite region. Allegedly, the Marines were being given control of this area, which included Al Hillah, Karbala, An Najaf, Ad Diwaniyah, and Al Samawayah, which was considered crucial to the stability of the whole region. After chatting with Division, I was able to ascertain that all of 1st Marine Division was at the Ad Diwaniyah location. So my next logical question was, "Where's my husband and 11th Marines?"

"They're here, too," Staff Sergeant Berrios told me at 1st Marine Division headquarters. "See, I told you I'd look out for you."

Our camp was packed in a day, and we had to sit in our vehicles, waiting for order for movement. How long it would take for us to go back home, no one knew. At least we were moving in some direction. There was also the slim chance that I would get to see my husband. But I didn't count on it in a place where expectations, any at all, are likely to be unfulfilled.

Another severe dust storm rolled through, and sand whipped around me. The night was unbearably long, and the sky never darkened. It was impossible to sleep. Half our squadron was sick, some hooked up to IVs and others rolling in pain, clutching their stomachs in agony. No one got to sleep before the convoy began to move in the morning. As first light drew across the horizon, we didn't need reveille to wake up. The sky was orange haze, and our convoy rolled alone through the sepia-toned land-scape. It was all a bad rerun of last month's odyssey. My driver, Corporal Reynolds, fought back sleep and the urge to throw up. We didn't speak. Sand pelted my face and flew into my lungs. I just didn't care anymore. Caravans of camels looked at us through the haze of the dust. Despondently we sat, watching the distant Ottoman domes of the mosques and the mud-encrusted ruins of towns. A hush had fallen over all of us. There seemingly was no end. Then, finally, we saw a checkpoint of Marines guarding a bermed-in area. Beyond it was 1st Marine Division's consolidated point—a small pocket of freedom in an otherwise disordered country.

We arrived at a position that housed the entire division, reinforced—tens of thousands of troops reconstituting themselves within a couple of klicks. As we pulled into the position, we entered an abandoned Iraqi mili-tary academy. The wall-sized fresco of Saddam in military attire had already been defaced like some ancient god fallen out of favor. Scattered barbed-wire fences, guardhouses, and military signs were everywhere. When at last we pulled into our position, we set up along a small road that would be our runway, near one of the buildings that was part of the military academy. The academy was in ruins, having been bombed by the coalition early in the war. A small cluster of buildings was our combat operations center, and strange Iraqi graffiti illuminated the rooms. Hospital-green tiles lined the remains of the interior building that we claimed as our own. After we had set up, Major Cepeda, the XO, came over and looked at me strangely.

"Well?"

"Well what, sir?"

"Well, what are you waiting for? Go find your husband." The XO gave me his blessing and lit up a cigarette, while I pulled out my lensatic compass and map to calculate the distance from my husband's position to ours—only seven hundred meters? That was within view. As I looked up across a graveyard of burned-out vehicles and hulks of metal, a misty view of rows of howitzers appeared, a prodigious symbol of the renewed life that suddenly surged within me.

Dropping my map in the truck, I made my way through the maze of the metal cemetery. Vehicles, parts of aircrafts, missiles, chairs, tables, and large weapons systems all lay in tangled piles along a well-worn dirt trail that weaved through the hulks. Marines in pairs passed me intermittently along the strange trail, a shortcut to their unit's position. The vehicle cemetery was bathed in reddish clay dirt that covered everything, blan-keting the area and turning it into an alien world. A reddish mist covered the ground and trails, obscuring the view. I passed a pack of feral dogs;

they looked at me, keeping a cautious distance. The alpha male gave me a pensive, cool stare as he lay in front of the pack and watched me weave through the obstacles. From the solitude of the metal graveyard, the path opened up and continued to ascend, leading to a muddy clay area, well worn by a trail of Marine boots that had been temporarily stamped into the earth. Approaching the units ahead, the smell of burning shit filled the air. I walked past several metal buckets of burning human feces and some newly erected plywood heads where lines of men waited for their turn to piss and shit in them. They were all male grunts, and they stared at me. As I turned away, I looked up to find a regiment of artillery parked in front of me. I read the unit markings on the sides of seven-tons: 2/11, K 2/12. Men urinating on the side of the path, near where I passed, were oblivious to my approach. Several men sat, with their pants down, shitting on the pots in plain view. Quickly, I turned away, pretending that sight had never entered my mind. My eyes focused on what was ahead. The words 11th Marines were in view.

I counted the unit markings on the sides of the vehicles: 2/11, 1/11, 11th Marines Headquarters, and finally 3/11. Edging forward, familiar faces emerged—Lieutenant Robertson and Lieutenant Ruehl greeted me with open arms. Others in Peter's unit came to greet me. Everyone looked emaciated, just like those in my unit. Staff Sergeant Sexstone smiled and shook his head. "You again?"

"That's right."

"He's in the FDC. Good to see you again, ma'am."

An olive-drab command tent was a few paces away. I walked into the tent and saw Peter at a field desk. His back was turned to me. There he was, and he was alive. I approached, touched his back, and he turned to look at me. Our eyes met, but military protocol kept us from emotion. We had changed. There were no tears left in my eyes, no sentiment. My greeting was as if from one Marine to the next. But inside, I was filled with relief.

"Are you all right?" I asked tentatively. "Uninjured?"

"Yes, fine, and you?"

"I'm fine." He motioned for us to walk outside, and I followed him. We walked without speaking, toward bombed-out buildings littered with filth, trash, and Arabic graffiti. Inside the cool brick shelters, urine and excrement stains marked the way. Pictures of Iraqis holding AK-47s, the Dome of the Rock, and strange images of people being tortured were everywhere. Unexploded mortar and AK-47 rounds, magazines, and rifles lay discarded, abandoned in piles. Marines appeared at every angle we turned, some seeking privacy to relieve themselves, some showering, others jerking off in the distance. This was not how I imagined my first meeting with Peter in combat.

"Don't look that way!" he said as I laughed.

"Why not?"

"Because there's a naked man's ass!" We both howled in laughter, but he took me into his arms and kissed me.

"Happy honeymoon."

"Honeymoon? What? That last view wasn't mentioned in the brochure!"

"Neither was the fact that we've spent most of our marriage and our engagement away from each other."

But there were few words to say. Here we were in the aftermath of the war, in a military academy long since abandoned, we wandered through the curious empty buildings, exploring. We found a land navigation room painted black, with celestial maps on the walls showing the phases of the moon; a shooting gallery where the targets were horrific fanged-face images crowned with stars of David, representing Jews as demonic creatures; an auditorium with murals of Qur'anic revelations and past Arab battles; a sand-table exercise room; and a gymnasium. We walked through a world that once trained men to fight against us. Epitaphs of hate were immortalized on the walls, in portraits of Saddam victorious over the United States and Israel, which lay trampled below. The Al Asqa Mosque, Dome of the Rock, floated on a cloud like a Valhalla painted on the wall. We saw strange iconic images of a border prison camp, which in Arabic told of a Zionist presence on the border between Jordan and Israel. It was hard to believe this was all real, that Peter and I walked together through this bizarre place. This was no ordinary military academy: it was a terrorist training camp for Iraqis fighting jihad in Palestine.

We walked through its corridors, where haunting remnants of a vanquished military lay scattered and dusty. Diplomas, field manuals, NBC weapons handbooks, propaganda, and personnel records littered the ground. As I walked with Peter, I picked up some papers with photos of women in chadors and military men. Hundreds of martial records and records of service were scattered over the floors. Immaculate, handwritten school journals contained charts and battle plans for a war not yet fought. Disturbing images of Saddam's regime were painted inside auditoriums. There were images of the triumphs of the people, women and children in Bedouin garb, carrying AK-47s that were tokens of tyranny that was no more. The images of demon-faced Jews we had seen in the shooting gallery were painted everywhere. We walked through the buildings silently, as if in a gallery. Our silence spoke of all the stories we would share later, and the unified knowledge that we both had been in the fight and seen worse horrors.

In the warm twilight, we walked through a once-tranquil courtyard now piled high with AK-47s, mortar shells, mortar tubes, and shattered AAA pieces. Arches of bougainvilleas, once tended, grew wild, breaking the line of the arch and overgrowing the walls. The spring had brought flowers throughout the ruins and the gardens, and walkways were filled with crimson hibiscus and pastel lantana. We walked into a small garden with an Islamic tiled fountain that had stopped running. We sat on the twisted log of a tree that had fallen and looked at the roofless sand-table room, where Iraqis once sat listening to their military instructors plan operations. But for an hour, we forgot about Iraq.

★   ★   ★

First Marine Division's consolidated Ad Diwaniyah position was a time for reunion, and in the strangest way, it was one of the happiest periods of my life. I hadn't expected to live to this point, let alone to see my husband and my friends. Classmates from my officer training were everywhere. Everyone had a story about getting shot at. I ran into Lieutenants Carlson, Stone, and Bock, all of whom humbly told me what their units had done. Most of all, we had the shared experience of having just occupied a foreign country. Saddam's rule was over, and I MEF, the "Imperial" Marine Expeditionary Force, was responsible for a major part of this. Yes, the Army played a part, as did the Air Force and the Navy, but I didn't share in their stories. Our legacy, whether in Guadalcanal, Belleau Wood, Iwo Jima, or Hue City, was forged from our shared stories, our remembrance of those decisive moments that shaped the battle space. Unit leaders and friends visited us, and the war unfolded before our eyes. We had the picture from the sky; they had the picture from the ground. There were a lot of moments of, "So that's what happened!"

I wandered back to my unit's position, and my CO gave me "the eye."

"Boots . . . what have you been up to?" He knew what I was up to.

"Just getting my bearings of the area, sir."

"Well, we're not that busy over here today, I'm sure you can find something to do." He gave me the eye again and smiled. That evening, I wandered back to my husband's position. Many of our peers joined us from different units, and we sat around and told stories about our friends. Some of the grunts described the insurgents they saw and shot as reminiscent of the zombies in *Night of the Living Dead.*

"Dude, they just kept coming."

"What the fuck do you mean?"

"We kept shooting them, and they kept coming. It was like they were inhuman or something. It turns out, when we got close to some of the wounded Fedayeen, they were all pumped up on PCP and heroin. They were on drugs, man! One hajji had about ten rounds in him, and he was still walking, even when we shot his arm off!"

Marines were still taking fire in other sectors of the city, and some stories involved our friends. Second Lieutenant McNair, a close friend of Peter, was attached to 1st Battalion, 5th Marines as their forward observer. His Amtrac Company had come under serious fire going through Baghdad. At the same time that the Army was being greeted in Baghdad with roses, our friends were greeted with RPGs and small arms fire. RPGs whizzed past him at a cyclic rate. After turning another corner, an RPG round landed on the Marines' gear hanging off the sides of the vehicle. The troop packs stopped the RPGs but were catching on fire. Lieutenant McNair raised the turret of his Amtrac, attempting to find out where the majority of fire was coming from so that he could call for fire upon them. But the enemy rounds were coming too fast. As he fired against snipers, an RPG impacted the side of the vehicle near him. McNair dipped his head in, and when he raised it out of the top of the armored vehicle again, a round flew at him. They all heard a large impact, so loud that when McNair opened his eyes, he could barely hear and was completely disoriented.

"Fuck, sir, are you OK?" the Private next to him called out, but Mc-Nair couldn't hear him. He looked over to see the Private shouting.

"I'm OK. I'm OK." McNair had been lucky; the RPG had impacted the side of the armored vehicle. But he felt blood on his neck where he had been hit by shrapnel.

"Sir, sir, *You're not OK!*" The Private was staring at the dark blood that was shooting out in jets from McNair's neck. The Lance Corporal next to him threw up. He had seen burning blood on the side of his Lieutenant's right arm, and then he looked up and saw that the right side of his face was ripped open, and blood was pouring down into the turret opening. A steady stream of blood flooded into the Amtrac below.

"No, I'll be fine." He applied pressure to his neck and then collapsed.

He had been my husband's best friend in artillery school at Fort Sill, Oklahoma. The medics thought he was going to die. But McNair pulled through; he went on convalescent leave and would be getting plastic surgery. On his hospital bed he said he wished he could go back to the fight.

From Alpha Battery, 1st Battalion, 11th Marines, our friend Lieutenant Whaley told us about his Captain. The Captain and First Sergeant had been in a tank with the turret open, and the Captain took an RPG round. The Captain looked down at his right arm, which was now gone, and said matter-of-factly to the First Sergeant, "Well, I guess I'm left-handed now."

A battalion tank commander in 2nd Tanks visited our CO. He told us about his unit. While assaulting through An Nasiriyah, one tank became mired in the sandy mud near the Tigris. A tank tread had come loose, and an industrious Private dutifully fixed the tread and managed to free the tank, oblivious to the fire coming from the bridge.

"It was beautiful and terrifying thing to watch a Marine under fire perform his job so well," the Battalion Commander told us. "For that I wrote him up for a Bronze Star!"

In the midst of all the deaths and stories that began to form about the war, we were thankful for our lives. No story diminished the happiness and joy I felt those days in Ad Diwaniyah. With my husband by my side, little else mattered. Stories unfolded before us on our long, daily walks. As we busied ourselves with writing awards and fitness reports, we rewarded ourselves with time together. There was no guilt for us; we both knew my unit might be one of the last units to leave. Worse news followed—Peter's unit would go on a nine-month UDP float a couple months after he got back to CONUS, and then he would be redeployed back to Iraq, Afghanistan, or Japan. The news hit me hard.

"Nine months? I might not even be home in time to see you before you are gone again?" My world didn't exist that far into the future. But I didn't want to go home if he wasn't there. I was so pissed off. What did I have to hope for? To return home and not even know where my husband was again? There was no relief from this feeling of dread. One deployment was long enough, but two or three? This war did not let me plan or hope. As General Mattis had told us, "Hope is not a plan!"

Late at night, I sneaked into Peter's tent to spend the night. Only the officers had private tents, and the enlisted Marines shared tents with one or two others. We didn't have tents in my unit; I usually slept in the bed of my truck. So this night, from inside his tent we listened to his Marines talk about their wishes and dreams. They didn't know I could hear them. I heard men's uninhibited talk for the first time in my life, and Peter and I found ourselves suppressing giggles as his Marines took turns talking about masturbating.

"Hey, Jones, what's taking you so fucking long? Are you still masturbating to that photo of your mother?"

"Fuck all y'all. I actually have the picture of your wife, and she's so goddamn ugly I can't get it up."

"Whatever, just hurry up, I want to get back in my tent to get some sleep!"

★   ★   ★

Peter and I lay silently, holding each other, unknown to anyone but each other. Sporadic sniper fire echoed in the nearby streets. We held each other as husband and wife as if for the first time. This was the only time we had. We could expect nothing else. Our lives were too uncertain. At 0430 every morning, I would awaken and slip out, invisible in the predawn light, past the junkyard and feral dogs, into my unit's area. I would slip back into my five-ton truck and count the minutes until I would see my husband again. So passed ten days as quickly as a flash.

The next thing I knew, his unit, like many others, got word that they were to retrograde, meaning they were on the list to go back to CONUS. We were told we were to remain until the end. But when was the end? August? September? Eternity? And Peter's unit would leave almost immediately on a nine-month deployment after its return to the States. I watched his unit in travel lock, pull out, and disappear. My heart felt bitter and angry. All of 11th Marines pulled out, leaving us suddenly exposed and alone.

Day after day was the same nothingness. The frustration was so intense that I wanted to clench my fists tight enough to draw blood, just to feel like my outward anguish matched my inner despair. The day, 7 May, was bitterly freakin' hot. I counseled myself against becoming overwhelmed in my own misery and tried to talk myself out of the black void that that my world had become. There was so much I could do to help the Iraqis, but here we were, ordered to button up and do nothing. They wouldn't let us out of the wire to help the Iraqis. We were forced as a unit to just sit there and wait until higher headquarters found a use for us. They were keeping us on standby. If you think something is all fucked up, it probably is.

We didn't know what to do except douse ourselves with water. There seemed to be no relief for us—we were told we would be here indefinitely. Days soared into the 100° to 140° range, and walking around in the sweltering heat could quickly lead to dehydration. As we watched more units begin the long convoy back to Kuwait, our squadron plunged into the depths of postwar despair. We pounded water and never relieved ourselves. It was so hot that when you were in the sun, your entire body would become drenched in sweat. After we dried in the shade, the sweat crystallized with salt and dirt, forming white, shiny stains on our gear and clothing.

I walked over to sit with Doc Casey and Captain Piper; this had become our morning ritual. We sat around the combat operations center and laughed because we thought life couldn't get worse. But it had. Sand picked up and whipped across our faces and turned the world into a Martian wasteland. Our wet bodies were now covered with powdery sand, turning us into veritable sand monsters. We looked at each other and laughed.

And then, across the road to the berm area near my husband's old position, we saw dozens of Iraqis running. They could see us and knew we were watching them behind our fortress of barbed wire. They merely taunted us, coming just close enough not to get shot, circling us like birds provoking cats. Our perimeter was now woefully unsecured; when 11th Marines had pulled out, they left behind a porous border. We now were the security for 1st Marine Division's northern flank.

I heard through a letter from my mother that Peter had arrived safely back in America. Although I tried to feel happy for him, I felt that this situation was somewhat messed up. I still had deep fears about arriving to find no one there. I imagined him arriving home to that empty place and wondered how strange it felt for him not to have anyone to greet him. But ultimately I tried not to think of him at all.

★ ★ ★

Things calmed down. The occasional sniper and suicide bomber threats were still present, but for the most part, pro-coalition feeling improved as humanitarian aid poured in. Across Iraq, the first commercial flights landed in Baghdad and Basra, carrying more aid, and dead Ba'athist party members were brought to the guard posts of the Marines, killed by the Iraqis who were now unafraid of their former regime. We were told that mobile biological weapon facilities were found, eighteen total, capable of making enough bioweapons to kill thousands in less than a month of production. Was this the justification to go to war that we had all been waiting for? Despite finding the facilities, no one had found the weapons yet. If that was not enough to justify the war, then maybe the children's prison, found by an infantry unit, was. We never learned why those children had been detained by the Ba'athist party, only that they had found children's corpses chained up. Men without ears were a common sight in An Nasiriyah, as

Saddam had the ears of military deserters surgically removed during the Gulf War. Without their ears, they were outcasts in their own culture and ineligible for marriage. Other Iraqis had different wounds, electric-shock scars and missing limbs, while some had been killed outright.

Postwar stabilization continued with the plan of incorporating the newly arrived international coalition forces into specific regions in Iraq and higher headquarters subdividing the country into distinct areas—Poland and Romania to the north, the United States in the middle, and the British to the south. Eleven countries would be part of the "coalition of the willing" and would have forces in Iraq.

★ ★ ★

To boost unit morale and to keep us from killing ourselves, I proposed to my CO that I lead a trip to Babylon for some of the troops in my unit. After coercing my upper echelon to buy into the trip, I took fifty Marines to this ancient historical spot, which was now secured by I MEF forward. Only a month after the war, Iraq had changed. Here we were, all fifty-one of us, passing through Ad Diwaniyah and Al Hillah in a convoy, and Iraqis carried on with their lives. Small children still chased the vehicles and waved, but now the adults displayed a passive indifference. We passed through the center of Al Hillah, busy with city activity, rusted taxis (some riddled with bullet holes), donkey carts, markets, and fuel stations so packed with traffic that the lines were a couple kilometers. Women veiled from head to toe in black carried objects on their heads; men in dishdashas screamed out sale prices to potential customers. Shrewd capitalist Iraqis sold cold sodas in the medians to the coalition troops. Souvenirs, such as headdresses, Republican Guard items, war trophies, flags, liquor, cigarettes, and RPGs were offered by eager, smiling teenagers. A single $5 sale was worth a week of waiting, since a good Iraqi salary was $20 a month. We threw money out to them eagerly. We didn't care what they charged. It was the only thing we had money to spend on anyway, and for them it meant a different life.

★ ★ ★

When we reached Babylon, we saw that Saddam's fingerprints had destroyed history. He left his mark by rebuilding Babylon in a way that made it look like some half-assed Disney World park. On top of the hill where the tower of Babel may have once stood was one of Saddam's palaces, an extravagant eyesore in an otherwise poor area. Immediately outside Babylon's walls, most of the houses in this area, typical mud shacks, didn't even have roofs. Only the trees were full of life, bathed by the waters of nearby streams. Palm trees and flowering plants stretched their way across the horizon, making the place seem beautiful. Saddam's palace stood aloft in adobe brown. Inside, glorious chandeliers, marbled floors and walls, gold-plated fixtures, and ceilings adorned with ornate Islamic patterns evoked an entirely different life than that which took place outside its doors. Below, the remains of Babylon lay stretched out, with the beautiful Ishtar Gate intact, awaiting us. All the Marines walked to the gate, where we were met by some locals. Eshmiel Jasem, the local curator and archaeologist who had been there thirty-four years, welcomed us. He was a kind man and seemed genuinely glad we were there.

"This is a unique moment in history," he said to us. "For the first time in history, American troops have entered the city of Babylon." A group of Marines formed around him. Eshmiel continued, "We welcome you here, and we welcome you back home!"

"Home? This is not my home," one of the Marines said, causing laughter among a number of the Marines.

"But it is. This is the home of our ancestors. This is the home that once was shared by all of us. And so you have the rare privilege of returning to the oldest civilization on earth." The Iraqi curator had become very dramatic. The Marines looked at each other and nodded in acceptance.

"Have you ever seen Saddam?" one of the Marines asked.

"Many times! Many times, friend. On three occasions, I spent several hours with him and his guests. But he did not let many people come here. For $500, a tourist could buy access, but seldom were there Americans. He denied many access here but often would come with dignitaries." Eshmiel Jasem spoke in a refined British accent, and I later learned he was college educated. He and the two Iraqi women with him were fascinated by the females in the military. Samira, the woman to his left, was a college-educated schoolteacher who worked in Babylon. She was middle-aged and had an attractive, motherly look. She wore the traditional chador. I saw her look at me and whisper something to the other woman. After the Marines were sent off on a tour of the ancient city, Samira asked me, "How is it that you are a female in the military?"

"Females are part of all the branches of service in the U.S. military. But there are not many females in the Marines."

"But you are a female leader? Do you have a college education?"

"Yes. All officers do, but not most of the enlisted. Most of my Marines do not."

"And are you conscripts?"

"No, no. We are an all-voluntary force."

"Is that so?" They acted amazed. They talked amongst themselves. "All of you?"

"Yes, we are an all-voluntary force. That is why we have such high morale." Samira didn't understand, but Eshmiel translated, and she nodded in understanding.

"So you . . . you joined on your own? What did your family say?"

I smiled. "They thought I was crazy at first, but then they were proud." Both the women smiled and shook their heads. She asked Eshmiel to translate her next sentence.

"So, you . . . are unique—it is not common for females in your role?"

"No, it is unique, there are only a few." She smiled along with the other woman after Eshmiel translated. They then asked him to tell me something else.

Eshmiel said, "She wants you to know that she is a pioneer, too. There are not many women who do what she does."

"She is very brave woman, then."

"Yes, Samira is brave!"

She asked then if I was married. I pointed to my ring and said, "Just married. We were married only a couple weeks before the war."

"Beautiful!" Her face became illuminated. "Ma sha Allah! Then, you are a bride!" My face turned red with embarrassment, but I said yes.

"It is customary for Iraqis to offer a gift to new brides." She pulled out a crisp Iraqi dinar. I put up my hands, insisting that I couldn't take anything from her.

"Here. This is not much, but please, take this as a token of happiness and success in your new marriage!" I refused again, but she insisted.

I held up the Iraqi note and said my thanks, holding my hand over my heart as a token of respect. She did the same. I didn't know at the time how important that dinar would become to me. My first wedding gift had been from an Iraqi.

★ ★ ★

The Ishtar Gate, despite its former splendor, was, as it turned out, only a mere copy in modern azure-colored paint, which had been slathered over it to resemble how it looked in antiquity. The walls of the three-story structure were not the originals, but duplicates decorated with friezes of Marduk lions and dragons, symbols of immortality. The real gate had been taken by the Germans some years earlier.

Eshmiel walked with us through the old city. Farther on, the main road into the kingdom of Nebuchadnezzar had been rebuilt as it once must have been. Saddam had fixed the princely walls of this edifice, and it stood as a city upon a city, with most of the original structure buried under four hundred years of dirt. Everything here had been changed by Saddam. In the courtyards of Nebuchadnezzar's palace, bricks inscribed with cuneiform read, "I am the immortal one, and may God show favor on me forever." But at the end of the passageway, Saddam's new bricks read, "Thank God for Nebuchadnezzar's victories, and show favor on his kingdom but may God make me immortal, too."

The Marines and I walked around, exploring. We stood on an overlook, looking over this once-proud kingdom.

"Can you believe this shit?" one of the Marines said to fellow Lance Corporal.

"This ain't Saddam's place no more!" the other Marine responded. It occurred to me only then that this place was, in fact, no longer Saddam's. I wondered if one day others would walk here and marvel over how Saddam's rule ended here. Would the Marines be remembered? Would they speak of our victory? How did we get to this point, when we walked over thousands of years of history and marveled at the possibility that the new kingdom had in store? Like Gilgamesh, we had walked the warrior's path and found indeed that life continues at any cost. Our will and struggle to survive as humans were remembered here. Where once Daniel, Abraham, Nebuchadnezzar, and Saddam had been, now here we stood. This was our past, not just the Iraqis', as Eshmiel had said it so well. It was our time, and one day someone would walk over our graves and our cities and remember us, perhaps, as the audacious nation.

★   ★   ★

When we convoyed back to our camp, an advanced party of twenty Marines from our squadron was getting ready to leave for the States. All the Marines in the unit who would reach their EAS, or end of active service, by September would be routed back ASAP. The stop loss had finally been lifted, and Marines were allowed to leave the Corps again and thus leave the combat zone. The other 150 Marines all carried on with their jobs. Sergeant Beaty, Sergeant Leppan, and Sergeant Young played cards by the vehicles, passing time. Sergeant Young was humming something again, but

I couldn't make out the tune. I stopped to talk to them for a while and then went about my business. On that day my CO was called back to Al Jaber, Kuwait, and we waited despondently, hoping his return would bring a good word: a date of departure. I looked across to that empty distance where my husband had been only a couple weeks earlier. We all watched and waited, too hot to be productive as the oppressive sun moved higher in the sky. Lisa hung out by herself most days and talked to me less and less. Debucher spent his time chatting with some of the Staff NCOs, and I also saw him less and less. Despite this, I was finding my place among the officers and enlisted in the unit, and the officers were beginning to accept me into the fold.

Although I had bonded with the officers, it was still not enough to dampen my hopes of returning home. When the CO returned a few days later with no word, my hope had all but dried up. Dreams of a real wedding were gone, and I didn't know how my marriage would survive another year of separation. My wedding dress, unworn, would lie in the closet forever. My only wedding gift was the Iraqi dinar handed to me by the woman in Babylon. My honeymoon was confined to the putrid, bombed-out rooms of the military academy at Ad Diwaniyah.

But just as our hopes are dashed and our fortunes seem dismal, things sometimes do change. My CO called me over.

"Boots, I want you to keep this under wraps, but I'm sending individuals back piecemeal who need to get back. I understand your husband is getting deployed in November, so I'm going to try to get you back earlier. I have my own selfish reasons, too—I need a remain-behind element, an officer in charge back in the States to manage things for me. The place has gone to pot, and all kinds of things are missing, and I'm worried nothing's going to be at our unit when we return."

"When would I leave, sir?"

"It could be weeks; it could be a month, but be prepared to leave in a moment's notice."

The CO later summoned us all into a circle. The Marines mumbled to each other, placing bets on what the word would be.

"Marines, how are we all doing?"

"Oorah!" was the crowd's response.

"I just went down to Al Jaber, as you all know. I met with the wing CG."

The CO continued his brief, "We may be moving again soon, Marines. I know, I know, we don't have a glamorous mission like we did during major combat operations, but MEF wants us here longer. We need to focus on the mission, even if we don't think the mission warrants it. We did a shit-hot job in war; now we need to continue do a shit-hot job. Remember what I said before: everyone will be OK if you stay close to me and do what I tell you to do. I'll get you all home."

There was some low grumbling among the Marines, but the CO continued. "I know you all feel like you have your face in a cheese grater now, and you keep rubbing and rubbing, wondering when it's going to feel better. Well, it's not! It really does hurt, and I know it sucks being out here. I can't tell you when you're going home, but just know I'm doing all I can. Everyone up to the MEF CG knows our mission is not glamorous now. But just focus on the mission, and we'll go home soon."

23

STRATEGIC CORPORAL

Who watches the watchmen? —Juvenal

There were a few people who weren't listening to our CO. Some Marines get through boot camp without ever really learning what it is to be a Marine. It's not about a perfect physical fitness score or the expert rifle score. The Corps values—honor, courage, and commitment—aren't just empty words. Without integrity, sound judgment, tact, and other leadership principles, the Marine is just a human in a uniform, not a leader. There's a special leadership concept coined by former Marine Commandant Charles Krulak called the "Strategic Corporal," which means that leaders are training subordinates to lead at all times so that the subordinates can step in if their leader is killed. Lance Corporals learn how to be Corporals; Corporals learn how to be Sergeants or Staff NCOs, and so on. The Strategic Corporal therefore has the ability to make decisions that could affect everyone because he is entrusted with authority. Modern combat has made it essential for small-unit leadership to be decentralized and able to make decisions away from a central core. This is part of what makes the Corps so fluid and maneuverable.

In the morning, the unit was up in arms. A line of Marines was waiting to see the CO, who was pissed off. I went over to talk to one of the Staff Sergeants.

"What's going on?"

"One of the Marines decided to get drunk on duty and disappeared somewhere, going UA. Gunny knows more. Ask him." I saw Gunny Wilson in the distance and went over to talk to him.

"Hey, Gunny, I heard one of the Marines went UA. Is this true?"

"Well, not exactly, ma'am, it's even worse. A couple of Marines had duty last night, and they weren't relieved by the oncoming duty. I happened to pass them and asked who the oncoming duties were supposed to be. 'There's only one missing—Gonzalez,' they said. When I was walking back from the showers earlier, I remembered thinking I heard her voice by the Army unit. So, on a hunch, I went back to that spot, and I saw a small fire in the distance with about six Army guys sitting around. And guess who was sitting in the middle? Lance Corporal Gonzalez. I chewed some serious fucking ass to those Army guys and let their boss know what was happening, and then I grabbed Gonzalez, who, at that point, was too drunk to stand. Can you believe that shit? She was more fucked up then a football bat. She couldn't even understand what kind of trouble she was in. She just kept laughing and throwing up on the walk home. I sat her down and tried to tell her, but she didn't seem to understand. When she wakes up this morning, she's in for the shock of her life."

A couple of hours later, the CO assembled the squadron in the bombed-out courtyard of the building we had been using. Pastel green tiles, once probably very pretty, had been badly damaged. Our boss never needed to yell to let us know he wasn't happy. His expressions were subtle, powerful, and effective. He walked to the front of the room and used a broken column as a podium. Lance Corporal Gonzalez, the Hispanic female, stood stone-faced at the position of attention.

"Attention on deck," one of the Marines shouted as the CO entered the courtyard. We all stood at attention. The CO cleared his throat and began.

"Marines, today a very serious violation of the UCMJ has occurred. Lance Corporal Gonzalez, you have been charged with the following: abandoning your post while in combat, dereliction of duty, drunkenness while on duty status, unauthorized absence. According to the UCMJ, during combat, these charges are punishable by death. You have put the safety of the entire squadron at risk because of your disregard for order and discipline."

There was complete silence among the entire squadron, and we all wondered what the CO was actually going to do. We all waited in a curious horror to see if he was going to pull out his pistol to shoot her.

"Because no Marines were injured due to your negligent and selfish acts of disobedience, however, I am not going to punish you by death. Instead, I am holding this public NJP so you may understand the seriousness of what you have done and your squadron will watch so that they, too, can learn. You will be reduced to Private and will have max NJP charges. Do you understand?"

"Yes, sir," she said, but she seemed confused. She didn't cry or get angry. Instead, she stared off into the distance. After the proceedings were over, the unit went about its business, and the security posture was revised. Private Gonzalez spent the rest of the deployment policing the area for trash. But that wasn't the end of her saga. After attacking an officer and getting more disciplinary action, she managed to get pregnant and then falsely accused various Marines at one time or another of being the father. It turned out the father was a married Marine from another unit.

★   ★   ★

Not far from my position, modern Al Hillah surrounded what remained of the ancient city of Babylon. In this sizeable city of more than a half million, Al Hillah citizens were waiting, as all of Iraq was, to see if the coalition forces would change anything for the better. First Battalion, 4th Marines was responsible for securing this area and was conducting missions in and out of the city. Second Lieutenant Seth Moulton was a platoon commander during the invasion and was then given the job of "information operations officer" for the battalion by the CO of 1st Battalion, 4th Marines. Moulton wasn't exactly sure what that job entailed. So, like a squared-away lieutenant, he asked his CO what he wanted him to do.

"First of all, go downtown and figure out what media we have to work with."

Moulton wasted no time. He was given no instructions and there was no plan for reconstruction, just "go work the media." He took Mohammed, one of the best translators in the battalion and, with a single Marine named Corporal Nickey accompanying him for security and assistance, drove down to the Hillah City Hall.

Searching for Iraqis who were willing to help reach out to the local media, Moulton's team asked many people to assist, but no one seemed willing. Time and time again, they were met with reluctance from the locals. On this day he immediately headed to the city hall in Hillah and ordered his team to stop at the steps leading up to the building. This seemed to be the place to get people's attention.

"What are you doing, sir?" one of the Marines asked.

Moulton ran to the top of the building's stairs where many locals passed on their way to the market. Moulton called for the translator. As he stood at the top of the city hall stairs he shouted, "Anyone who works with the Iraqi media, come work with me." But the Iraqis stared at him strangely as they walked by. Moulton continued, "Who wants to help?"

Mohammed translated word for word. Extraordinarily, the Iraqis actually stopped to listen. They were not sure what he meant, but they listened.

He told them he wanted to speak with someone who knew about the radio or television station. Moulton had gotten quite heated, and as Mohammed translated, the crowd offered help.

"We will help!" one of the locals shouted in Arabic, but he didn't come forward. Two other Iraqis, a man and a woman, who had come out of a building made their way through the crowd.

"We can help you. We run the local radio and television station," the Iraqi woman said in English. Although she wore a colored chador, there was something distinctly modern about her. She told them her name was Mona.

Moulton agreed to accompany the woman and the man, who told him to follow them to the television station, which was located outside town. The man and woman got into a car and urged Moulton and Mohammed to follow them. While Moulton wasn't sure these guys were legitimate members of the media, they decided to follow them in their vehicles. They drove until they were outside the city and continued driving south. Ready to turn around after about forty-five minutes of driving, Moulton saw in the distance a towering antenna on the horizon. It didn't look real and seemed to dwarf the surroundings. Moulton had never seen such an unusually large antenna before. Finally, they had arrived at the television station. The building looked as though it had been built in the 1970s and was just a vestige of a studio that looked as if it had fallen out of use. They entered a studio, where a crew of surprised employees greeted Moulton enthusiastically. The workers, it turned out, had been holding off looter from the place and hoped that the Marines were there to help.

Moulton walked into a primitive television studio. There was no camera or broadcast equipment. The only piece of equipment was a VCR that was hooked up to a transmitter. The office had formerly been under the thumb of the Ministry of Information and thus the equipment was tailored to broadcast specific messages.

One of the Iraqis asked what Moulton wanted to broadcast and if he brought any equipment. Moulton explained that he wanted to get the message out that the Marines were there to help the local community not to cause harm.

"Well, that isn't possible without a video. Please, if you get us DVDs, we can play them here." The Iraqi said to them. Mohammed translated to Moulton and his Marines. One of the television station's employees pointed to the duct-taped, glued-together VCR. Moulton was surprised that it worked at all. Moulton asked if they had a news broadcaster. Mohammed translated again and they all laughed.

"No, we have only this VCR player. We do not do live broadcasting. We only aired the tapes that Saddam's Ministry of Information sent us. But we are very excited to have a broadcast here from our station!"

Moulton explained that while he didn't have any media experience, he would help them as best as he could. The station's personnel also had little experience. Few had studied to be technicians in the media, and it was clear there was no one in charge. The first thing Moulton decided to do was determine who would be in charge. But when he asked the workers, they argued about who should be appointed. Finally, he decided to hold a mini-election. He had the fifteen or so Iraqis cast ballots to see if they could elect someone to be in charge. Moulton thought that he had no right to choose a leader for them, and it was best to let them decide. They had never used this method before. They all scribbled a name on their piece of paper and threw it into Moulton's Kevlar helmet. An Iraqi named Haleen, a schoolteacher, started telling people what to do and was elected. After Haleen was appointed, Moulton met with him to come up with a plan. After some hours, Moulton left and returned the next day.

Many of the Iraqi workers started complaining that Haleen was too harsh to be a leader; they wanted to hold another election. They seemed to like the idea that they could have a chance to be the group leader if they won the vote. After Haleen started making decisions and acting like a leader, they decided they didn't want him bossing them around and asked if they could elect a new leader. But Moulton insisted that he wasn't going to hold another election and they would just have to get used to Haleen. During the next week, Moulton sized up what he had to do with Haleen in order to start broadcasting messages. Haleen told Moulton it was important for the people to see what was going on and to try to fix the problems that they saw, such as those with electricity, which was by far their biggest issue: each night, for three or four hours, power went out in the whole Hillah region, and people could not refrigerate food or do their work.

After working for hours to fix the situation, both with Haleen and how to broadcast messages using the limited equipment available, Moulton went back to his CO to explain that he needed equipment that could be hooked up to the station's minimal facilities. Moulton told his CO about the problems with the TV station facilities and the electricity issue and suggested they tell the local population that the U.S. forces would try to improve the power situation. But the CO, who was focused on the main strategic mission, instructed Moulton that once he got the right equipment to broadcast, he was only to broadcast messages that were drafted by the Coalition Provisional Authority. He was insistent about this.

When Moulton returned to the station the next day, he explained to the Iraqis the necessity of establishing a free and independent press. The Iraqis were interested in hearing Moulton's ideas about how to make this happen, as well as his ideas about democracy and freedom. Freedom of the press, as it turns out, was a very difficult concept for them to understand. They had never known freedom of the press. In the past, all they had known about televised media came from the three stations in Iraq: theirs and two Iranian channels. Over the course of a few weeks during the late afternoons, the Iraqis that Moulton worked with would ask questions about what freedom of the press was. At first it was just one or two but soon the whole group of Iraqis would gather around and listen to Moulton. Moulton explained what the responsibilities of a reporter were and that they had the duty to report the truth despite the situation or their own beliefs about the situation. "The truth will prevail," he told them. But after Moulton showed the Iraqis the messages he had brought them from the coalition forces, they weren't exactly happy. Moulton was ordered to bring these messages from his CO, who had in turn gotten them from the Coalition Provisional Authority. They were the authorized messages that the CPA wanted to deliver to the Iraqis.

"How is this different from the Ministry of Information?" one Iraqi asked.

"With all due respect, sir, Iraqis are going to see through this," another Iraqi told him.

Moulton was torn about this information. Martial law in Iraq made it difficult to show news in any form, and the CO urged Moulton not to produce anything that could be misconstrued about the Coalition. When Moulton again discussed this with his CO, they got into a heated debate about what content to broadcast. After all the discussions about freedom of the press, he was now forced to push what the Iraqis likely saw as basic propaganda messages.

The following day, Moulton and Mohammed went back to the station and got a detailed tour of the equipment inventory from the Iraqis, who were very proud of their rather humble facility. Moulton had already supplied them with a DVD and the Iraqi technicians sat around the DVD player and transmitter and showed Moulton how they could play American movies. The Ba'ath party forbade it before, but now they pushed in a movie for the first time. When they came to a racy scene, the Iraqis simply stopped broadcasting until the scene was over and then continued the movie after the scene had passed. When Moulton returned the next day, the public was upset, complaining that the movie was shut off before it got to the good parts.

After seeing the station's capabilities, or lack thereof, Moulton was ready to start with a simple public service announcement. Moulton had gone out to town to find the equipment the station needed, but no one in Hillah or Baghdad had what they needed. So, Moulton left with a group to go to Kuwait to buy a Mac computer, camera, microphone, and equipment. He procured a video camera and DVD equipment, and after a couple days, he was ready to start. When he brought the new equipment to the station, Moulton quickly learned that his little experience in broadcasting surpassed that of most of the technicians. It was as if the average American's experience living around multimedia put him technologically ahead of the professionals in Iraq. Left to his own devices, Moulton drew from his own experiences of how to set up multimedia equipment, including a camera and a recording device and editing software. He sat down with Mohammed after they had edited the tape.

One of the first public service announcements was a short piece called, *Don't Pick Up the Bomblets*. They taped this message to warn civilians about the dangers of picking up bombs. They received positive feedback, and soon Iraqis were requesting that the station make the messages into a television show. Soon, they added other messages to assure the public that the Iraqi military would continue to get paid, and that they should continue to show up for work.

After the public service announcements started airing, Mohammed suggested to Moulton that, while the messages were informative, the Iraqis wanted to hear the truth, and they should tell them what they needed to hear. After hooking up the new video camera, they started filming one program at a time. As they learned how to operate the equipment, they began broadcasting a news commentary show three times a week. They interviewed schools, Iraqis, and American military members. The first stories they broadcast were what Moulton's CO had dictated: positive, pro-American stories, but the Iraqis on the ground weren't buying it. They complained that it wasn't news; it wasn't what was happening to the Iraqis. Moulton knew it needed to change.

Moulton protested to his CO, who had just met with the Iraqi provisional governor and the powers that be. They agreed that they wanted to continue with the propaganda messages. Moulton was outnumbered.

The following day, the convoy pulled up to the television station, and the Marines patrolled the area while Moulton and Mohammed readied themselves to spend the day interviewing the citizens of Al Hillah. Moulton and the Iraqi media team wanted to look at the overall problem in Iraq.

Every day, Moulton would ask Mohammed, "What's going on and what are the rumors on the street?"

"Electricity. That is the biggest problem," the Iraqis always said.

Moulton, Mohammed, the film crew, and the Marines all set out on a patrol along the city's main square. Unorthodox as the patrol was, the citizens seemed friendly and curious. Moulton had spent the previous night developing ideas about what he wanted for the show, and the first step was to find out what the people needed.

Moulton asked a man walking by in a dishdasha if he could interview him. Mohammed translated, and the man agreed to be interviewed. Moulton started with the big question: "What do you think is the largest problem for the people of Al Hillah?"

"We have many problems, some even more than when Saddam was here. But, most of all, the people need electricity." Mohammed thanked him, and he walked away.

Moulton then asked a woman what she thought was the biggest problem in the region.

"Thank you for coming to free us from Saddam," she said. "But the people of Al Hillah live in the dark. We cannot cook, we cannot see, we cannot live without electricity. The Baghdadis are stealing the electricity from us. They have gone to the power plant and diverted the electricity for their use! It is an outrage!" the woman's arms were flailing wildly.

As they continued interviewing, most people said the same thing: electricity was the big concern, and they were certain it was being diverted to Baghdad.

After an afternoon of taping, Mohammed turned to Moulton and asked, "What now?"

Moulton said they should go to the power station to find out if the electricity was being routed to Baghdad. They went to the electric power station, which was very modern, but the problem wasn't there. They were told the problem was at the switching station.

The television crew knew exactly where on the outskirts of town the switching station was. Unlike in America, the Iraqi switching station was a mess of huge gray wires and towers in all directions. In the center, a young, professional Iraqi in Western clothing came out to see what they were doing.

"Marhaba, may I help you?" he asked in English.

Moulton explained they were investigating why the power was out in the city and wanted to know if they could interview him. The man agreed and explained that he was the main switch operator there. After Moulton explained that the people believed the power was being routed to Baghdad, the Iraqi looked at him curiously.

"You know, sir, I am glad you have come. No Iraqi has come to ask me this, and I will be happy to explain everything." First, the switching station operator explained in layman's terms how the power switches worked and how the power was routed. He then took them to the switching room and explained how the system worked, moving from one switch to another.

"So you see, it is not as they say. These switches do not reach Baghdad—it is impossible. The problem is simple: the connectors are bad, and we need replacements. But we cannot get them, and so we cannot provide the people with power."

When Moulton returned to the television station, Mona, the woman who had originally approached him in the town square, was ready to show the film they had recorded that day.

"Well, it needs to be edited."

Moulton didn't know how to edit but he sat down with the Iraqis, and they figured it out together. But Moulton knew more than he thought, and he spent the rest of the night with the crew, both learning and teaching how to edit film. The Iraqis had never used computer-editing software before, so it was easier for Moulton to convert analog video into digital format back at his unit position. Moulton taught them how to do their own reporting, and he edited the tapes himself, exporting them to DVD back at his unit's position at night and then returning the edited DVD to the station. When they finished, Moulton taped a brief introduction, including an actual title screen announcing the *Moulton and Mohammed Show.*

The following day, Moulton provided a back brief to the CO. After learning of the dire state of electricity problem, the CO made some calls and promised Moulton funds or equipment to fix the electricity problem as soon as possible. Moulton was sent to Kuwait with $10,000 to purchase equipment. After the Marines returned to the power station with the replacement parts, electricity was restored within days. Moulton reported this, along with the significant events of the day. The Iraqis in turn were watching, listening, and responding to the new, improved *Moulton and Mohammed Show.*

However, the translators and the Iraqis were still very critical of the media they were broadcasting. Moulton had to maintain a careful equilibrium between following his CO's orders and not inciting violence on the street by airing propaganda. It was a delicate balance of reporting truth and following orders. But after the electricity story aired, things changed. The show's popularity increased, and Iraqis as far away as Baghdad were watching. As Moulton's patrol made its way back to their unit position after another day of taping and editing, a little girl in a chador ran across the street, waving to the convoy. She ran straight to Moulton and said something in Arabic. He asked Mohammed what she wanted.

"She wants our autograph!"

"Are you serious?" The little Iraqi girl smiled sweetly. He signed her paper, and she ran back to her mother and several other women in head-to-toe black, who waved and thanked him. He remembered how, just a short time ago, these same women wouldn't approach or speak to him. Moments later, a small mob of preteen Iraqis ran after the patrol. They were mostly girls.

"Moulton! We love you! Autography!" Moulton and Mohammed eagerly signed away.

They hadn't gone ten feet before yet another person approached to thank them or request their autograph. The entire town waved to them. In fact, it seemed as though every Iraqi who passed by knew who they were. One man approached Moulton and kissed him fervently on the cheek, saying something in Arabic.

"What is he saying, Mohammed?"

"Thank you, we have electricity!" Mohammed smiled.

Moulton must have realized that he had become a bit of a celebrity in Al Hillah. In fact, the show not only made Moulton and Mohammed celebrities throughout Al Hillah, but their show became the number-one program in Iraq. Moulton was amazed that they would repeat the same program several times a day, and people would watch it over and over. They continued the taping as planned, and their show gained more support from the people.

When Moulton returned to base camp, it was an entirely different world. The other Marines didn't have the same exposure to the Iraqis that he did. Moulton was making a considerable impact on the people of Al Hillah, and they were responding positively to the show. There were not just one or two hundred people watching the show, Haleen told them it was the most watched show in all of Iraq.

Moulton really was a celebrity. Everyone in Al Hillah and people throughout much of Iraq knew who he was. The people began to recognize that the Marines were sincere about helping them. That is, until

Mohammed found a note left at his house saying he would be killed if he continued working for the coalition.

The next day, Mohammed approached Moulton and said, "Moulton, I can't do this anymore. For you, you don't have to live here. But people know me and my family. They will come after me again."

Moulton said he understood and that he should do what he had to do to keep his family safe, but Moulton also tried to persuade Mohammed to stay on.

The next night, masked men approached Mohammed near his home and told him he needed to stop working on the show or they would kill him and his family. Even though Moulton convinced Mohammed to stay, when Moulton asked the Marines if they could protect Mohammed, they said they didn't have the manpower. Before they had a chance to fix the problem, Moulton was told that his unit would be pulling out of the area within the next week or two. Moulton fought to stay with the show and to continue broadcasting, but the incidental coordination between the military and civilian authorities wasn't flexible enough to allow for such an out-of-the-box request, despite the enormous success of the show.

Unfortunately, that was the end of *The Moulton and Mohammed Show*. But for a brief instant, things had been working—the Marines were helping the Iraqis, and there was a mutual understanding between the Iraqis and military that we were working together. That was to fade when broadcasting ended and the military withdrew, leaving the Iraqis to their own fate in the bombed-out chaos we had just created for them.

24

NO BETTER FRIEND, NO WORSE ENEMY

Life without liberty is like a body without spirit. —Kahlil Gibran

Days rolled slowly by in the desert, and I was caught between boredom and insanity, trying to find the median. What made the days bearable were the trips down to the water treatment area where we got our clean water. It was the only time we left the safe area past the wire. Staff Sergeant Gorman, the motor-T officer, in charge of all the vehicles in my unit, had discovered Ali and Kasim, college-educated brothers who were the water plant's engineers and spoke some broken English.

When we arrived, we saw the area the local Iraqis called the "Ali Babas"—a large area of project-like homes filled with what some Iraqis called "undesirables and suspected criminals."

Children screamed and held out their hands for candy. We threw coveted care package items out, and they fought each other for the handouts. As we drove farther, two little girls of about eight and ten smiled and waved. I fell in love with them instantly. We threw out more candy and food. We reached a secured area near the river and parked the humvees. I got out and walked over to where Ali had set up a business for himself. A two-story, government-style white building was the designated water treatment plant, but it was no longer operational. Instead, the Army was helping them fix the water for the city. Ali was a medium-sized man who had a recently acquired gut after the coalition came to the country. He had a sideline—selling cold sodas and food to the military units who passed through here. He consumed a substantial amount of his wares, which accounted for his weight gain.

"He's making $1,000 a day," Staff Sergeant Gorman told me.

"A thousand? That's a fortune! What's he going to do with all that money?"

"He says he's going to buy the city of Ad Diwaniyah!"

"Good to go! I love capitalism."

By the river, the American military water purification system's bladder, a large rubber container, sucked up water from the turgid, charcoal-colored Euphrates. The water passed through a series of bladders until it was fit to drink and then decanted into a cistern. Towed military water tanks would pull up and pump water from the cistern through giant hoses. Vehicles from the Army, Navy, and Marine Corps lined up for hours to get drinking water for their units. In the distance lay a small village, unmarked by any changes throughout the centuries, sheltered by sorghum, tall date palms, and eucalyptus trees. The mud homes had no electricity, but the town was lovingly maintained, with no trash or debris lying about. I looked curiously behind the elaborate layers of barbed wire that separated me from the rest of Iraq. Just then, several children, who had been playing in the river, ran over. I was horrified by how the children swam in and drank the water from this festering river that probably had enough bacteria and malaria to wipe out all of Manhattan. But the children, apparently unharmed by the water's effects, stood by us, separated only by the barbed wire. They looked curiously at the Sergeant to my left, a handsome light-skinned black man, and started giggling. One of the taller older boys pointed at him and said, "Michael Jackson!"

The Sergeant's face turned bright red, but we all laughed with the children. I asked them as best as I could what their names were. The two girls had nutmeg-hued complexions and wore brightly colored handmade chadors. The five boys, who had been swimming, wore bathing suits and half-buttoned shirts.

"My name is Jane," I said in botched Arabic.

"Ani isme Miriam," the taller girl in orange said.

The oldest boy, the comedian of the group, said, "Hassan—Ani Hassan." The rest introduced themselves so fast that I didn't catch most of their names. They turned back to the Sergeant to my left and giggled, "Michael Jackson!"

It was impossible not to feel sympathy and love for these smiling, impoverished children. Hassan and his pack were impeccably good-natured, and his smile held no reservations and no lies. Anyone would be won over by his guilelessness. But there he stood, behind the barbed wire near where he lived. It was only then that I realized that even though I was American, this was where I lived, too. We were not unlike him, and he and his brothers and sisters would determine the future of this place someday. We were part of their future. Our fates were intertwined by the brief intersection of two foreign worlds. And, just for a moment, we stood there together laughing.

Their mother, who obviously wasn't comfortable with her children talking to Americans, screamed for them to come back. I snapped a couple of photos of them, and they had to go. We said our good-byes, but Hassan's eyes lingered for a moment, watching us walk away. He studied the incredible contraption that pumped water out of his river. Hassan must have thought it curious that the Americans had to go through all this to purify water that he swam in and drank his entire life. His eyes lingered on this marvel of technology, and then he turned and ran back to his village.

★   ★   ★

As we walked back to the main building, Ali came over to meet me. He shook my hand and then placed his right hand over his heart as a sign of respect. I did the same, so as to not insult them. Ali wore blue coveralls and sandals. His English was broken, but as with most Iraqis, he pretended he understood more than he actually did. He brought a cold soda for me to drink.

"How much?" I asked.

"No, no. No money."

"Thank you." It was my first cold soda in a long time, and I drank it fast. Ali's son was sitting in a cheap plastic chair but was quickly booted out and the seat was offered to me. I declined at first, but they insisted, so I politely sat down. Ali's father sat in front of me. He looked like he was in his sixties or seventies and wore the traditional dishdasha gown and black-and-white headdress. He did not look at me, but stared into the distance, oblivious to the fact that we were there.

Staff Sergeant Gorman had struck all kinds of deals with Ali, purchasing hookahs, teapots, rugs, and other ornamental items. Ali made daily runs to the souk, where he purchased all the items and undoubtedly made ten times the profit on what he sold. I was more than eager to feed the economy after what I had seen. Ali offered me falafel and vegetables. It was my first non-MRE meal in about three months. I scarcely had time to swallow. Food never tasted so good. I sat there, smugly satiated. Kasim, Ali's brother, whom Staff Sergeant Gorman had described as crazy, now joined us and asked if we would like some tea. Kasim was a thin, attractive man in his thirties but covered in sweat and sand from working. We agreed and followed him back into the water treatment building. Inside was a small room with a table, some chairs, and a small teapot.

Ali's son accompanied us and put little shot glasses in front of us, emptying copious amounts of sugar into them. Some Marines from another unit who evidently knew Kasim joined us. One gave Kasim his Sergeant rank insignia. He jokingly placed the metal insignia in the center of his gray dishdasha. Someone had already given him a boonie cover, one of the soft hats the Marines wore while on deployment. Kasim wasn't really crazy—in fact, he seemed very clever; he just liked to talk and smile a lot.

He spoke very little English, but Kasim was good at pantomiming with his hands. Through his version of charades, he got across the message he was trying to convey, and we had a reasonable conversation. The little pocket dictionary Kasim produced was a lot of help, too, as my Arabic was worse than Kasim's English. A Corporal walked in, and Kasim pointed to his new Sergeant rank insignia. Then he motioned at the Corporal, clapped his hands together, and said, "You! You bring water!"

We all laughed. The Corporal was shocked at first but then caught on, playing along by pretending to stand at the position of attention. Kasim was having fun playing Sergeant. Kasim told us, "See, I am American soldier now!"

He looked at the Lance Corporal who had come in with the Corporal. He gestured, asking who was higher in rank, the Lance Corporal or himself. The Lance Corporal motioned that Kasim was higher ranking. Kasim immediately said, "Push-ups, now!" as he mimicked the motion with his hand.

We all rolled in laughter. Next he pointed to Staff Sergeant Gorman. "No, I don't think so—I'm higher!"

Kasim laughed and said, "Yes, sir!" Next he motioned at my gold bars. Staff Sergeant Gorman shook his head and made the crazy gesture with his hand, then added, "She's an officer!"

"Oh!" His face lit up, and he immediately lifted his hand, stood up, and gave me an Iraqi salute. We again burst out in laughter.

Kasim and I discussed Iraqi politics and the fact that most Iraqis were not happy with Ahmed Chalabi, leader of Free Iraqi Fighters and Iraqi National Congress. They felt he was interested only in money and fame. As for Muhammad Baqir Al Hakim, who was apparently one of the foremost Twelver Shi'a Muslim leaders in Iraq, Kasim liked him a great deal, although he was not necessarily popular with everyone. All Shi'ites, however, revered Ayatollah Sistani—he was their holy father, their guide through the darkness, as Kasim tried to explain. I liked Sistani from what I had read about him, and this made Kasim very happy. Sistani and Hakim were part of the *marjiya*, the most respected of four senior Shi'ite clerics in the country. Sistani was the leader who issued the fatwa instructing Iraqis not to attack or resist coalition forces. He had in many ways created the momentum for us to win the war with minimal casualities. Hakim brought influence from Iran. Kasim's face beamed with joy. He liked talking politics and religion. He went into the other room and came back with a poster of Al Hakim.

"For you!"

"Thank you, Kasim!"

"For you, thank you." We finished our tea and left for the camp. Kasim walked us out of the building. He hoped I would come back another day. But that was the last I saw of him. Staff Sergeant Gorman told me that every day after that, Kasim and Ali asked when the blond-haired woman would return. Apparently, I had made quite the impression—probably because I was the only female officer they ever met. Now, I was stuck in the camp. Higher command had been getting word about increased attacks on convoys, so leaving the wire was out of the question. That night, after my encounter with Kasim, it was especially hot. Nights were no relief from the weather—sometimes the coolest point in the night would be 100°. Sweat poured off me at midnight as I lay under the bivy sack trying to sleep. Without the bivy sack, malaria-carrying mosquitoes attacked, and I was no longer taking my anti-malaria medicine. Nearby gunfire echoed through the night. The war wasn't over, not really.

★   ★   ★

Back at our camp, other units were pulling out around us. Where once there were thousands of Marines, now only a handful remained, including 130 from my squadron. Although our plan was to go to Al Kut, we still had to wait for word. Our whole squadron had packed up and was prepared to move, but we waited and waited. Lieutenant Colonel Mykleby was getting severely pissed off. The seven battalions of the Marine Expeditionary Brigade remained. 1/7 and 2/5 were going to leave soon, though, leaving only five dedicated units behind. Then there was us—UAV grunts. We were now 1st Marine Division's northern security, a kind of provisional rifle company. We were left, we imagined, to rot in the dust of this god-forsaken place.

Near the last remaining elements of 1st Marine Division was a big sign with their logo on it—a blue diamond with stars and a big number 1 in the center indicating they were 1st Marine Division. Flanking the sign was their slogan, "No better friend, no worse enemy." To me, this meant we could be professional and courteous world diplomats, but if you showed hostility, we'd kill you. Former President Ronald Reagan once said that Marines can hold a small child in one hand and shoot an enemy with the other and know the difference between the two. I would learn later that Iraqis didn't fully understand the meaning of the slogan and thus found it offensive. They took this Janus-like motto to mean that we were duplicitous and could turn from friend to enemy at a moment's notice. To many Iraqis, it meant that we pretended to be their friends but knew them to be enemies. Just as much of Arab culture didn't translate well for Americans, this slogan definitely was outside Arab ideology.

Back inside the wire, the MEF CG and the MAW CG had come to visit Division Headquarters. They were the last unit left besides my own before they, too, pulled out. Strangely, they brought the band with them. I never figured out what a band was doing in combat. Their band, part of Division Headquarters, played the solemn sound of "Waltzing Matilda" in the distance. The sadness of the song fit with the dismal surroundings. I listened to the melody, remembering the words in my mind:

> Once a jolly swagman camped by a Billabong
> Under the shade of a Coolabah tree
> And he sang as he watched and waited till his billy boiled
> "Who'll come a-waltzing Matilda with me?"
>
> Down come a jumbuck to drink at the water hole
> Up jumped a swagman and grabbed him in glee
> And he sang as he stowed him away in his tucker bag
> "You'll come a-waltzing Matilda with me."
>
> Up rode the Squatter a-riding his thoroughbred
> Up rode the Trooper—one, two, three
> "Where's that jumbuck you've got in your tucker bag?"
> "You'll come a-waltzing Matilda with me."
>
> But the swagman he up and jumped in the water hole
> Drowning himself by the Coolabah tree,
> And his ghost may be heard as it sings in the Billabong,
> "Who'll come a-waltzing Matilda with me?"

Lieutenant Colonel Mykleby, in an attempt to find out what was going on, walked over to Division and found the group of upper echelon officers and the wing CG. He told them, "We're ready to leave; we just need the word to go."

"Have at it, Mick!" said the wing CG. "Al Kut is a good place. You'll like it there. You'll have your own hangar, maybe air conditioning."

"Great."

But while the CO was walking back to our unit area, a message had come from MEF, and Major Cepeda, my XO, told him, "Sir, Division wanted to relay from MEF that we can't leave until we have a FragO."

"What kind of bullshit is that? The wing CG said we could go!"

You could see from his expression he was caught in a bind. He struggled with calling MEF up and chewing them out. It made me realize that the power struggle never gets easier, no matter what your rank is. There's always someone who will use their rank, even if they don't know better, to try to call the shots.

The Major Cepeda pulled out a fresh cigarette from his stash and lit it. Calmly, he asked, "So what else did the Generals have to say?"

"Well, I asked them when we're going home."

"And what did they say?"

"Funny you should ask. One of the Generals who shall remain nameless said, 'Don't worry about that, just focus on your mission, and you'll go when you're no longer needed.' That seemed understandable, I thought, but as I was walking away, I heard the same General get on the phone and say, 'Can you please tell me at what time my plane leaves today to go to CONUS?'"

"The bastard!" one of the officers chimed in.

"Jesus!" said another.

The rest of us just shook our heads. Even though he wasn't happy, our CO always kept us in the loop of exactly what was happening. He wanted us to know where we stood and what was going on at every level. My CO walked around and talked individually to all the officers. He came over to me, and we made small talk.

As we talked, I looked out into the distance and saw a group of Iraqis in the truck graveyard about two hundred meters away. It looked like they were just looting, but I said, "Sir, it looks like our Iraqi neighbors are back."

"Someone call the watch officer, and let's get a patrol out there immediately to push them back!"

The Sergeant Major got up and started walking toward the nearest Iraqi. Since he was alone, I decided he needed backup. I got up and started walking. The CO said, "Where are you going, Boots?"

"I'm going to watch Sergeant Major Rew's back, sir," I said with a smile. He laughed, and I walked off.

By the time I caught up with Sergeant Major Rew, we were about fifty or seventy-five meters away from the Iraqis. They all edged away from us, never really looking at us but sensing we were there. We watched as about ten of them picked up everything they could carry, from wooden shitters to empty oil barrels.

"Good lord, they're just scavengers!" said the Sergeant Major. "What brings you out here, by the way, ma'am?"

"I didn't want you getting all the action on your own."

He smiled. The Sergeant Major was very much the embodiment of what you'd imagine a Marine, grunt, and prior drill instructor to be like. Sergeants Major are like legends or the backbones of units—they are the grandfathers of the family. If the CO is the father of a unit, they are the experience behind it—the authority, the adviser. They are the gray-headed, bearded ones to whom all defer. They say every great man has a great woman behind him. I'd say in the Marine Corps, every great CO has a great Sergeant Major behind him. That's why the Commandant gets to pick his own Sergeant Major. It's that dynamic team of leadership and experience that forges the swift and deadly weapon at the tip of each command's power.

"So what do you think, ma'am?"

"Looks like a bunch of teenage punks. It's not them I'm worried about; it's the crazy one they tell who comes by himself and decides to pull a suicide bomb attack."

We crouched down behind some shrubs and waited for them to come closer.

"Let's see what they'll do," the Sergeant Major said.

"Probably scream when they see the likes of you!"

"Thanks, ma'am!" He smiled. As the Iraqis drew closer, they spotted us and began moving away, still carrying the junk they had acquired. Only two weeks ago, this had been the site of my tryst with my husband. How different it had been then.

It was the hour of the call to prayer. Usually the muezzin's voice was disquieting and urgent. But this voice was haunting, gentle, and siren-like, beckoning the faithful to come to prayer. The voice softened the heat and the surroundings. It stilled the evening. The Iraqi teens walked with a slow methodical pace. But they got too close, so I arose and screamed in Arabic, "Hallas! Mu zen! Emshee!" ("Stop! Not good! Go away!")

They took off running, but they weren't scared enough to drop all the gear they took. The Sergeant Major and I laughed, watching them run off with their hands full.

"Ma'am, you've got a lotta fire!" He chuckled again and added, "It's good to have you here with us; you're a good player in this unit."

As the Sergeant Major was speaking, we turned around, and a squad of Marines from our unit came up behind us in full patrol attire. We debriefed the squad, and they went storming ahead.

"They'll chase them out," I said.

"You know, this reminds me a lot of Beirut."

"You were there, Sergeant Major?"

"Yup, and we can't get too complacent. We were complacent in Beirut. I got there right after the Beirut bombing. There was so much the Marines could have done to prevent it. But higher told the Marines they could not keep ammo in their weapons. The Marines assumed they were secure because they were in condition 4, and the threat was thought to be low. But they were wrong. It was all a misperception."

"This place is totally unsecured. It would be easy for someone to slip through our guards at night. We're right next to the city. You're right, Sergeant Major Rew, we need to move. The only thing we can rely on right now is that this town seems not to mind us too much. Just one more night, that's all." We started walking back toward the camp.

"You know, ma'am . . ."

"Yes?"

"You never forget those you go to war with. We'll remember this always. All of us will probably lose touch at some point, but we will never forget. One day you'll see one of them, and it will seem like not a day has gone by. My buddies I went to Beirut with, I saw one at the Walmart and we didn't care, we hugged each other right there in front of everybody. There's no brotherhood or sisterhood like the bonds we form in combat."

25

RIBBONS

A soldier will fight long and hard for a bit of colored ribbon.

—Napoleon

As far as I'm concerned, there are only two types of people who want to go to war: the insane and the naive," Captain Piper said as we sat around philosophizing. "The insane want to go because they either don't care about anything in the world, or they're just freaking sociopaths! The naive—they want to go because they're young. They're your eighteen-year-olds who are too fresh to have experienced anything: the pain of death or injury."

The rest of us, we didn't like war and didn't want anything more than for things to resolve so we could go home. Sure, we, too, had been thrilled by the glamour of war. We had been excited by the prospect of killing. We had wanted to feel the rush of the bullet whizzing past our faces as we imagined ourselves heroically firing back. We wanted to come home with all the new ribbons on our chests or at least with the knowledge that we had done right. Of course, we were told that we weren't getting the coveted Combat Action Ribbon because we were a wing unit, even though all the units around us, and some behind us, were getting the ribbon. We didn't really understand why wing units didn't rate the ribbon, or why we specifically didn't. But we didn't really care because in our hearts we knew what we had done.

But ribbons are not what war is about. Much of war is the painful process of waiting for those decisive movements. War is the execution of convoys, logistical training, the Pentagon's lengthy deliberations, the endless months of waiting, and the cleaning up afterward. It is all the unglamorous things. It is being part of a chaotic flash in history over which you have no control, and all you can do is sit, wait, and watch until you are summoned to perform your role in combat. For some, that means a moment of sheer adrenaline and then a muzzle flash from the enemy. For others, it means the ecstasy of flying an F–18 over Baghdad and the memory of dropping bombs over a target. For the unfortunate, it means living a life with the scars, either mental or physical, from battle—never returning to the former way of life again. For some, it would be flag-draped coffins, watched by their crying families and friends as they were lowered into the ground. For me, it was a whirlwind tour of Iraq through the eyes of a UAV's camera lens, and now the never-ending and useless wait to get home.

Someone cut the wire to the feed on the UAV, so we could not receive images. That meant our flights were down for a couple days. Who did it, and why, no one knew. Maybe it was someone who thought we would go home if we couldn't fly. Sergeant Leppan and Sergeant Beaty took to reading reports on the computer and keeping to themselves. Sergeant Young, as chipper as ever, volunteered for patrols around the city. It was around that time that Lieutenant Lisa Bishop stopped talking to me. She stopped talking to everyone. She either slept or disappeared to do her own thing. She wouldn't tell me what was wrong, and we had slowly grown apart. Admittedly, I had abandoned her for the selfish reason that I had realized she was very different from me. Lately, she had seemed to be going rather "equal opportunity" crazy. What got me was when she spray-painted over some abstract Arab graffiti on the walls of the abandoned administration building we were using. Lieutenant Colonel Mykleby asked her what she was doing.

"It's offensive and obscene, sir. I'm not going to work in these conditions." The graffiti on the wall looked like bodies, but it was too abstract to tell for sure. All the officers took turns staring at the graffiti on the wall that had offended her so much, and no one could figure out exactly what she was seeing.

"Offensive and obscene? After all we've been through, this is offensive to you?" It had appeared irrational to most of the officers, and after that event I began to distance myself further from her. I didn't do it deliberately; it just happened. I felt bad that the rest of the officers and I made fun of some of the irrational things she would do. The strange thing was, I had become buddies with a number of the male officers, and the more I distanced myself from her, the more they seemed to accept me. Even though she was senior to me by a year, she was much younger than I was. I tried to talk to her several more times, but she didn't want to have anything to do with me. Yet her distancing from me and other members of the unit still bothered me. Toward the end of my time there, I asked her if I had wronged or offended her, and she simply said, "Since you asked, there were rumors going around that a Marine saw a female Lieutenant having sex in a seven-ton."

"What?"

"Yeah, and guess what? They came to me and asked if it was me. I was so humiliated. How could you do that, Jane? People thought it was me, but it was really you!"

"What the hell are you talking about?"

"Don't deny it."

"First of all, if it had been me, I wouldn't deny it. But more importantly, how could you do to me what you were complaining people were doing to you?"

"What am I doing?"

"You're assigning blame about something you have no proof for and assuming it is true. Think of this logically: I wouldn't even drink water on the convoy for fear of someone seeing me going to the bathroom. Why would I expose myself in the middle of camp by doing something so flagrantly indiscreet?"

"Well, it wasn't me."

"Did you ever think that maybe the source is wrong?" She shook her head and walked away. The accusation pissed me off—obviously, some Marine was passing around rumors, and people believed them. Moreover, having another female blatantly make assumptions was enough to make me not want to deal with her. Lisa and I never really spoke, apart from exchanges related to our duties, after that. I was professional and polite, but I found her entirely irrational. What made it worse was that this was so trivial in the larger scheme of things. We were in combat, after all, not high school. Had she been holding this grudge the entire time? No one else ever said anything to me, which I assume is because they knew that the Marine was doing what all Marines do: making shit up for fun.

★   ★   ★

The next morning, we pulled out of Ad Diwaniyah and moved to Al Kut. Al Kut was reported to be better, since the wing had taken the area over, but I had my doubts. Farther north, that's all I knew. So once again we were on the road for hours until we reached our new area. We reached our hardened hangars, giant concrete structures that once must have housed MIGs. We set up and moved 130 cots into the main bunker area like a giant squad bay. My despair had reached an all-time low. I put my new cot down and wished I would wake up on some Caribbean island.

A mass graveyard of dead mosquitoes was strewn across the deck near my rack area. I stared down at the sweat collecting on my pants. Psychotically, I waited with sniper-like silence to get the next perpetrator with my fly swatter. I had fifty-three confirmed kills. My boredom and rage were running deep. I stared down at my dirty, sweat-stained trousers, which were now also covered with mosquito guts and blood.

Our sister squadron, which had been at this location for a month and was about to leave, told us they hadn't flown in two weeks. So now we would be on standby. I wished I could at least go on patrols, but we weren't allowed. We wouldn't even be flying. No one could tell us why we were still here, no one could justify it, no one was responsible, and no one cared. This endless waiting was the military purgatory. I saw myself growing old in this hardened bunker, sitting here with gray hair, never to know what real life was like again. One day, someone would happen upon us, as in *Heart of Darkness*, and wonder why we had all gone insane. A lot of the Staff NCOs didn't even smile anymore. One just stared into the distance, a cigarette burning, unsmoked and wasting away between his fingers. How did they manage during World War II? Vietnam? I wanted to smash something with my fist.

I got up to sit with Doc Casey and Captain Piper, my usual breakfast buddies. I watched Sergeant Leppan and Corporal Warseck mock sword fighting in the distance. I flipped through some magazines from care packages as I waited for my MRE meal to heat up. I had purchased, from Ali's black market, a pound of Arabic tea from a local market, but I had resolved not to become dependent on caffeine again if I couldn't get it regularly. But that morning, I was ready to begin my addiction again. Doc Casey had gotten a portable water heater when the mobile PX passed by our unit the day before. After offering them all some tea, I eagerly poured an enormous cup for myself. We sat around talking about the news of the day.

"This tea tastes good, but I'm not feeling anything," I said. "I don't think it's very strong." I kept drinking. The mint tea had the strong aroma of smoky herbs.

"That's strange. That stuff is usually concentrated," Doc Casey said. I drank about half a cup more, and then I suddenly started feeling light-headed.

"Are you OK?" Doc Casey asked.

"Yeah—I'm just a little dizzy." I started feeling queasy, like I was going to throw up. Doc Casey looked at me curiously. I was expecting the doctor to do something, but he just sat there passively gazing at me. My face contorted from the nausea, and I tried to conceal it. Oh God, I was going to throw up. No, no, I was actually poisoned and I was about to die. I went through about twenty different emotions in twenty seconds.

"You're turning green, Jane," Captain Piper said, amused.

"Are you sure you're OK?"

"I think . . . I'm starting to feel the caffeine a little."

"Yeah, no shit! You sure are!"

I threw up around the corner, and I threw away the rest of the tea leaves.

★　★　★

There was a bit more freedom of movement at Al Kut's Blair airfield. It was late May or June now, but time blended together. We were completely detached from the Iraqis and the rest of the Marine Corps. We seldom interacted with the local population. So much for winning the hearts and minds. We knew the majority bore us goodwill and seemed positively affected by our coming, but with no contact, how were we expected to keep the peace? The services in Al Kut, at least, had now improved since we had arrived, or so we were told. When restrictions were lifted, we finally took convoys into town; where once we had seen riots and protests, now we saw hands upheld in praise and thumbs-up. As a female, I got air kisses from young boys, who shouted, "I love you, madam!"

One day a group of Marines and I drove to what we called the B-2 building. This was where local leaders met with military leaders only a month and a half ago. The building, which looked nice from the UAV, was not what we had expected. Instead, like all buildings in Al Kut, it was rundown and decrepit. Coalition forces had secured all the buildings in the area. Civil affairs occupied the buildings and were working with the locals to put the city back together. Inside was an Iraqi-run restaurant. We had driven to the building with a seven-ton so there were about twenty Marines with me. I was with the XO, Major Cepeda, and he asked the owners if we could eat. They said no—the restaurant had not yet opened for business. As everyone was about to give up, I decided to give it a shot. I went up and asked again, and they smiled and said, "For you, madam, we will open early."

I went back to my XO and the Marines with a grin on my face. "They are going to let us eat."

"So much for rank!" one of the Staff Sergeants said.

We dined on local cuisine—vegetables, pita, tamarind sauce, meat—and french fries. We were famished, but our shrunken stomachs couldn't digest all the food on front of us. For $1.50 each, we had feasted. As we rode back, I noticed the concrete murals that once displayed images of Saddam now were being painted over to display Al Hakim. Al Hakim was not their leader, just a religious figurehead. Apparently there was a lot we didn't understand about the Shi'ites. His importance was due to his role as part of the *marja'yiat,* a council of the most senior imams in Iraq. These images, these spaces in their lives, would need to be filled. They did not understand the idea of democracy and did not understand that the Ba'ath party no longer controlled them. Only three months later, it seemed as if Hakim might be the Shi'as' new hope. But that hope was soon crushed as Hakim's convoy was attacked by Muqtada al-Sadr's minions, and he was killed. Al-Sadr was the son of a prominent cleric, the late Grand Ayatollah Mohammad Mohammad Sadeq al-Sadr, and the cousin of Musa al-Sadr, the well-respected Iranian-Lebanese founder of the Amal Movement, who had disappeared. Al-Sadr's father was believed to have been killed by Saddam Hussein, and his whole family was a prominent Shi'ite family with strong connections to Iran. He and his fighters would create enormous problems for American forces, more so than we had known at the time. Many times we watched Muqtada al-Sadr through the eye of the UAV camera and wondered if he would be another al-Reef or something much more.

Coalition forces along the way busied themselves teaching the Iraqi police force how to patrol and manage this zone, rather than abandoning their posts at night when they got tired and bored. Similarly, the Iraqi people were taught by civil affairs how to reconstruct their utilities, although many of their citizens were trained professionals in those fields. But they weren't used to making decisions and would abandon projects if not supervised the whole way through. Everything was taking on a Persian influence. All of the flyers, murals, and recent signs had a mild Iranian undertone. I wasn't sure what to make of it.

★   ★   ★

At last we reached our camp and airfield again, only a few miles out of town. We pulled up at our hardened bunker, where the overhead lights were full of nesting birds that fiercely scrambled for food to feed their young. Owls, hawks, and other birds made this place home along with our UAV bird. It looked like an aviary. Our new location was on an airfield, with gigantic concrete hangars across the runway. The place hadn't been in use since the Gulf War. Iraqi jets had been housed here before; our entire squadron fit underneath the football field–length hangar.

The doctor had begun issuing a number of Marines "happy pills," which were purple pills with smiley faces on them. I saw the doctor bring them to Marines, but I didn't know if they were a placebo or a real drug. I never inquired as to what Doc Casey was giving them, as long as it helped bring their morale up. In a strange way, Iraq was growing on me. I stared out into an open field and got up to run around the bunkers in my boots. Exercising was a positive step. But when I returned, the CO called me over.

"Jane, we got a new flight for some of the Marines, and you are on it."

"Sir, I'm leaving? But when will you and the rest of the Marines be going back to CONUS?"

"Jane, we'll be joining you in a couple weeks. Get things set up for us back there so that we don't come back to a bunch of renegade Marines."

"How many Marines are back in the rear, sir?" I asked.

"Over forty-five. That's why we need an officer back there."

"But . . ."

"Go!" he said.

I said my good-byes to the XO and some of the officers. The XO, who was smoking, looked at me and said, "Drink one for me."

I didn't tell most of the Marines I was leaving, since they were expected to follow in a couple weeks' time. I didn't want all the gushy good-byes when they would be following me shortly. Not to mention that I felt guilty that I was leaving them.

★ ★ ★

From Al Kut, I took a C-130 with a Corporal from my unit back to Kuwait. Destination: Al Jaber, an Air Force base that was the lap of luxury—the true decadence of the wing in all its spoiled glory. And I couldn't wait to indulge in much-needed rest and relaxation. But until I got on the plane to America—rather, until I stepped *off* the plane *in* America—I wasn't getting excited. Anything could happen, especially while I was riding in a C-130 over Iraq, and the plane was encountering air turbulence. Just about everyone in the plane felt like throwing up. Some Marines held bags over their mouths in anticipation, while others put their heads in between their legs. The bumpy ride reminded me how terrified I am of flying. It wasn't just that—for the first time in months, I was on my own, and I felt surprisingly isolated. Then suddenly, I felt guilty and uneasy about leaving my unit. My eyes scanned the plane. About thirty-five Marines sat stoic, warrior-like, and silent as the plane edged south. For most of us, it was our first time out of Iraq since the war began. Everyone looked torn up. Some had been injured. I wondered if I looked as grim as they all did.

★ ★ ★

We arrived in Al Jaber without incident, and Staff Sergeant Gray was there to greet us. He was assigned to provide logistical support to our unit from the rear areas, and I was glad to see someone from my unit again. We arrived in Al Jaber just in time for dinner. I was looking forward to feasting for the first time in five months.

But once I got there, I was overwhelmed. It wasn't the vacation resort I had imagined. Well, it was, but I didn't enjoy any of it. They had a multitude of activities for the Air Force, Navy, and Marines: swimming pools, billiards, cable television, a twenty-four-hour movie theater, a huge PX, a gym. Air Force members luxuriated by the pool, catching rays in their bathing suits and playing in the pool with a giant colored ball. I couldn't identify with those women at all; it was as though I didn't understand them anymore. Female and male Navy personnel walked by, laughing among themselves, all done up in their clean uniforms. But I simply felt alienated. I was on my way to the armory, as it was on my check-in list of things to do and a requirement for all military members who arrive on base. When I got to the armory, I wasn't exactly sure why I was there or what I was supposed to do. The Air Force armorer, a young, honest-looking boy with a fresh haircut, told me to hand over my pistol in exchange for a ticket receipt. He handed me a piece of paper with the base rules for weapons. Apparently, you were allowed to keep your weapons if you were on base for short, unspecified periods of time, though no one was clear about how long that amount of time was. According to the paper, most people elected to turn their weapons in because you couldn't go to the gym, PX, and certain other buildings with weapons.

"I'm not giving you my pistol," I said after reading the paper.

"But everyone turns their weapon in," said the armorer. He reached over to grab my weapon.

"Get the fuck off my weapon," I said.

"OK, no need to get hostile, ma'am. You can keep your weapon if you want."

I didn't care if there was a rule or if this was the safest fucking place on earth. I was keeping my weapon.

26

THE TWILIGHT'S LAST GLEAMING

May it be my privilege to have the happiness of establishing the commonwealth on a firm and stable basis and thus enjoy the reward that I desire, but only if I may be called the architect of the best possible government, and bear with me the hope when I die that the foundations that I have laid for its future government will stand deep and secure.

—Caesar Augustus

Some historians speculate that if North Korea invaded South Korea, they would be unable to fight once they reached the streets of Seoul because they would be overwhelmed by stimuli and activities they had never seen or heard before. The starved and deprived North Koreans would be so in awe of the lights, shops, smells, and taste of food that they would simply go into shock. They called this the "mall theory."

When I walked into the chow hall in Al Jaber, this is how I felt. The fact that I had choices and was in a room with lights and doors and air conditioning was strange enough. But here was a hall filled with several hundred military, and a cafeteria with a soda machine, juices, milk, a cappuccino machine, fresh meat, vegetables, starches, choices of bread, and a cornucopia of desserts. Nothing unusual by American standards, but when you've been in the desert eating nothing but MREs and sand, food itself becomes astonishing. I had gone to chow with the Staff Sergeant, and I marveled over the wonder called food and piled my tray high. As I sat down to eat, food never tasted so good. To my surprise, however, I could barely eat anything. My appetite had so greatly diminished that I was full almost immediately. Fullness was followed by horrible stomach cramps. I stared at my nearly full tray of food.

Staff Sergeant Grey looked at me and said, "That's normal. For some reason, everyone who comes back gets sick right away."

"I wonder why that is . . ."

"All the preservatives in MREs or something. Your body forgets what real food tastes like."

"It's just strange." But I was sure it was partially due to starvation and that my stomach had shrunk.

★   ★   ★

After chow, I separated from the Staff Sergeant to go to my air-conditioned tent. This place was crazy. Even the laundry trailers were air conditioned. It made me angry to think that members of the Air Force were living in such excess and could do nothing for the forward units. I had become so serious. My CO was right; I had changed a great deal. Al Jaber and rear-echelon motherfuckers made me feel uncomfortable. I realized I didn't want to be like them after what I had been through in Iraq. I understood how the grunts felt when they returned to higher headquarters. How could these people justify getting all these luxuries when, at the front lines, my Marines barely had one MRE a day? I wanted to go back.

I wanted to deliberately separate myself from these people. My uniform, still dirty, my weapon, and my sleeves down made me look different. Marines wear their sleeves down in combat, and as far as I was concerned, there was still combat going on. On the way back to my tent, I stopped at the gym to see what kind of facilities they had and caught sight of my reflection in a mirror. I barely recognized myself. I stepped on the scale: ninety-seven pounds. I had lost fifteen pounds. I looked like a child in the mirror.

I walked out into the twilight, the air still sauna warm. I liked the warmth; I had gotten used to it. As I walked through the huge camp, I found myself behind a member of the Air Force. He was walking slowly, and it annoyed me. I kept trying to pass him, but the path was too narrow. He slowed down and kept turning around to look at me. Finally, he turned and said, "Ma'am, did I do something wrong?"

"No, why would you say that?"

"I just thought you were going to kill me!"

"No, no. Not this time." Good lord, what kind of person had I become?

The fact was that, more than ever, I felt like I no longer needed anything. I had done without luxuries; now they were superfluous. Truly, I was a stranger. I had abandoned my squadron, I couldn't get in touch with my husband, and the world of America was just a distant thought. How could I get life back in me? If Al Jaber was bad, how would the civilian world of America be?

I was almost apprehensive to go back to the United States, into the foreign world of America. The post-deployment brief I was forced to listen to said we would be distant, independent, changed. Would I ever learn to love the good things in life again, or would I be permanently scarred by this place? Would I find enjoyment again in the trivialities of life? Would I know my husband at all when I returned? Would he be the same loving person? Would I relate to civilians? For a moment, I wanted to turn around and go back to Iraq. Something sick inside me called me back to that place. Iraq had grown familiar and strangely safe. I had grown to know and, in a way, love those people.

At last it was time to get on the plane. After forty-eight hours at Al Jaber, a place I never wanted to return to, I began the painful forty-eight-hour process of going home. The Army ran the twelve-hour preboarding waiting period at the airport. We had no clue why, but likely just to torture us some more. All of our bags were emptied and searched thoroughly for war trophies or unexploded ordnance, and K-9 dogs sniffed our bags for drugs and explosives. When we moved into the final "sterile area," we slept again on the deck for many hours, waiting for an available plane. I wasn't the least bit bothered, because I knew I was on my way home.

We boarded a charter flight. They made the officers, including myself, board first and take the first-class seats. Since Kuwaiti International Airport was still considered a hostile zone, the entire flight crew was made up of volunteers. The flight attendants were bright and boisterous women, with their hair done up, lots of jewelry and perfume, grandmotherly types, who gave ample hugs to all the Marines on the flight. Our plane was a 777, so there were about four hundred people on the flight. A flight attendant, Barbara, came on the speaker.

"Welcome back, troops! Thank you for serving our country! It's a real honor for us to service this flight today! We just wanted to say, 'God bless America and God bless the Marines! We love you boys!'" All the Marines cheered, and we took off shortly thereafter. Barbara was the attendant for first class, and she had almost every conceivable rank insignia on her lapel. I gave her one of my Second Lieutenant bars. She didn't have one of those.

★　★　★

America was not at war on its home front. That was apparent when we landed, because life had returned to normal after 9/11. So much seemed forgotten in America, and it was hard to find news about the troops in Iraq. Signs saying "Thank you, troops" or "Welcome home" could be seen occasionally, as well as frayed yellow ribbons that had turned white from age. America was forgetting that more than one hundred thousand of its own were still in Iraq. At the time, in most civilians' minds, the war had ended on 1 May 2003, when Bush declared "major combat operations over."

I was flying over the world on my way back home. From my window I watched the world pass below, as though I was my little UAV passing overhead, spying on the world. We passed over Saudi Arabia, and I saw the pyramids in Egypt. Then we flew over Rome, and it was all there: a grand tour of humanity below. Something about seeing all that below made me not want to ever be on the ground again, but there is so much of the world that you can't understand by staring at it from above. The real truth was on the ground, talking to the people, seeing things eye to eye. I thought about my CO and the things he had said to me, and how I would be changed. I thought about the Iraqis and how they had shown compassion in a time when they should have been feeling fear or hate. There was so much I couldn't see from so high above.

★   ★   ★

I was picked up when the plane landed by some of my squadron mates who had returned on an earlier trip. Banners and food welcomed the Marines back at the hangar at Miramar Navy Base, near San Diego, California, about a two- to three-hour drive away from my base. Walking off the plane, I shook a bunch of high-ranking officers' hands as I deboarded and walked to the reception area, where I quickly seized the initiative and downed a half a beer. I was instantly and effectively drunk. It was perhaps the fastest high ever achieved.

The thought of returning straight home made me happy. The Marines from my unit drove the Corporal and me back in their government vehicle, but they told us along the way that they had orders to take us back to the base, not my actual house. This was apparently SOP for all returning Marines. The Marines told me they had already let my husband know that the rendezvous point had changed. As we entered the darkness of the desert on the three-hour drive back to Twentynine Palms, the terrain around us was eerily similar to Iraq.

It was 0300, the middle of the night. Pulling into the base, we were driven up to the gym, where, to my surprise, hundreds of people assembled, including the Marine Corps band and base CG. But I didn't see my husband. As we got out of the vehicle, the few Marines and I got a round of applause from the crowd, the band played "Waltzing Matilda," the base CG shook our hands, and the Marines and their families were all cheering. It was a lot to take in. After saying the necessary niceties and reluctantly surrendering my 9mm and M16, I greeted the Marines from my unit who had come home earlier. They all said I looked starved.

I laughed, "Well, get the hell out my way so I can eat!"

I wasn't really hungry—I really just wanted to go home. Looking around, I didn't see my husband, and I kept searching the crowd, but I had some business to square away with my Marines. But when I turned around, Peter was standing by himself across the parking lot. I dropped everything, walked over, and instantly, his arms surrounded me. The warmth of his touch flooded me. And then, suddenly, everything seemed normal. Iraq, at least for that moment, became a dim and distant memory.

27

HOME OF THE BRAVE

*We used to wonder where war lived, what it was that made it so
vile. And now we realize that we know where it lives . . . inside
ourselves.*

—Albert Camus

Saddam and his sons had fled, their whereabouts unknown until a later
date. Uday and Qusay's bodies would be found later following a raid.
Saddam would be captured by Army units in Tikrit, his great kingdom now
crumbled like the ruins of Babylon, his infamous legend extinguished. He
was a man who was used to fleeing, having escaped death in assassination
attempts, military raids, bombs, and three wars. He was a master of disguise,
with multiple body doubles, trains of bodyguards, secret meeting places,
underground bunkers, torture chambers, and elusive convoys that ferried
him away at a moment's notice, always leaving a serpentine trail of vehicles
to throw anyone off his lead.

The first time I thought about going to war was when I was in the
movie theater with a friend watching the beginning of *Saving Private Ryan*,
where they're storming the beach at Normandy. My friend turned to me
and said, "You know, if there is one regret in my life, it's that I'll never
get to experience that."

At the time, I was thrown by his comment.

"Are you crazy?" I said. "Why would anyone want to do that?" What
I failed to understand at the time was that my friend was not marveling over
the horrors of war, but the heroic acts of soldiers in battle. That feeling,
which was barbaric to me as a civilian, now was obvious. People want to go
to war because they know others are depending on them. No longer do I
witness courageous acts of war as blind obedience and slavery. Although war

is neither beautiful nor joyous, the men and woman who defend this nation against hostility are selfless and admirable. I will never feel the regret that my friend had felt. I will always understand why someone would go to war.

As for the "enemy," most of the Iraqis we fought were not interested in fighting. They wanted a better life. The Iraqis' future, in fact, was very much tied to my own future. After all, as long as the war went on, I would be part of it. At home, I felt alienated. I thought about Iraq a lot and felt guilty that I wasn't there with the rest of the Marines left behind and the Iraqis. I wondered what it would be like to spend my whole life living under the conditions in which the Iraqis lived. It was so easy for us to feel superior to them. Meanwhile, during New York's power outage in August 2003, Americans behaved like savages. Many were panicking after just a few short hours without air conditioning, refrigerators, elevators, and television. Iraqis would endure this, and worse, for months and years to come.

During the transition, I felt responsible for what would happen in Iraq's future. If only I had done more. As United Nations and U.S. forces labored to create a better Iraq, it was obviously going to be a long struggle ahead. This wasn't some easy domestic fix; it was reconstructing the entire way of life of the Iraqi people. Who was going to do this? What was clear from my end is that I never really was able to leave Iraq behind in my mind. Something was different in my life; part of my old life would never be re-covered. I thought back to everything: the gas drills, the Scud attacks, near ambushes, the dead Marines, the artillery barrages on the Iraqis, refugees, nightmares, sickness, and the ongoing war. I thought about how lucky I had been to survive it, but how I would never be the same person again. There was sadness inside me now that I couldn't shake loose.

I returned to America and to a place that I no longer knew. I felt like I stepped into a culture where I had no commonality and no interest. I had become a stranger, and that existential emptiness I had felt during my rebellious teenage years returned. I didn't want to talk to anyone. Conversations with old friends focused on trivial problems in their own lives, and I found it hard to care. I wanted only to stay home and listen quietly to the sound of rain or read a book. Civilian frivolity alienated me. Everyone moved about in a slow, oblivious state, and I wanted to push them all out of the way. Civilians seemed like nothing but obstacles in the way of progress. If I was driving, they were preventing me from getting home. If I was walking, they appeared unaware of anything but themselves. They were ignorant and totally absorbed in their petty little lives. I was not home. The emptiness of this realization made me comfortable only in a military setting. It was hard to venture out into the civilian world. I began to wonder if my perception of the world would ever return to what it had been. I wanted to jump on a plane to a deserted island and live out a quiet existence. I had serious doubts that life would ever return to the way it was when I left.

Peter left for a second deployment within a couple of months after returning home. He would be gone for another nine months. I found it so hard to sleep while he was gone that I kept a .45 under my pillow. I had to adjust my sleep cycle so that I slept in the afternoons and woke up in the middle of the night. If someone knocked on the door, I could only answer it with the pistol behind my back, even if it turned out to be a Girl Scout selling cookies. The majority of Marines had returned now to the United States, and many were not the same. Post-traumatic stress disorder isn't just flipping out and killing someone: it is a failure to adjust to normal society. Every Marine had it. Some admitted it. Some drank and drank until they were pulled over for drunk driving. Some came home and used drugs. Others got into fights, while others left the Corps in pursuit of some boring, low-stress job. A few committed suicide. Some volunteered to go back to Iraq as soon as possible. Every Marine dealt with it differently. Eventually, I adjusted, but I'd never be quite the same person I was before.

My story is just one among the countless stories of Marines in combat. I can't help think back to the 250 Lieutenants with whom I went to The Basic School and who I will always count as my friends. Not all of them came back alive, and most of them didn't come back the same. We graduated together and were instantly put in a combat zone. Iraq had become the war that defined the Corps most of us knew. And although our war was different from Vietnam, from World War II, from the Korean War, there are many who hold stories that will become legend in the Corps, becoming part of its history. And many stories will be lost. Unless those stories are told, their history and their deeds will be forgotten.

Appendix A

RANKS IN THE UNITED STATES MARINE CORPS

OFFICER RANKS (FROM JUNIOR TO SENIOR)

Second Lieutenant
First Lieutenant
Captain
Major
Lieutenant Colonel
Colonel
Brigadier General
Major General
Lieutenant General
General
Commandant of the Marine Corps

WARRANT OFFICER (FROM JUNIOR TO SENIOR)

Warrant Officer 1
Chief Warrant Officer 2
Chief Warrant Officer 3
Chief Warrant Officer 4
Chief Warrant Officer 5

ENLISTED RANKS (FROM JUNIOR TO SENIOR)

Private

Private First Class
Lance Corporal
Corporal
Sergeant
Staff Sergeant
Gunnery Sergeant
Master Sergeant or First Sergeant
Master Gunnery Sergeant or Sergeant Major
Sergeant Major of the Marine Corps

Appendix B

STRUCTURE OF THE 1ST MARINE DIVISION

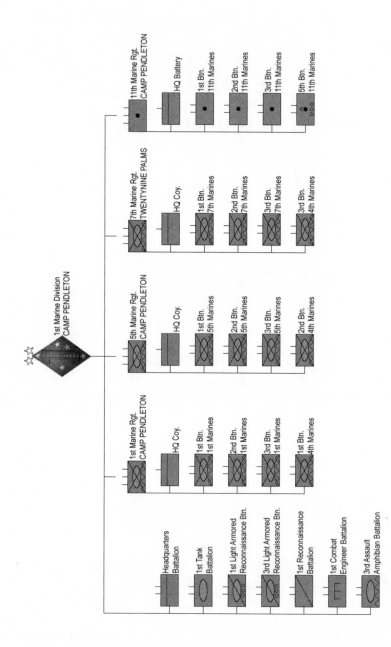

1st Marine Division
CAMP PENDLETON

1st Marine Rgt.
CAMP PENDLETON

HQ Coy.

1st Btn.
1st Marines

2nd Btn.
1st Marines

3rd Btn.
1st Marines

1st Btn.
4th Marines

5th Marine Rgt.
CAMP PENDLETON

HQ Coy.

1st Btn.
5th Marines

2nd Btn.
5th Marines

3rd Btn.
5th Marines

2nd Btn.
4th Marines

7th Marine Rgt.
TWENTYNINE PALMS

HQ Coy.

1st Btn.
7th Marines

2nd Btn.
7th Marines

3rd Btn.
7th Marines

3rd Btn.
4th Marines

11th Marine Rgt.
CAMP PENDLETON

HQ Battery

1st Btn.
11th Marines

2nd Btn.
11th Marines

3rd Btn.
11th Marines

5th Btn.
11th Marines

Headquarters
Battalion

1st Tank
Battalion

1st Light Armored
Reconnaissance Btn.

3rd Light Armored
Reconnaissance Btn.

1st Reconnaissance
Battalion

1st Combat
Engineer Battalion

3rd Assault
Amphibian Battalion

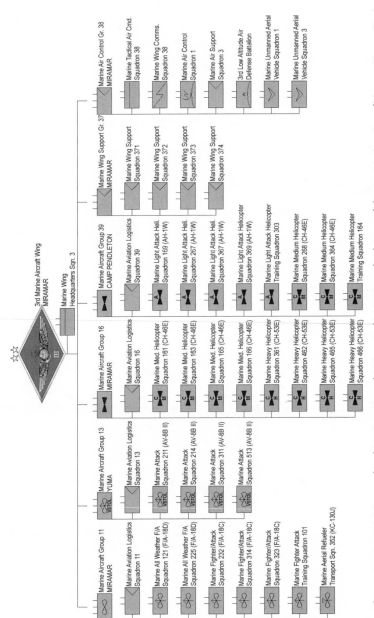

The 1st Marine Division and 3rd Marine Aircraft Wing (3rd MAW) are both part of the 1st Marine Expeditionary Force. During times of war, elements of the 3rd MAW sometimes become integrated into 1st Marine Division in order to support operational needs. Source: These charts were created by Noclador and are reproduced here under CC BY-SA 3.0.

GLOSSARY

15th MEU	The 15th Marine Expeditionary Unit. One of seven Marine Expeditionary Units in the United States Marine Corps. When operational it consists of about 2,200 personnel.
.50 cal gunner	The operator of the M2 .50-caliber automatic, crew-operated machine gun. It is primarily mounted and used as an anti-personnel and anti-aircraft weapon. The gunner is usually selected for the ability to understand the weapon system and carry it.
AAA	Anti-aircraft artillery; commonly known as "triple-A." A weapons systems specifically designed to target aircraft.
ACE	Aviation combat element or air combat element. Part of the Marine Air-Ground Task Force (MAGTF). It consists of rotary-wing, tilt-rotor, and fixed-wing aircraft, support equipment, pilots, and maintenance personnel, as well as command and control assets.
actual	Radio communication: call sign for commander of a unit.
adjust-fire mission	In an artillery unit, if the artillery rounds are not landing at the desired location, the artillery officer or forward observer can "adjust fire." This allows the artillery officer a chance to adjust where the final impact will be when the full battery fires on the target.

A-driver
Assistant driver. The driver whose task is to assist and provide security for the driver, often acting as "sniper bait" for any enemy observer looking for an easy target.

Amtracs
Armored tracked vehicles. A variety of landing vehicle tracked (LVT), which is a type of amphibious vehicle used as an assault troop and fire support vehicle to carry troops by land or sea to the fight.

AO
Area of operations. An operational area defined by a commander to delineate the area of his responsibility or control. These areas are usually chosen after thorough battle-space analysis to ensure that subordinate commanders can achieve their goals, objectives, and missions, and protect their forces.

AOR
Area of Responsibility. A region assigned to commanders that is used to define an area with specific geographic boundaries where they have the authority to plan and conduct operations.

arty
Artillery.

back brief
A term used to describe a military member's obligation to provide information to his commander after an execution of an order. The idea is to increase understanding of orders by providing the commander with feedback on the results of an operation or exercise.

B billet
A short-term duty assignment (usually two to three years) outside of the primary job of a Marine, designed to give experience or a rest from the operational forces, or help out the overall needs of the Marine Corps. Some B billet assignments include Drill Instructor, Recruiting Duty, or an instructor at Officer Candidacy School.

BDA
Battle damage assessment; the after-requirement of an aircraft or artillery operation to provide an assessment of damage inflicted on a target through observation of the target area.

bivy sack
Bivouac sack; a semi-waterproof, individual shelter, used by the Marine Corps instead of a traditional tent system.

BLU-109s	Bomb Live Unit; a hardened penetration bomb used by military aircraft intended to penetrate through concrete and other hardened structures before exploding.
boonie cover	A wide-brimmed hat commonly used by military forces.
CAAT	Combined Anti-Armor Team, which consists of a platoon in a weapons company with heavy machine guns and TOW missiles and whose mission is to provide quick reaction support to combat armored vehicles in addition to providing security for convoys.
CAX	Combined armed exercise; Marine Corps training on combined arms tactics, which incorporates different branches in order to provide mutual support and force the enemy onto the horns of a dilemma.
CENTCOM	The United States Central Command (US-CENTCOM) is a theater-level Unified Combatant Command unit of the U.S. Armed Forces.
CFLCC	Coalition Forces Land Component Command; directs all land forces on behalf of a combatant commander or Joint Task Force commander.
check	radio communication: O.K. or I'm following.
CG	Commanding General; a general officer appointed to a specific billet where he is commander of forces within his appointed duty.
class B mishap	An accident where the resulting total cost of reportable property damage is $200,000 or more but less than $1,000,000 or results in an injury and/or occupational illness leading to permanent partial disability.
clear	radio communication: I have finished talking and am shutting off my radio.
close air support	An action by fixed- or rotary-winged aircraft against hostile targets within close proximity and requiring detailed communication and deconfliction to coordinate fire and movement.
Cobra	The AH-1 Cobra is a two-bladed, twin-engine attack helicopter used by the USMC.

COC	Combat operations center; an area designated as a commander's centralized command and control facility for all combat tactical and operational operations conducted.
CONUS	Continental United States or America. OCONUS is describes the areas Outside of Continental United States.
copy	radio communication: I understand (said after receiving information).
crew-served weapons	Weapons requiring more than one person to operate, with the exception of squad automatic weapons (SAW) and sniper rifles. With crew-served weapons there is usually an operator and an assistant to carry ammunition or assorted parts.
CSSB	Combat Service Support Battalion; the old name for Logistics Combat Battalion whose job is to provide all support functions not organic to the ground and aviation units. Functions include communications, combat engineers, motor transport, medical, supply, maintenance, air delivery, and landing support.
cyclic rate	The rate of fire of rounds from a weapon, specifically the fastest possible rate at which rounds exit the chamber.
dark-green Marine	An African American Marine
DASC	Direct Air Support Center; the USMC aviation command and control center and the air control group responsible for the direction of air operations directly supporting ground forces.
donning and clearing	Ensuring a gas mask is correctly sealed and properly fitted.
DPICM	Dual-purpose improved conventional munitions; an artillery warhead designed to burst into sub-munitions at a specific altitude and distance from the desired target. Sub-munitions are used for both anti-armor and anti-personnel attack.
DRASH	Deployable rapid assembly shelter; a military tent or shelter.
EAS	End of active service; the period at which a military member reaches the end of his or her enlistment.

EOD	Explosive ordnance disposal. EOD technicians perform duties that include locating, accessing, identifying, rendering safe, neutralizing, and disposing of hazards including chemical, biological, radiological, nuclear, and high yield explosives (CBRNE), unexploded explosive ordnance (UXO), improvised explosive devices (IEDs) and weapons of mass destruction (WMD).
EPW	Enemy prisoner of war; a civilian or combatant who is held in custody by a military power during or immediately after an armed conflict.
FAC	Forward air controller; an officer who assists in providing coordination to close air support missions and to aircraft and who ensures that their attack hits the intended target and does not injure friendly troops.
FDC	Fire direction center; the brains of the artillery unit and where the fire missions and data received are transformed into calls for fire.
fighting hole	Military slang for a dug-out trench area where a Marine can lie or stand to shield himself from small arms fire.
fitrep	Fitness report; a periodic written assessment of the performance and professional moral fiber of Marines from the grades of sergeant through major general.
Five Paragraph Order	A military report or issuance of orders used for small unit tactics and based on an METT-TC analysis (mission, enemy, terrain & weather, troops & fire support, time, and civilian considerations) on how to conduct a specific tactical operation.
float	A tour of duty aboard a Navy vessel usually as part of a Marine Expeditionary Unit deployment.
FLOT	Forward line of troops or front edge of battlefield area (FEBA); an imaginary line that designates the forward-most friendly and hostile forces on the battlefield during a conflict or war.
FOB	Forward operating base; any secured, temporary, forward military area that is used to support tactical military operations.

FragO	Fragmentary order; used to send timely changes of existing orders from higher commanders to subordinate and supporting commanders.
FSC	Fire support center; the heart of an artillery unit where there is central communications in order to coordinate and execute fire missions.
GCS	Ground control station; the central operating systems, co-located in or near the battlefield with the UAVs (unmanned aerial vehicles), that control both the aircraft movement and the UAV camera or payload.
gedunk	Military slang for junk food.
GHN-45s	The GHN-45 (gun, howitzer, Noricum) is an Iraqi howitzer that can be used as a chemical-carrying artillery system. This was one of the Iraqis' most common artillery systems, especially during the Gulf War.
GOSP	Gas oil separation plant; a type of industrial facility used primarily in the oil industry to process crude oil, separating gases and contaminants, making the crude economically viable for storage, processing, and export.
ground combat element	Also known as GCE; the land force of a Marine Air-Ground Task Force (MAGTF).
grunt	An infantry Marine.
guidon	A military flag signifying a garrison's unit designation and affiliation.
Gunny	An abbreviation for the rank of Gunnery Sergeant.
head	A Naval and Marine Corps term for a bathroom.
higher	Military slang used to reference the higher command element.
HLZ	Helicopter landing zone; an area designated and approved as safe for helicopters to land.
hooch	Military slang term for a military tent.
Huey	The Bell UH-1 Iroquois or "Huey" is a military helicopter powered by a single, turboshaft engine, with a two-bladed main rotor and tail rotor, used for assault support in the Marine Corps.

HUMINT	Human intelligence; the collection of intelligence by means of contact with other people, as opposed to the more technical intelligence collections such as SIGINT (signals intelligence) and IMINT (imagery intelligence).
ICS	Internal communications system; a system that allows the internal UAV pilot and operator to communicate via radio uplink with the associated UAV.
I MEF	I Marine Expeditionary Force; a Marine Air-Ground Task Force (MAGTF) of the United States Marine Corps primarily comprised of the 1st Marine Division, 3rd Marine Aircraft Wing, 1st Marine Logistics Group, and a command element.
INC	Iraqi National Congress; former Iraqi opposition group led by Ahmed Chalabi. It was formed with the aid and direction of the U.S. government following the Gulf War for the purpose of encouraging the overthrow of Iraqi leader Saddam Hussein.
intel	Intelligence; refers to the military intelligence field, which uses information collection and analysis to provide guidance and direction to commanders in support of their decisions.
IR	Infrared light; electromagnetic radiation with a wavelength between 0.7 and 300 micrometers. The military uses IR cameras in order to find heat-emitting objects especially during low-level light or night-time operations.
ISR	Imagery/surveillance/reconnaissance; also known as ISTAR (intelligence, surveillance, target acquisition, and reconnaissance), which is the process of using intelligence usually collected from imagery and the gathering and managing of information from sensors, satellites, UAVs, or aircraft.
JAGMAN	Manual of the Judge Advocate General; the military legal manual, which the military uses for purposes such as determining if a case should be

	referred to a court martial based on the NCIS investigation and any additional factual evidence.
JDAMs	Joint direct attack munitions, also known as or smart bombs; a guidance kit that converts unguided bombs or "dumb bombs" into all-weather "smart" munitions.
KA-Bars	A fighting knife issued to American armed forces.
KIA	A military abbreviation used to designate those military members who are killed in action.
KISS	An acronym meaning "keep it simple, stupid."
klick	Military slang for kilometer.
LAVs	Light armored reconnaissance vehicles (LAV-25); the primary weapon system of the Light Armored Reconnaissance Battalion (LAR) in the Marine Corps. LAVs are specially designed as a light, nimble track vehicle that can transit faster and further than a tank and used primarily for reconnaissance but not heavy fighting.
leaving the wire	also left the wire; Marine slang meaning that someone is stepping outside the secured perimeter area, usually to go into a hostile fire area.
libo	Marine slang meaning "liberty," that is, time off from duty or a period of rest.
line of departure	The initial position for an attack on enemy positions and the point where attacking forces cross from a friendly area to an unsecured hostile zone.
LOC	Line of communication; a route connecting an operating military unit with its supply base, which allows for communication between forward and rear units.
MAG	Marine Aircraft Group; a subordinate unit of the MAW that is comprised of combat-ready squadrons that can include fixed-wing, rotary, tactical aerial refueling, logistics, or tilt-rotor aircraft.
1MARDIV	1st Marine Division, nicknamed "the old breed"; the oldest and largest marine infantry division of the United States Marine Corps located at Marine Corps Base Camp Pendleton, California. It

	is a subordinate unit of the I Marine Expeditionary Force (I MEF).
MAW (3rd MAW)	3rd Marine Aircraft Wing; the major west coast aviation unit of the United States Marine Corps, which is headquartered at Marine Corps Air Station Miramar, California, and provides the aviation combat element for I Marine Expeditionary Force.
MEB	Marine Expeditionary Brigade; a special deployed unit used primarily for global crisis response that is part of a Marine Air-Ground Task Force consisting of approximately 14,500 Marines and Sailors. A MEB is constructed around a reinforced infantry regiment, a composite Marine aircraft group, a logistics group and a command element.
MEF	Marine Expeditionary Force; the largest type of a Marine Air-Ground Task Force and the largest element of United States Marine Corps combat power.
MEPS	Military entrance processing station; a military center that screens and processes applicants into the United States Armed Forces at various locations throughout the United States.
MOPP	Mission-oriented protective posture; protective gear used in a toxic environment, i.e., during a chemical, biological, radiological, or nuclear (CBRN) strike.
MOS	Military Occupational Specialty; a code used by the United States Marines to identify a specific job that a Marine is assigned to do throughout his service.
motor-T	Motor transport; a subunit of Marines responsible for the operation and maintenance of wheeled non-combat and non-engineer vehicles.
MREs	Meal, Ready-to-Eat; a standard U.S. field ration.
MSR	Main supply route; the route or routes designated within an area of operations used by units to transit from one area to another in support of military operations.

NBC | Nuclear, biological, chemical. More recently, the term chemical, biological, radiological, and nuclear weapons (CBRN) is used.

NCO | Non-commissioned officer (NCO); in the Marine Corps the term usually includes all grades of corporal and sergeant and designates a small unit leader (enlisted), who usually has leadership responsibilities over other subordinate Marines.

NGO | Non-governmental organization; an organization operating independently from any government and usually providing some humanitarian service or social or political aim.

NJP | Non-judicial punishment; a form of military justice authorized by Article 15 of the Uniform Code of Military Justice. NJP permits commanders to administratively discipline troops without a court-martial, offering a lighter punishment that will not later interfere with a civilian legal record.

NVGs | Night-vision goggles; an optical device, usually in the form of binoculars, which allows images to be produced in levels of light approaching total darkness.

OCS | Officer Candidates School; where all Marine officers (with the exception of United States Naval Academy graduates) train in order to gain a commission as officer in the Marine Corps.

ops | Slang term for operations.

OpsO | Operations officer; the third in command of a Marine Unit and in charge of planning all operations for that unit. Often referred to as the "S-3" or "G-3."

order | Operations order; a report describing a military operation. It will describe the situation facing the unit, the mission of the unit, and what activities the unit will conduct to achieve the mission goals.

out | radio communication: I have finished talking and do not expect a reply.

over | radio communication: I have finished talking and am listening for a reply.

parade rest	A military drill movement in which the military member is called from the position of attention to a position of modified rest, where the hands are clasped behind the small of the back, and the legs are shoulder width apart.
PFC	Private First Class. In the United States armed forces, it is a rank held by junior enlisted persons. The only lower rank is Private.
Phase IVB	Upon the U.S. military establishing the Coalition Provisional Authority in Iraq after major combat operations were declared over, U.S. forces entered Phase IVB, which transited the mission to recovery operations, and overall war authority was transferred from the CFLCC to the Combined Joint Task Force 7 (CJTF-7).
POG	Persons other than grunt; a Marine not of the combat arms (infantry, armor, and artillery), sometimes seen as "Pogue."
PT	Physical training; activities necessary for all Marines to maintain proper strength.
PX	Post exchange; a store where military members buy food, clothes, electronics, etc.
racking out	Marine slang meaning to sleep.
RCT	Regimental combat team; formed by augmenting a regular infantry regiment with smaller tank, artillery, combat engineer, mechanized cavalry, reconnaissance, signal, air defense, quartermaster, military police, medical, and other support units to enable it to be a self-supporting organization in combat.
relief in place	Reassignment of combat forces (often a swap for other combat forces to take control of the area held by the current combat forces) to better respond to changes in mission such as from combat to occupation functions.
retrograde	The deliberate withdrawal of forces from an operation after combat operations are over.
ricky-tick	Marine slang meaning as soon as possible. Often seen following the word "most" as in "most ricky-tick."

ROE	Rules of engagement; the rules that determine when, where, and how force shall be used in any military engagement.
roger	radio communication: information received.
RPGs	Rocket-propelled grenade. A shoulder-launched, anti-material projectile equipped with an explosive warhead, used by Iraqi forces against U.S. forces during the Iraq campaign.
S-2	The Intelligence Section of a unit.
S-3	See OpsO; the Operations Section of a unit.
S-4	The Logistics Section of a unit.
SALUTE report	Size, Activity, Location, Unit, Time, and Equipment; used to describe a military situation report.
Sam Browne belt	A wide belt, usually leather, which is supported by a strap going diagonally over the right shoulder. It is most often seen as part of an officer's uniform.
SAM	Surface-to-air missile; a missile designed to be launched from the ground, usually to destroy aircraft. It is one type of anti-aircraft system.
sand-table exercise	A military exercise, sometimes referred to as a TEWT (tactical exercise without troops), designed to rehearse military operations on a small scale to simulate how an operation could be conducted, sometimes just for war-gaming purposes. This type of exercise is often demonstrated by a large box scale model where war fighters can use sand, models, and symbolic devices assembled on a miniature diorama to plan operations.
Scorpion	A.K.A. the Akrep; a light armored reconnaissance vehicle produced in Turkey and previously used by the Iraqi military.
SERE	Survival, Evasion, Resistance, and Escape; a program providing military personnel with training in evading capture, survival skills, and the military code of conduct.
shave tail	A nickname for newly assigned officers with no prior enlisted experience.
SNCO	Senior noncommissioned officer; an enlisted member who has a high enlisted rank but has not

	been given a commission. NCOs obtain positions of authority by promotion from the lower ranks.
SNCOIC	Senior noncommissioned officer in charge; holds a billet of responsibility enabling him to carry out orders of the commander and carry out many orders as an officer.
SOP	Standard operating procedure; used to describe the routine and expected procedures to perform a given operation.
SPOT report	An abridged intelligence report used to send timely intelligence or an update on the status of events that could have an immediate and significant effect on current planning and operations.
standby	radio communication: pausing for the next transmission; usually means staying off the air until the operator returns after a short wait.
stand down	A temporary stop of offensive military action.
stand to	An order given by a unit commander when he wants his troops in a state of readiness when the expectation of an attack is imminent.
stop loss	U.S. military policy requiring military members to remain in service beyond their normal discharge date.
TBS	The Basic School; where all newly commissioned United States Marine Corps officers are sent to learn the art and science of being an Officer of Marines. The course lasts about six months.
TFT	Task Force Tarawa; the name given to the 2nd Marine Expeditionary Brigade during the 2003 invasion of Iraq. It was named after the island Tawara in the South Pacific, best known by outsiders as the site of the Battle of Tarawa during World War II.
third-generation warfare	Tactics focused on using speed and surprise to bypass the enemy's lines and collapse their forces from the rear.
T/O	Table of organization; each unit in the military has a table of organization describing in detail what weapons or equipment should be given to

each military member based on their billet and assigned unit.

TOT

Time on target; refers to the estimated length of time it takes a round, missile, artillery shell, or other munitions to reach the intended target.

TOW

Tube-launched, optically tracked, wire-guided missile; anti-tank missile used by the Marine Corps.

TPFDD

Time-phased force deployment data; the estimate of transportation requirements that must be fulfilled in order to move arriving or departing units to a different location.

tracking

Military slang indicating that you understand what someone is saying, as in "I'm tracking you."

TRAP

Tactical recovery of aircraft and personnel; a military mission performed by specifically trained units to rescue downed pilots or recover aircraft.

T-rations

A.K.A. T rats; larger versions of MREs, which are prepared food from containers.

travel lock

The preparation of units for movement or relocation during a very limited period of time.

UA

Unauthorized absence; the missing of a movement or absence from an appointed place of duty. Long-term unauthorized absence can lead to desertion: the abandonment of a "duty" or post without permission with the intention of not returning. Absence Without Official Leave (AWOL) can refer to either desertion or a temporary absence.

UAV

Unmanned aerial vehicle, also referred to in slang as a bird; an aircraft flown by a pilot or a navigator without a human crew on board the aircraft.

UCMJ

Uniform code of military justice; the foundation of military law in the United States. It applies separate laws to U.S. military members that are not applicable to American civilians.

UDP

Unit Deployment Program; a policy established in the Marine Corps to reduce the number of unaccompanied tours, specifically overseas, of units to the Western Pacific (WESTPAC). UDPs generally run for periods of approximately six months.

up on personnel

When all personnel in a particular unit are accounted for, meaning their whereabouts are known. Commanders are responsible for maintaining control and accountability of all members assigned to their unit.

VX

Nerve gas. An extremely toxic substance whose application is used solely in chemical warfare as a nerve agent.

Warning Order

An order given to military units to initiate development and evaluation of courses of action by a supported commander. This order requests a commander's estimate of the situation and initiates subordinate unit mission planning.

WIA

Wounded in action.

wingers

Slang used to describe those who are assigned to "Wing" or Aviation units. Often used derogatorily by grunts, or infantry Marines, to mean that aviation Marines lack the same "marshal spirit" as them.

weapons conditions

The four weapons conditions for an M16A2 service rifle. Condition 4: Weapon on safe, bolt home on an empty chamber, no magazine inserted, ejection port cover closed. Condition 3: Weapon on safe, bolt home on an empty chamber, magazine inserted, ejection port cover closed. Condition 2: Does not apply. Condition 1: Weapon on safe, round in chamber, bolt home, magazine inserted, ejection port cover closed, weapon ready to fire.

XO

Executive Officer; the second-in-command, reporting to the Commanding Officer.

Yellow footprints

The spot where Marine recruits stand when they first step off the bus to begin recruit training at Parris Island or San Diego.

BOCA RATON PUBLIC LIBRARY, FLORIDA

3 3656 0563568 1

956.704434 Bla
Blair, Jane, 1972-
Hesitation kills

AUG   2011